The Inclusive, Empathetic, and Relational Supervisor

Supervisors are the bridge between line employees and middle/upper management. Therefore, they must effectively communicate across the organization to be responsive and thoughtful leaders. With work being more global, organizations are taking advantage of remote work, and the workforce is now more diverse and decentralized, making the workplace more dynamic and complex. However, diversity can be one of the most controversial and least understood business topics because of the issues regarding quality, leadership, and ethics (Anand & Winters, 2008).

An inclusive supervisor will ensure that their direct reports are treated fairly and respectfully but never made to feel less than anyone else. They will be a critical success factor in supporting the business case for diversity, equity, inclusion, and belonging (DEI&B) as a critical strategy in a globally competitive market.

This book builds on the belief that people are the most valuable resource and that everyone should be treated with dignity and respect. The authors will provide tools to self-assess intrapersonal/interpersonal communication, develop a positive work environment, and evaluate listening skills.

A list of competencies to be an effective communicator will be provided. Key concepts such as cross-cultural competence, generational cohort, critical race theory, emotional intelligence, emotional contagion, social exchange theory, and interpersonal competency will be explored.

This book provides strategies for building solid relationships with team members; uses positivity as a foundational practice to lead and encourage other employees; provides guidelines on how to hold employees accountable and set high expectations; presents strategies to engage, coach, and develop employees by creating a positive environment to influence attitudes and behaviors; and offers various approaches for managing time and increasing productivity.

Successful Supervisory Leadership

Series Authors: William J. Rothwell, Behnam Bakhshandeh & Aileen G. Zaballero

Successful Supervisory Leadership: Exerting Positive Influence While Leading People
2023
William J. Rothwell, Behnam Bakhshandeh & Aileen G. Zaballero

The Inclusive, Empathetic, and Relational Supervisor Managing Diverse Employees through Interpersonal Relationships
2024
Behnam Bakhshandeh, William J. Rothwell & Aileen G. Zaballero

The Inclusive, Empathetic, and Relational Supervisor
Managing Diverse Employees through Interpersonal Relationships

Behnam Bakhshandeh, Ph.D.,
William J. Rothwell, Ph.D. &
Aileen G. Zaballero, Ph.D.

Routledge
Taylor & Francis Group

A PRODUCTIVITY PRESS BOOK

First published 2024
by Routledge
605 Third Avenue, New York, NY 10158

and by Routledge
4 Park Square, Milton Park, Abingdon, Oxon, OX14 4RN

Routledge is an imprint of the Taylor & Francis Group, an informa business

ISBN: 9781032537696 (hbk)
ISBN: 9781032537689 (pbk)
ISBN: 9781003413493 (ebk)

DOI: 10.4324/9781003413493

Typeset in Garamond
by Deanta Global Publishing Services, Chennai, India

Behnam Bakhshandeh

I am dedicating this book to all hardworking supervisors in all industries. Thank you for all your hard work, wisdom, experience, and dedication to training, developing, and empowering your workforce.

William J. Rothwell

I am dedicating this book to my wife, Marcelina Rothwell. She is the wind beneath my wings.

Aileen G. Zaballero

I dedicate this book to my mother, Aleli, and in loving memory of my father, Alfredo, for a lifetime of continuous support and encouragement. In addition, I wanted to acknowledge my cousins David and Tita Lori for their continuous love and support.

Contents

Preface

Supervisors are the bridge between line employees and middle/upper management. Therefore, they must effectively communicate across the organization to be responsive and thoughtful leaders. Book II of the *Successful Supervisory Leadership* series, *The Inclusive, Empathetic, and Relational Supervisor: Managing Diverse Employees through Interpersonal Relationships*, will be the second book of a five-book series.

The Inclusive, Empathetic, and Relational Supervisor: Managing Diverse Employees through Interpersonal Relationships will build on the belief that people are the most valuable resource and everyone should be treated with dignity and respect. The authors will provide tools to self-assess intrapersonal/interpersonal communication; develop a positive work environment; and evaluate empathy, inclusion, and listening skills.

As work becomes increasingly global, firms capitalize on remote work opportunities, resulting in a more diversified and dispersed workforce. This, in turn, makes the workplace more dynamic and intricate. Nevertheless, diversity remains a very contentious and enigmatic subject in the corporate world due to its implications for quality, leadership, and ethics. A supervisor who embraces inclusivity will guarantee equitable and courteous treatment for subordinates, ensuring that no one is ever made to feel inferior. *The Inclusive, Empathetic, and Relational Supervisor: Managing Diverse Employees through Interpersonal Relationships* shows them a path to a better understanding of their crucial role in bolstering the business case for diversity, equality, inclusion, and belonging (DEI&B) as a vital strategy in a highly competitive global market. Organizations face evolving demands as customers and workers want greater responsibility and diversity.

What Does This Book Do for Readers?

Readers of *The Inclusive, Empathetic, and Relational Supervisor: Managing Diverse Employees through Interpersonal Relationships* will learn the following:

- the dynamics of working with teams and groups,
- the elements of effective communication and active listening,
- the role of human resources in establishing an inclusive working environment,
- the elements of Human Relations and their effect on interpersonal relationships,
- individuals' motivations and how to delegate the workload effectively and responsibly,
- to understand employment conflict and the disciplinary process,
- to effectively supervise diversity, equity, inclusion, and belonging (DEI&B),
- to supervise with interpersonal and intrapersonal relationship skills, and
- to be a relational supervisor with and through people.

The Purpose of the Book

Supervisors are the bridge between line employees and middle/upper management. Therefore, they must effectively communicate across the organization to be responsive and thoughtful leaders. The demand for soft skills, namely the capacity to comprehend the emotional and cognitive requirements of others or to exhibit empathy, is steadily increasing—empathy centers around interpersonal connections. Research conducted by the Center for Creative Leadership indicates that there is a favorable correlation between empathy and work success. Supervisors who demonstrated empathy toward their subordinates received more favorable evaluations. A supervisor who possesses empathy may identify the needs of their subordinates, establish unambiguous expectations, and encourage actions that foster a favorable work atmosphere. *The Inclusive, Empathetic, and Relational Supervisor: Managing Diverse Employees through Interpersonal Relationships* will shed light on some critical issues of lacking essential skills, such as empathy, inclusion, and interpersonal relationships.

The Target Audience for the Book

The Inclusive, Empathetic, and Relational Supervisor: Managing Diverse Employees through Interpersonal Relationships provides a comprehensive and detailed approach to becoming an effective supervisor who is inclusive, empathetic, and able to relate to others. This book is full of information, approaches, methods, and tools that would be useful to:

- Human Resources and human resources development professionals and practitioners,
- Organization development and workplace learning and performance practitioners,
- Business owners, business managers and supervisors,
- Professional business coaches and consultants,
- Management and Business school students,
- Organization Development, Human Resources, and Human Resources Development students,
- Employees who are committed to learning more about being professionals and
- Technical and trade schools and vocational facilities faculty and staff.

The Organization of the Book

This book provides theories and concepts focused on successful supervisory activities. Presenting methods, models, practices, and tools to guide you and your teams to increase success and effectiveness. The contents are for all supervisory positions, managers, business coaches, consultants, high-performance coaches, and managers-as-coaches.

In more detail, this book consists of a **Preface** to summarize the book, **Acknowledgments** to thank contributors, an **Advance Organizer** to help readers assess which chapters they wish to focus on, and a summary of the **Authors' Bio-sketches**.

Continuing the theme that supervisors play a central role in positively influencing their teams and organization, this book is the second part of the Successful Supervisory Leadership Series. Book II, *The Inclusive, Empathetic, and Relational Supervisor: Managing Diverse Employees through Interpersonal Relationships*, continues to build on the fundamental belief that people are the most valuable resource and that every individual should

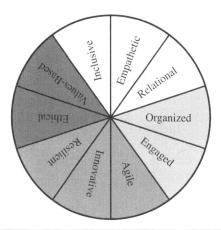

Figure A.1   Positive and influential supervisor framework. *Note:* Authors' original creation.

be treated with dignity and respect. This book will focus on three of the ten characteristics in the *Positive and Influential Supervisory Framework* (see Figure A.1 for the slices in white). The framework, first unveiled in Book I, *Successful Supervisory Leadership: Exerting Positive Influence while Leading People*, is depicted as a pie chart (see Figure A.1). These characteristics, however, are not static. Each slice is a "characteristic that can fluctuate based on environmental (internal and external) conditions, the team, and the supervisor's strengths. The magnitude of each slice may vary based on the industry, work environment, organizational structure, and current circumstance" (Rothwell, Bakhshandeh, & Zaballero, 2023, p. 183). This flexible approach underlines the importance of adaptability and contextual awareness in modern supervisory roles, two qualities indispensable for any successful leader.

Book Structure

This book follows the structure illustrated in Figure A.2, *Supervisory Leadership Series Book II Structure.* Starting with the frame of the book, **Chapter 1**, *Overview and Background*, examines the central role of inclusive, empathetic, and relational supervisors in today's evolving workplace environment. We will investigate the World of Work, where paradigms are shifting, and there is an increased focus on collaborative work groups as the supervisory role evolves. Teamwork and communication are more important in this new World of Work as the traditional hierarchical supervision model begins to break down. The second part of the frame is **Chapter 2**,

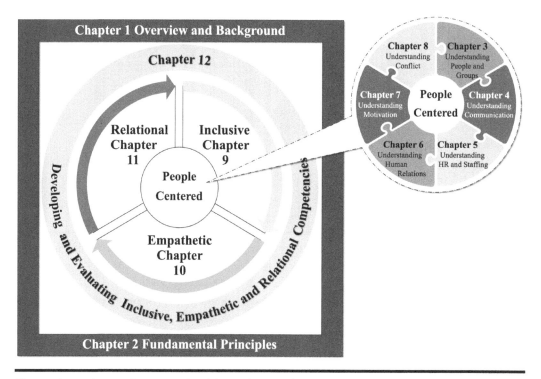

Figure A.2 *Supervisory Leadership Series Book II Structure.* Note: Authors' original creation.

Fundamental Principles for the Inclusive, Empathetic, and Relational Supervisor, which sheds light on concepts that shape dynamic work environments. It focuses on the nuances of cross-cultural competence, the power of emotional intelligence, and the intricacies of social exchange theory.

Chapters 3–8 are dedicated to better understand the person-centered approach from a supervisory perspective (puzzled pie slices in Figure A.2). **Chapter 3**, *Understanding Working with Teams and Groups*, builds on our understanding of individual and group dynamics, exploring the subtle complexities that define and influence organizational behaviors. In **Chapter 4**, *Understanding Communication*, we explore effective communication in greater detail, offering insights into bridging gaps, fostering understanding, and nurturing positive interpersonal interactions. By delving deep into organizational dynamics, **Chapters 5**, *Understanding Human Resources and Staffing*, and **Chapter 6**, *Understanding Human Relations*, provide a comprehensive overview of human resources—the structures and systems that facilitate effective personnel management—and human relationships, the intangible bonds and interactions that define workplace culture. **Chapter 7**, *Understanding People's Motivation and How to Delegate*, explores the realm of human motivation, exploring theories and practices that ignite passion, drive, and commitment among team members. **Chapter 8**, *Understanding Employment Conflicts and the Disciplinary Process*, addresses the inevitable challenges of team and employee conflicts, offering strategies and insights for resolution, and ensuring a harmonious and productive work environment.

The subsequent chapters examine the essential qualities of inclusivity, empathy, and relational supervision (inside the frame of Figure A.2). **Chapter 9**, *The Inclusive Supervisor: Supervising Diversity, Equity, Inclusion, and Belonging*, explores the nuanced strategies required to cultivate a truly diverse and inclusive workplace. **Chapter 10**, *The Empathetic Supervisor: Supervising with Interpersonal and Intrapersonal Skills*, focuses on the critical soft skills that underscore effective leadership, emphasizing the importance of self-awareness and interpersonal savvy. **Chapter 11**, *The Relational Supervisor: Supervising with and through People*, highlights the art of leading by example and the power of collaborative success.

Finally, **Chapter 12**, *Developing and Evaluating Inclusive, Empathetic, and Relational Supervisor Competencies* (outside circle in Figure A.2), provides a holistic and systematic exploration of the competencies essential for leaders to embody a leadership style that's inclusive, empathic, and relational. It offers a list of competencies to develop, complemented by evaluative tools designed to ensure that supervisors not only adopt these skills but continue to develop and utilize them, thereby ensuring their effectiveness and adaptability in an evolving workplace.

In the end, **Appendix A** reviews sources for education and implementation of practices drawn from the book, which will take you to other sources that can broaden and deepen your understanding of the Inclusive, Empathetic, and Relational Supervisor.

Acknowledgments

Behnam Bakhshandeh

I would like to thank my two partners, Dr William Rothwell, for his original research, knowledge, supervisory leadership work, and valuable input on this wonderful book, and Dr Aileen Zaballero for her collaboration and serious efforts in partnership with us to develop this book project.

William J. Rothwell

I want to show my gratitude to my two partners and co-authors, Dr Behnam Bakhshandeh and Dr Aileen Zaballero, for their wisdom, experience, and collaborative efforts in generating this book as the second volume in this series.

Aileen G. Zaballero

I am grateful to Dr Rothwell for his continued support and guidance and for giving me the opportunity to be part of this seminal book. Furthermore, I would like to thank Dr Bakhshandeh for his patience, persistence, and continued hard work. This publication would not be possible without Dr Rothwell's expertise and Dr Bakhshandeh's vision.

Behnam Bakhshandeh
Greenfield Township, Pennsylvania
November 2023

William J. Rothwell
State College, Pennsylvania
November 2023

Aileen G. Zaballero
Marietta, Georgia
November 2023

Advance Organizer

Complete the following Organizer before you read the book. Use it as a diagnostic tool to help you assess what you most want to know about *The Inclusive, Empathetic, and Relational Supervisor* and where you can find it in this book fast.

The Organizer

Directions

Spend about ten minutes on the Organizer and read each item thoroughly. Think of *The Inclusive, Empathetic, and Relational Supervisor* as you would like to practice it for yourself, and how you want to develop others in a leadership position. Be honest and indicate your level of knowledge on a Likert scale of 1–5, with "1" having little to no knowledge and "5" being very knowledgeable. When you finish, score and interpret the results using the instructions appearing at the end of the Organizer. To learn more about any item below, refer to the right-hand column referencing the specific chapter.

I would like to develop myself on:						
Level of knowledge No knowledge ------- knowledgeable						Book chapter in which the topic is covered
1	2	3	4	5	*The area of knowledge, understanding, and development*	
					Introduction and overview	1
					Fundamental principles for inclusive, empathetic, and relational supervisor	2
					Understanding how to work with teams and groups	3
					Understanding aspects of effective communication and active listening	4
					Understanding elements of human resources and staffing	5
					Understanding human relations	6
					Understanding people's motivation and how to delegate	7
					Understanding employment conflicts and the disciplinary process	8
					Supervising diversity, equity, inclusion, and belonging	9
					Supervising with interpersonal and intrapersonal skills	10
					Supervising with and through people by building relationships	11
					Developing and evaluating inclusive, empathetic and relational competencies	12
Total						

Scoring and Interpreting the Organizer

Give yourself 1 point for each Y and a 0 for each N or N/A listed above. Total the points from the Y column and place the sum in the line opposite to the word TOTAL above. Then interpret your score:

Score

- **1–15 points =** Congratulations! This book is just what you need. Read the chapters you marked 2 or 1.
- **16–30 points =** You have great skills in *Inclusive, Empathetic, and Relational Supervisor* already, but you also have areas where you could develop professionally. Read the chapters you marked 2 or 1.
- **31–45 points =** You have skills in *Inclusive, Empathetic, and Relational Supervisor*, but you could still benefit from building skills in selected areas.
- **46–60 points =** You believe you need little development in *Inclusive, Empathetic, and Relational Supervisor*. Ask others—such as mentors—to see if they agree.

Authors

Behnam Bakhshandeh, Ph.D., MPS

Behnam's formal education includes a Ph.D. in the Workforce Education and Development (WFED) with concentration on Organization Development (OD) and Human Resources Development (HRD) from the Pennsylvania State University, a master's degree in Professional Studies in Organization Development and Change (OD&C) from the Pennsylvania State University, World Campus, and a bachelor's degree in Psychology from the University of Phoenix.

He is also the founder and president of Primeco Education, a coaching and consulting company working with individuals, teams, and organizations on their personal and professional development since 1993. He has authored and published five books in the personal and professional development industry. His recent books include *Building Organizational Coaching Culture: Creating Effective Environment for Growth & Success in Organizations* (2024), *Successful Supervisory Leadership: Exerting Positive Influence while Leading People* (2023), *Transformational Coaching for Effective Leadership, Creating Sustainable Change through Shifting Paradigms* (2023), and *High-Performance Coaching for Managers: A Step-by-Step Approach to Increase Employees Performance & Productivity* (2022), and before this title, he published *Organization Development Intervention* (2021). The other two titles are *Anatomy of Upset; Restoring Harmony* (2015), and *Conspiracy for Greatness; Mastery of Love Within* (2009). Besides these books, he has designed and facilitated 17 coaching modules for individuals, couples, the public, teams, and organizations; 9 audio/video workshops; 16 articles on personal and professional development topics; and 21 seminars and workshops.

He is an accomplished business manager, known widely as a dynamic writer, speaker, personal and professional development coach, and trainer. Implementing his skills as a passionate, visionary leader, he produces extraordinary results in record time. Behnam brings his broad experience and successful track record to each project, whether it involves personal development, implementing customer-focused programs, integrating technologies, redesigning operational core processes, or delivering strategic initiatives.

Before designing Primeco Education technology, Behnam led educational programs and later managed operations for a global education organization based in two major US cities. During these seven years, Behnam worked personally with tens of thousands of participants. He was accountable for expanding customer participation, training program leaders, increasing sales, and improving the finance department's efficiency and management of the overall operations for the staff and their team of over four hundred volunteers, who together served an annual client base of over 10,000.

Behnam designed the Primeco Education technology in 2001. Since then, he and his team members have helped countless businesses and individuals not only to achieve their goals but also to transform their thinking. His proven methodology and approach are based on his extensive experience in business and human relations. Behnam enjoyed expanding into psychology as an addition to his already strong background in philosophy and ontology. He particularly enjoyed and was inspired by Applicative Inquiry, Positive Psychology and the work of many psychologists who used the Humanistic Psychology approach for empowering and treating their patients. Behnam finds these two psychological approaches like his own work, methodology, and approaches.

William J. Rothwell, Ph.D., DBA, SPHR, SHRM-SCP, RODC, FLMI, CPTD Fellow.

William Rothwell is President of Rothwell & Associates, Inc., Rothwell & Associates, LLC, and Rothwell & Associates Korea. As a consultant he has worked with over 50 multinational companies and countless governments and nonprofits. In addition to the three consulting companies he founded, he also founded 3 small businesses (a vacation rental home company employing three people, a personal care home for the elderly licensed for 50 beds employing 27 people, and an 18-unit motel employing 9 people).

As Distinguished Professor at Penn State University, University Park, where he has taught for 30 years, he is co-Professor-in-Charge of an online and onsite academic program that offers a master's degree in Organization Development and a Ph.D. in Workforce Education and Development with an emphasis in Talent Development/Organization Development. Before joining Penn State in 1993, he had over 15 years of executive-level work experience in human resources, talent development, and Organization Development leadership in government (the Illinois Office of the Auditor General) and in business (Franklin Life Insurance Co., a wholly owned subsidary of a multi-national company, #48 on the Fortune 500 list).

With a combined total of 50 years of work experience in HR, OD, and Talent Development, he has published 159 books in the Human Resources field. He was given a special award in 1998 from the American Society for Training and Development for his leadership on *ASTD Models for Human Performance Improvement*; in 2004, he was awarded the Best Book Award from the Academy of HRD for *The Strategic Development of Talent*; in 2004, he was given Penn State University's Graduate Faculty Teaching Award (only one per year is given on Penn State's 24 campuses); in 2011, he was given the Association for Talent Development's (ATD) Distinguished Contribution to Workplace Learning and Performance Award and also the UNICEF and Kiwanis International's Walter Zeller Medal (Award) for International Service; in 2016, he was given the Distinguished Researcher Award by the College of Education at Penn State; in 2022, he was given the Organization Development Network's Lifetime Achievement Award and also Penn State University's highest award for international work; and in 2023, he was inducted into the International Adult and Continuing Education Hall of Fame (hosted globally by the University of Oklahoma). He has conducted training on training, Organization Development, Talent Development, coaching, and much more on every continent except Antarctica and has taught in universities globally including 83 trips to China and 32 trips to Singapore.

His recent books since 2020 include *Building an Organizational Coaching Culture* (2024); *Mastering the Art of Process Consultation and Virtual Group Coaching Simulation* (2023); *Successful Supervisory Leadership* (2023); *Transformational Coaching* (2023); *Succession Planning for Small and Family Businesses* (2022); *High-Performance Coaching for Managers* (2022); *Rethinking Diversity, Equity, and Inclusion* (2022); *Organization Development (OD) Interventions: Executing Effective Organizational Change* (2021); *Virtual Coaching to Improve Group Relationships* (2021); *The Essential HR Guide for Small Business and Start Ups* (2020); *Increasing Learning and*

Development's Impact through Accreditation (2020); *Adult Learning Basics*, 2nd ed. (2020); and *Workforce Development: Guidelines for Community College Professionals*, 2nd ed. (2020).

Aileen Zaballero, Ph.D., CPTD

Aileen G. Zaballero, Ph.D., CPTD, is a senior partner of Rothwell & Associates, Inc. (R&A) with a dual-title Ph.D. in Workforce Education and Comparative International Education from Pennsylvania State University. She has been a Certified Professional in Talent Development since 2009. Aileen has over 25 years of experience in the learning and development field and more than 10 years researching what adults learn, how they know it, and the value placed on types of knowledge. As an instructional designer and learning consultant, she created various educational and training materials, including online videos and webinars. As a practitioner and researcher, Aileen believes it is critical to bridge academic discourse in workforce education (theory) with industry best practices (application) to address complex issues. She led a project to examine instructional design competencies; was a researcher and subject matter expert (SME) in competency modeling for the Advance Commercial Building Workforce (ACBW) project, funded by the US Department of Energy, aimed to develop a competency model and career map; and was part of the team that developed ATD's Talent Development Framework.

Aileen has authored and co-authored chapters in Performance *Consulting-Applying Performance Improvement in Human Resource Development* (2013); co-authored a book on supervisory leadership, *Successful Supervisory Leadership: Exerting Positive Influence while Leading People* (2023); co-edited and co-authored *Optimizing Talent in the Federal Workforce* (2014); co-authored a chapter in *Organization Development Fundamentals: Managing Strategic Change* (2014); co-edited *The Competency Toolkit*, 2nd ed. (2014); and co-authored *Increasing Learning & Development's Impact through Accreditation: How to Drive-Up Training Quality, Employee Satisfaction and ROI* (2020).

Introduction

Supervisors serve as intermediaries between frontline staff and middle/upper management. Hence, they need to engage in good communication within the business to exhibit responsiveness and thoughtfulness as leaders. The second installment in the *Successful Supervisory Leadership* series, titled *The Inclusive, Empathetic, and Relational Supervisor: Managing Diverse Employees through Interpersonal Relationships*, will be the second book out of five volumes in the series.

Researchers increasingly recognize that adopting a "person-focused" strategy has a greater impact on performance. Modern employees seek greater emphasis on cooperation rather than rivalry and prioritize building connections over focusing on productivity. They want improved work relations. Relational supervisors must possess the necessary skills to actively listen, offer constructive comments, and engage in respectful discussions that successfully communicate the value of workers to the firm. The supervisor prioritizes building and maintaining relationships rather than focusing just on tasks or transactions. By prioritizing interpersonal connections, the supervisor may foster a sense of belonging and inclusion among the team members.

Organizations are facing difficulties due to the unprecedented surge in employee resignations. Employees desire a work environment that fosters a more cohesive community characterized by enhanced social and interpersonal bonds with their colleagues and bosses. They prefer meaningful interactions, even if they do not necessarily occur in person, rather than just transactions. This needs a work environment in which individuals are motivated, involved, and recognized. Organizations must enhance their comprehension of their people, while leaders should cultivate a more profound empathy for the experiences and challenges faced by their personnel.

The Inclusive, Empathetic, and Relational Supervisor: Managing Diverse Employees through Interpersonal Relationships will build on the belief that people are the most valuable resource and that everyone should be treated with dignity and respect. The authors will provide tools to self-assess intrapersonal/interpersonal relationships and communication; develop a positive work environment; and evaluate empathy, inclusion, and listening skills.

Chapter 1

Overview and Background

Introduction

The traditional boundaries of work have changed significantly in the modern workplace. With the increasing diversity, decentralization, and digital interconnectedness of organizations, how employees interact, teams collaborate, and leadership styles have had to change. More than ever, there is a growing recognition of the profound need for an inclusive, empathetic, and relationship-oriented work environment. A company that wants to be successful in the 21st century cannot simply put on a facade of inclusion; it must be embedded in the corporate culture. An inclusive work environment ensures that every individual feels valued and can contribute authentically, regardless of background. Empathy enables leaders and teams to understand and address the unique challenges and needs of their colleagues, promoting a culture of mutual respect and understanding. Fostering a relational environment encourages open communication, collaboration, and a shared sense of purpose, elevating collective performance. Organizations that prioritize inclusion, empathy, and relationship building will attract and retain top talent and drive innovation, productivity, and sustainable growth.

As a supervisor, you may have observed the traditional models that prioritize hierarchy and directive leadership. However, such approaches appear outdated and not suitable for today's constantly changing environment. By navigating your role as the primary interface with employees, you have a profound and decisive influence on organizational relationships. Your leadership style, your ability to listen, and how you address and manage both challenges and successes directly influence the collaborative atmosphere and team dynamics. Remember that employees often see the values, ethics, and

DOI: 10.4324/9781003413493-1

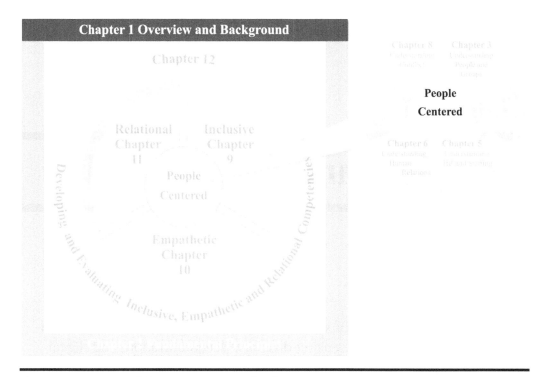

Figure 1.1 *Successful Supervisory Leadership Series Book II Structure.* **Note: Authors' original creation.**

culture of the company in tangible form through your lens. Every decision you make, the strategies you use, and the empathy you show are not just managerial practices. They become the linchpin, defining and refining organizational relationships and culture.

As outlined in Figure 1.1 of the *Successful Supervisory Leadership Series Book II Structure*, we begin at the uppermost frame that sets the stage with a comprehensive backdrop, emphasizing the primary need for a supervisor who is inclusive, empathetic, and competent at building relationships. We investigate the changing World of Work and how it has influenced traditional paradigms, changed the way we interact with our colleagues in the workplace, and emphasized teamwork, which is a central evolution in the supervisory role. In this context, the core of this book is devoted to a people-centric supervisory approach.

Key Concepts

This chapter will cover the following key concepts:

- Changing World of Work
- Evolution of the Supervisor's Role
- People-Centered Supervisor

Definitions

The following definitions of key terms will help to better understand the main elements of this chapter:

- ***Fourth Industrial Revolution***: popularized by Klaus Schwab, founder and executive chairman of the World Economic Forum (WEF). According to Schwab, the Fourth Industrial Revolution is characterized by a fusion of technologies that blur the boundaries between the physical, digital, and biological domains. This revolution is marked by emerging technologies, such as (Schwab & Davis, 2018):
  - Artificial intelligence (AI) and machine learning.
  - The Internet of Things (IoT).
  - Robotics and autonomous vehicles.
  - 3D printing and advanced manufacturing.
  - Biotechnology, including gene editing.
  - Quantum computing.
  - Advanced materials and nanotechnology.
  - Blockchain and distributed ledger technology.
- ***Scientific Management (Taylorism)***: Frederick Winslow Taylor developed the theory of Scientific Management, also known as Taylorism, in the late 19th and early 20th centuries. The goal of this management style is to improve economic efficiency and labor productivity. It involves (Taneja et al., 2011; Taylor, 1911):
  - *Time and Motion*: Analysis of work processes to determine the most efficient way to perform tasks.
  - *Standardization*: The creation of standardized methods and procedures to complete tasks efficiently.
  - *Task Division*: Breaking down tasks into simplified, repetitive actions.
- ***Human Relations Movement***: The human relations movement emerged in the early 20th century as a reaction to the traditional, mechanistic approach to management and the efficiency-focused principles of Taylorism (Scientific Management). It emphasized the importance of understanding the social and psychological factors that influence employee performance and satisfaction. The movement shifted organizational thinking from task orientation to people orientation (Carson, 2005).
- ***Management by Objectives (MBO)***: A management technique in which managers and employees collaborate to set, discuss, and agree

upon specific, clear, measurable objectives for a particular period. Once the objectives are established, they are used as benchmarks to measure performance and evaluate outcomes (Drucker, 2012).

■ ***Total Quality Management (TQM)***: A management approach that focuses on continuous improvement in all functions of an organization, with the aim of enhancing product quality and delivering superior value to customers (Golhar, 1997).

Changing World of Work

Carroll and Conboy (2020) have pointed out that the pandemic has brought about sudden and profound changes in workplace practices and organizational operations. Many workers globally had to adapt their work patterns too as the virus spread quickly throughout the world (Davison, 2020; Matli, 2020). From a business perspective, employers were compelled to find innovative ways to maintain productivity while their workforce operated remotely from home. This shift, although not a new idea, became a new operating norm for many employees. Furthermore, there has been a significant impact on mental health in our broader social context. More people experience anxiety, stress, depression, and other mental health challenges.

As a supervisor, you are at the confluence of many of these workplace shifts, which will influence your management practices, team dynamics, and role as a leader. These changes have led to new organizational conditions, policies, and strategies, all of which you must understand, adapt to, and utilize. Furthermore, it's imperative to recognize the various benefits but also to proactively mitigate the challenges. The following section will discuss a few emerging issues that greatly impact your role as a supervisor, as illustrated in Figure 1.2.

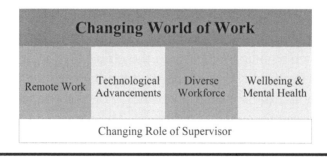

Figure 1.2   Changing World of Work. *Note:* **Authors' original creation.**

Remote Work

Remote work is not a novel idea. It dates to the 1960s, when telecommunication networks allowed employees to work from home (Nilles, 1975). Over the years, as technology has advanced, particularly with the proliferation of the internet and various collaboration tools, remote work has become more feasible and surged in popularity. Its myriad benefits have made it an increasingly alluring option for employees and organizations.

One primary advantage is the elimination of daily commutes. It not only saves time but also reduces stress. Furthermore, the research underscores that customizable workspaces tailored to individual preferences have been proven to elevate distress and enhance productivity (Popovici & Popovici, 2020). Organizations are more appealing to top talent and potentially increase retention rates when employees have more autonomy and control over their work environment and schedules.

As the World of Work continues to evolve, many organizations have opted to implement hybrid work models, enabling your team to balance remote and on-site work effectively. This approach provides flexibility while ensuring a certain level of physical presence in the office. However, whether fully remote or hybrid, there are certain prerequisites. Companies need to invest and upgrade their digital infrastructure and technology, including robust IT systems, secure remote access solutions, collaboration tools, and cloud-based platforms (Graves & Karabayeva, 2020; Thomas et al., 2020). These enhancements facilitate seamless communication and data sharing between you and your team members. You may also want to consider the necessary security to protect sensitive data during remote work. This requires prioritizing cybersecurity measures, implementing data encryption, requiring multifactor authentication, and providing your team members with training on cybersecurity best practices to ensure the protection of critical information (Flores, 2019; Matli, 2020; Ozimek, 2020; Fialho, 2022).

While the advantages of remote work are evident, it's equally crucial to acknowledge and proactively address the associated obstacles. One primary challenge is the potential for reduced face-to-face communication and collaboration. Because you're not physically present with your team, working remotely can sometimes lead to feelings of isolation. Additionally, it can also lead to decreased team morale. If you want your team to communicate effectively, resolve conflicts, and foster a sense of cohesion with remote team members, you may have to put in some extra effort. Consider scheduling regular virtual meetings, implementing collaboration tools, and providing clear guidelines for remote communication. In addition, facilitating virtual team activities can help you connect your team by fostering unity, trust, and understanding. It is important to note that it goes beyond just engaging in activities. It's about creating opportunities for team members to share and learn about each other on a personal level (Flores, 2019; McDaniel et al., 2021; Gong et al., 2023).

Another challenge many supervisors face is monitoring the performance of remote individuals. Tracking the progress of the work, assessing the quality of the work, and ensuring everyone is held accountable for their work is not as straightforward as on-site assessments. In contrast to on-site work, where productivity and work quality can be readily assessed through direct observation and in-person interactions, remote work requires a more intricate approach to performance management (Flores, 2019; Ozimek, 2020). It is essential to establish clear and objective performance metrics, but aligning these metrics with remote employees' tasks and responsibilities can be complex. As a supervisor, an effective strategy for addressing these challenges is to schedule regular one-on-one check-in sessions with your team members. These meetings provide you with a valuable opportunity to monitor their progress, address any challenges they may face, and collaboratively set goals. These interactions play a crucial role in enhancing communication within your team and promoting greater accountability among team members.

Technological Advancements

One of the most significant changes we have seen in recent years is the integration of technology in almost every facet of work. As a supervisor, it's crucial to understand that the *Fourth Industrial Revolution*, a concept coined by Klaus Schwab, signifies a new era of technological advancement that directs profound transformation across industries, reshapes established business models, and redefines the essence of work itself. The convergence of advanced technologies like artificial intelligence (AI), the Internet of Things (IoT), 3D printing, blockchain, biotechnology, and more are interconnected and can significantly enhance each other's capabilities (Barley, 2020).

As you navigate this revolution, be aware that automation and AI technologies are advancing at an unprecedented pace, which will have significant implications for your team. Technological tools can automate routine and repetitive tasks, impacting various roles across all industries. However, it's crucial to recognize that technological advancement extends beyond task automation. With the rise of technology, some jobs that may have existed in the past may no longer be needed, while others will evolve or emerge, creating an increased demand for skills related to technology, data analysis, and problem-solving. What makes this situation even more challenging is that the rate of change is so rapid that skills and knowledge can become outdated and obsolete in a very short period. This reality places a significant responsibility on your shoulders as a supervisor.

As the team leader, one of your primary responsibilities is to encourage and facilitate continuous learning within your team. This involves encouraging but actively facilitating opportunities for growth and development. Continuous learning and adaptability are not mere buzzwords; they are the cornerstones of survival and success in a rapidly evolving work. Your role as a supervisor is pivotal in ensuring your team stays relevant, competitive, and ready to tackle the challenges and opportunities that the Fourth Industrial Revolution presents (Schwab & Davis, 2018; Barley, 2020). They need to be empowered to adapt and acquire new skills. Furthermore, competency development and training can equip your employees with the skills and knowledge they need to thrive in the ever-changing job market. It is not just an investment in their future—it's an investment in the future success of your team and organization, therefore, a strategic imperative.

Diverse Workforce

The impact of technology extends beyond just altering our work methods; it has also revolutionized our professional relationships and the composition of our workforce. One of its remarkable feats is the dissolution of geographic boundaries, allowing us to collaborate effortlessly with individuals and teams across the globe. On a broader scale, the workforce is undergoing profound transformations in the United States, marked by increasing racial and ethnic diversity. Factors drive this transformation, such as growing immigration and the rising number of women entering the workforce. According to Ozkanzanc-Pan, the United States is projected to reach a demographic milestone of becoming "minority white" by 2045 (2021, p. 2646). These demographic shifts are ongoing, presenting both fresh opportunities and challenges for organizations, many of which still predominantly have male and white individuals occupying leadership positions. "The lack of growth and leadership opportunities for women and minorities has been noted by executive themselves, who state that their places of work do not invest enough in leadership development for millennials, women or minorities" (p. 2646).

Many organizations acknowledge the advantages of having a workforce that is diverse in race, ethnicity, gender, sexual orientation, and other factors, placing more emphasis on diversity and inclusion. Chapter 5 will further discuss the role of the organization's HR in implementing DEI&B initiatives. However, as a supervisor, you play an important role in creating a work environment where everyone feels included and valued, and where differences are seen as strengths. Diversity, Equity, and Inclusion (DEI) practices are your compass in effectively managing a multidimensional workforce. Your responsibility extends beyond effective communication. You must be the watchdog to affirm that every team member is treated with fairness and respect, as well as inclusivity, regardless of their cultural background, race, gender, employment status, location, or nature of their work.

However, within this evolution of the workforce, we must address additional concerns regarding the ethical dimensions and enduring impacts on the job market. Scholars have aptly drawn attention to the concept of "automate[d] inequality" (Ozjazanc-Pan, 2019, p. 2646), shedding light on how various technologies, such as AI-driven surveillance systems, can inadvertently perpetuate societal biases. For example, many AI and machine learning systems heavily depend on historical data, which may include discriminatory practices or prejudices. These algorithms can perpetuate biases that may unintentionally discriminate against specific groups. This raises ethical concerns and poses challenges for fairness and equity (Houser, 2019).

The benefits of a diverse workforce are widely recognized to promote creativity, innovation, and improved problem-solving capabilities. Diverse teams offer a kaleidoscope of views and experiences and enrich the decision-making process with a broader range of ideas. However, DEI practices essentially come down to you as a supervisor. Regardless of the aim to create an inclusive organizational culture where employees feel valued and empowered to contribute their best, if the actions of management and supervisors do not align, DEI becomes a superficial concept. Your role as a supervisor is paramount in shaping organizational culture through your actions, decisions, and communication. You use the power to lead by example, to promote inclusivity through your recruitment and promotion decisions, and to passionately advocate for DEI initiatives within your organization.

Employee Well-Being and Mental Health

The COVID-19 pandemic has brought mental health and well-being into sharp focus, as people around the world grappled with unprecedented challenges, such as social isolation, blurred work–life boundaries, and heightened stress levels. This has underscored the critical need for mental health support, particularly within the workplace. Initiatives like Mental Health Awareness Month in May have played a pivotal role in raising awareness and reducing stigma surrounding mental health issues through increased media coverage. This cultural shift toward greater acceptance and understanding of mental health has seamlessly extended to the corporate sphere, encouraging more open dialogues about mental well-being (Yu et al., 2021; Hammer et al., 2022).

Employers are now increasingly cognizant of their ethical and legal responsibilities to cultivate a safe and healthy work environment that encompasses mental health considerations. Extensive research consistently demonstrates that neglecting mental health can have dire consequences, including reduced employee productivity, heightened absenteeism, and elevated turnover rates. Conversely, a mentally well workforce tends to exhibit enhanced focus, creativity, and innovation, thereby contributing substantial contributions to organizational success (Mohr et al., 2021).

The younger generations, such as Millennials and Generation Z, who are entering the workforce, are placing a premium on achieving a healthy work–life balance and nurturing their mental well-being. Recognizing that these generations will soon constitute most of the workforce, many companies are actively reshaping their workplace cultures to make them more appealing to these employees (Sánchez-Hernández et al., 2019). Organizations that wholeheartedly invest in and demonstrate unwavering commitment to employee mental health are often rewarded with a more positive and supportive workplace culture. This, in turn, fosters increased collaboration, improved communication, and a heightened sense of belonging among all employees.

As a supervisor, understanding the critical nature of mental well-being, especially in today's diverse workforce, is of the utmost importance. Your workforce is a mosaic of individuals from diverse cultural backgrounds, each bringing their unique values and beliefs regarding mental health. With cultural sensitivity and awareness at the forefront, you comprehend that different team members may possess distinctive ways of expressing and coping with mental health issues. In response, you foster an environment of open dialogue and engage in ongoing cultural competence training to navigate these differences with respect and understanding. Furthermore, recognizing that remote employees are often challenged by work–life boundaries, which can potentially lead to overwork and burnout. In your role as their supervisor, it is incumbent upon you to actively encourage a balanced work–life equilibrium and discourage excessive overtime, and you must remain vigilant for any signs of burnout. Equally vital is providing accessible resources for stress management and holistic well-being, as these can make a substantial difference. To effectively promote the well-being of your team members, you should adopt an empathetic leadership style tailored to their individual needs and well-being (Rothwell et al., 2023).

Evolution of the Supervisor's Role

As a supervisor, it is crucial to acknowledge the historical evolution of your role and how this evolution has shaped your present-day responsibilities. During the early stages of the Industrial Revolution, supervisors predominantly functioned as overseers within factories and manufacturing plants. Their primary objective was to ensure worker compliance and prevent time wastage. These early supervisors wielded authority to uphold stringent routines and production processes, fostering productivity by enforcing discipline and rule adherence. The evolution supervisor's role has been a progression of ideas and approaches to organizing work and leading people (see Figure 1.3).

Scientific Management (Taylorism)

One notable figure in developing supervisory practices is Frederick Taylor, an American engineer and management theorist. In his seminal work, "The Principles of Scientific Management" (1911), Taylor introduced a more systematic approach to enhancing production efficiency. He applied engineering principles to optimize work processes, significantly impacting the supervision of workers. Supervisors were responsible for closely

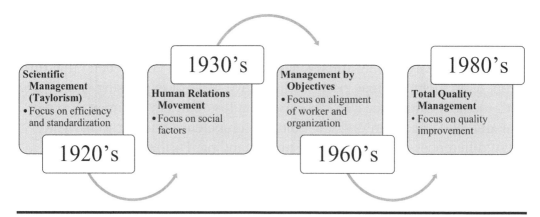

Figure 1.3   The evolution of the supervisor's role. *Note:* **Authors' original creation.**

monitoring, controlling, and assessing segmented work processes to iden-tify the most efficient and effective methods, thereby maximizing pro-ductivity and minimizing time and cost inefficiencies (Taneja et al., 2011; Taylor, 1911). This approach, often referred to as Taylorism, brought about the standardization of organizational processes and procedures. However, it received criticism for viewing humans as an extension of the machinery and overlooking social dynamics and the human aspect of work (Taneja et al., 2011; Carson, 2005).

Human Relations Movement

The *Human Relations Movement* emerged in direct response to the limi-tations of scientific management, a system that prioritized efficiency and task-oriented methods. This movement instead advocated for focusing on the relationships between employees and management, recognizing the inter-personal dimensions of work. It concentrated on understanding and effec-tively managing the social and psychological aspects of work. This evolution eventually led to the development of personnel work, which further evolved into the study and management of human resources within an organization, which we now know as human resource management (Carson, 2005).

One of the pioneering contributors to the *Human Relations Movement* was Mary Parker Follett. Her philosophy centered on considering human relations and recognizing the social dimensions within organizations as integral elements of effective management. In her view, organizations should be perceived as social communities, and managers should prioritize integrat-ing individual and group interests. She introduced the concept of "power with" instead of "power over," advocating for collaborative efforts between managers and employees to achieve shared goals, rather than relying on hierarchical control structures (Carson, 2005, p. 454). Follett made signifi-cant contributions to the evolution of management theory and supervisory practice, with a primary focus on group dynamics, conflict resolution, and integration. Her work had a profound and lasting impact, highlighting the pivotal role of individuals and their relationships within the workplace. Her ideas laid the foundation for more participatory and collaborative manage-ment approaches that are now widely acknowledged and adopted. Her con-tributions bridged the gap between the principles of scientific management (Taylorism) and the subsequent Hawthorne Studies (Carson, 2005).

The 1920s were marked by significant economic growth and prosperity in the United States following the end of World War I. The economic expansion was due to increased industrialization, technological advancements, and a booming stock market. One notable company was the Western Electric Hawthorne Works, which manufactured telephone equipment and employed about 40,000 people. A progressive workplace, they provided their employees with a company-paid pension plan, vacation days, and sickness disability pay. In 1924, the National Academy of Science conducted several studies to determine how factory lighting affects work productivity. However, the results were inconclusive. The original study was followed up by later studies, collectively known as the Hawthorne-Harvard Cooperative Inquiry or Hawthorne Studies. These studies were the first scientific inquiry into employee attitudes and the first formal employee interviewing program that allowed individuals to express their feelings about their jobs, supervisors, or working conditions. The results indicated that workers were more responsive to social factors—such as their manager and coworkers. The studies also found that although financial incentives are essential to worker productivity, social factors are equally important (Carson, 2005).

The Hawthorne Studies evolved into a comprehensive exploration of human relation–oriented management practices, illuminating the need to enhance interpersonal and communication skills when dealing with employees. Consequently, the Hawthorne Studies laid the foundation for the human relations movement in management, strongly emphasizing treating employees as unique individuals and acknowledging their social and emotional needs. Furthermore, these studies emphasized the pivotal role of supervisors in fostering positive work environments. Effective supervision, open communication, and adept leadership were recognized as critical components for enhancing employee morale and productivity. The Hawthorne Studies also challenged the belief that productivity was solely driven by external factors, such as technology and processes. Instead, they underscored the central role of human factors in determining organizational performance. This paradigm shift in management philosophy led to a heightened focus on employee welfare, motivation, and job satisfaction. Managers and supervisors began to recognize the profound significance of interpersonal skills and employee engagement as essential drivers of success (Carson, 2005).

Chapter 6 delves deeper into human relations, emphasizing the various facets of interpersonal relationships. This chapter sheds light on the significance of rapport in the workplace, the pivotal human relations skills required, and the responsibilities associated with upholding effective human connections. Additionally, it offers valuable tips for fostering and sustaining impactful human relations, outlines the primary goals of these relations, and provides insights into identifying and surmounting barriers to effective interpersonal interactions.

Management by Objectives (MBO)

As organizations grew in size and complexity, traditional command and control management approaches were perceived as inadequate for effectively managing large and diverse workforces. There was a growing recognition that employees' efforts should be aligned with organizational objectives. Management by Objectives (MBO) was a management philosophy and approach that gained prominence in the mid-20th century, especially in the 1950s and 1960s. Championed by Peter Drucker, a renowned management consultant, MBO was a desire to address the limitations of traditional management practices and foster greater alignment between individual and organizational goals. MBO introduced the practice of setting specific, measurable, achievable, relevant, and time-bound (SMART) objectives for employees (Drucker, 2012).

MBO encourages managers and supervisors to collaborate with employees to establish goals that align with the organization's broader objectives. Regular performance appraisals and feedback discussions are integral to the MBO approach, prompting ongoing conversations about progress, challenges, and adjustments required to achieve objectives. With MBO, employees understood their roles and responsibilities better, fostering accountability for their performance and contributions to organizational objectives. Effective communication is a cornerstone that requires open communication channels with employees. These channels were of the utmost importance to ensure that the objectives remained relevant and that obstacles were promptly addressed. This approach shifted the emphasis from micromanaging processes to evaluating outcomes and results. Focus is on what needs to be achieved, rather than dictating how tasks should be performed (Drucker, 2012).

Total Quality Management (TQM)

As international competition intensified, organizations were forced to reassess their quality strategies to maintain a competitive edge in the global market. In the late 1970s and early 1980s, the developed economies of North America and Western Europe faced economic challenges due to Japan's formidable competition, which earned a reputation for producing high-quality goods at competitive prices. In response, companies began to reevaluate quality control techniques and how Japanese firms had effectively employed them.

At this critical juncture, W. Edwards Deming emerged as a pivotal figure in the development of Total Quality Management (TQM). After World War II, Deming was invited to Japan to contribute to the nation's post-war reconstruction efforts. His teachings made an indelible mark on Japanese manufacturing and industry. Deming introduced innovative concepts, such as quality circles, that encouraged the active participation of employees in initiatives aimed at improving product quality. He underscored the significance of systems thinking, urging organizations to view themselves as intricate systems comprising interconnected processes. He argued that the attempt to improve isolated components of a system without considering the holistic picture could prove counterproductive. Furthermore, Deming's work significantly contributed to the widespread adoption of the Plan-Do-Check-Act (PDCA) cycle, also known as the Deming Cycle. This iterative framework involved planning, implementation, evaluation, and adjustments, serving as a foundational tool within TQM and continuous improvement practices (Golhar, 1997).

As a modern supervisor, gaining insight into the historical context of your role's evolution can be immensely valuable. It enables you to strike a balance between efficiency and your team's well-being effectively. Your role as a supervisor has evolved significantly. It has transitioned from the early principles of Taylorism, which stressed the standardization of organizational processes, to the human relations movement, which underscored the significance of interpersonal skills and employee engagement. Further development led to Management by Objectives (MBO), which shifted the focus from dictating task methods to achieving specific goals, and Total Quality Management (TQM), which strongly emphasized the iterative process of continuous quality improvement.

This historical perspective acknowledges the lessons of the past and underscores the need for a more holistic approach to leadership. The rapidly changing work environment and the evolution of work itself require organizations to seek solutions and strategies to equip you to be more effective in your role. However, it's important to note that what makes an exceptional supervisor can vary depending on the industry and specific situation. One such strategy gaining prominence is the people-centered approach.

People-Centered Supervisor

The evolution of management from Taylorism to TQM has laid the foundation for your role as a supervisor in today's business environment. Standardizing organizational processes and procedures, and the influence of social interactions, job satisfaction, and continuous improvement on employee performance and productivity, laid the foundation for a more people-oriented management approach. Concurrently, labor unions and worker advocacy groups were pivotal in advocating for improved working conditions, fair treatment, and employee rights, thereby pressuring management to pay further attention to employee welfare (Black & La Venture, 2017; Taneja et al., 2011; Carson, 2005).

As work evolved, employees began to expect more than just a paycheck from their jobs. They sought meaning, purpose, and personal growth in their work, prompting organizations to adopt people-centered practices to attract and retain talent. Influential figures in the development of people-centered management include Abraham Maslow, Douglas McGregor, and Frederick Herzberg (Rothwell et al., 2023). To learn more about their contribution, read the first book of this series, *Successful Supervisory Leadership: Exerting Positive Influence while Leading People.*

People-centered supervision is an approach that puts well-being, growth, and satisfaction at the forefront. This approach not only values employees as valuable assets but also recognizes that their commitment, motivation, and development are crucial to achieving organizational goals. The people-centered approach can be visualized as a framework with three essential segments: relationship building, inclusivity, and empathy (see Figure 1.4). These three components are foundational to creating a work environment that prioritizes the well-being and satisfaction of employees:

- Inclusive: Effectively Managing Diversity, Equity, and Belonging
- Empathetic: Managing Interpersonal and Intrapersonal Skills
- Relational: Managing with and through People

Inclusive: Effectively Managing Diversity, Equity, and Belonging

As a supervisor, adopting a people-centered approach is essential for effectively managing diversity, equity, and inclusion (DEI) and cultivating a workplace culture where your team members truly belong. When you, as

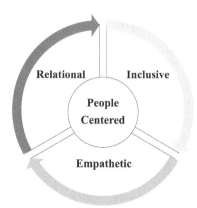

Figure 1.4 The inclusive, empathetic, and relational supervisor framework. *Note*: Authors' original creation.

a supervisor, ensure that your team members feel valued and respected for their diverse backgrounds, perspectives, and experiences, you create an environment where people can openly express themselves without fear of being judged.

Your role as an inclusive supervisor is to ensure that every team member consistently receives fair and respectful treatment, without ever feeling inferior to their colleagues. To achieve this, it's important to explore innovative ideas that leverage multiple perspectives, both within and outside your department. Strive for justice through impartial practices, encourage open and transparent communication to foster inclusivity, and employ emotional and social intelligence to foster a profound sense of belonging among your team members.

Chapter 2 will explore key concepts such as Cross-Cultural Competence, Generational Cohort, and critical race theory. These concepts provide valuable insights and tools to help you, as a supervisor, navigate the complexities of diversity, equity, and inclusion, ultimately contributing to developing a workplace where every team member feels valued, respected, and an integral part of the team.

Chapter 9 focuses on the intricacies of being an inclusive supervisor. We will address pressing questions, such as: "What challenges are contemporary organizations facing?" This chapter emphasizes the importance of managing diversity, equity, inclusion, and belonging (DEI&B) initiatives in the workplace. In this chapter, we will explore the crucial roles played by HR departments and senior management, and how your leadership as a supervisor is essential in promoting an inclusive environment and engaging staff in workplace DEI&B programs.

Empathetic: Managing Interpersonal and Intrapersonal Skills

As a supervisor, it's crucial to embrace inclusivity and prioritize empathy in your approach. When your team members feel you care about their well-being, they are more likely to be engaged and productive. An empathetic supervisor can not only understand the needs of their direct reports but also reinforce clear expectations and positive behaviors, ultimately fostering a positive work environment. It's worth noting that, as Shapiro (2002) suggests, empathy is a skill that can be learned.

Being an empathetic supervisor requires comprehending the emotions and perspectives of your team members and responding with compassion and support. This approach creates a safe and supportive workplace environment where everyone feels heard and valued. To achieve this, you must effectively manage interpersonal skills, which involve interacting, communicating, and collaborating effectively with others, and intrapersonal skills, which involve understanding and managing your emotions, thoughts, and behaviors. Incorporating empathy into your supervision is not just an option; it's a fundamental principle. This empathetic approach can yield numerous benefits, such as increased trust, improved communication, and boosted team morale. It also enhances conflict resolution and supports the emotional well-being of your team members.

In your role as supervisor, exploring key concepts such as emotional intelligence and emotional contagion in Chapter 2 will be instrumental. These concepts form the foundation for understanding what empathy truly means, and how developing this skill can greatly benefit your ability to connect with and lead your team effectively. By embracing empathy and its associated skills within a people-centered approach, you contribute to a workplace culture that values the relationships between team members and the well-being of everyone. Ultimately, this approach enhances teamwork, communication, trust, and a sense of belonging among your team, resulting in higher engagement, satisfaction, and productivity.

In Chapter 10, we'll explore the qualities of an empathetic supervisor in more depth by developing your interpersonal and intrapersonal skills. We'll distinguish between hard skills and soft skills, deepen your grasp of emotional intelligence, and offer additional insights to cultivate your interpersonal and intrapersonal capabilities.

Relational: Managing with and through People

As a supervisor, adopting a person-centered approach underscores the importance of building meaningful relationships within your team, firmly anchored in mutual trust. Trust, however, is an emotional bond that doesn't develop instantly. It's built over time through consistent, positive interactions and experiences. According to Serrat, the emotions associated with trust include "affection, gratitude, security, confidence, acceptance, interest, admiration, respect, liking, appreciation, contentment, and satisfaction, all of them necessary ingredients of psychological health" (2017, pp. 627–628). These emotions are essential to psychological well-being and fostering a productive and harmonious workplace. In essence, being a relational supervisor means valuing the human element in leadership. It involves treating team members as individuals, fostering trust and respect, and creating an environment where they feel heard, valued, and motivated. This approach contributes to a workplace culture characterized by positive relationships, teamwork, and a strong sense of belonging, ultimately leading to higher engagement, satisfaction, and productivity.

Chapter 2 of the book will delve deeper into key concepts that will further enhance your skills as a relational supervisor. Social Exchange Theory and Interpersonal Competency will provide invaluable insights and practical tools for building and nurturing robust, trust-based, and mutually beneficial relationships within your workplace.

In Chapter 11, we will further expand the idea of being a relational supervisor. We will introduce relational intelligence, a term that goes beyond mere interactions. It captures the essence of understanding, fostering, and leveraging human connections in the workplace. In this final chapter, we will coalesce everything that drives a people-centered approach to support you in a nurturing, inclusive environment built on relationships.

As a supervisor, you are the "keystone" of building a people-centered culture in a rapidly changing work environment that must adapt to new organizational challenges and technological innovations. Remember the First Industrial Revolution? At that time, the supervisor's role focused on ensuring compliance and discipline with the workers. But times have changed. Influenced by human relations movements, the push of labor unions, and worker advocacy groups, there's been a shift toward a more people-centric approach, emphasizing employee welfare. In today's business setting, it's crucial to foster an inclusive and empathetic environment. By ensuring that every team member feels valued and treated fairly, you pave the way for deeper trust, clearer communication, and a boost in team morale. Empathy, a skill you can cultivate, requires you to tune in to your team's emotions and viewpoints. As an effective supervisor, you must continuously develop your interpersonal skills, which enhance collaboration and communication, and intrapersonal skills, helping you manage your emotions and behaviors. Embrace your role as a relational supervisor, valuing the individuality of each team member and fostering trust and respect. By doing so, you'll cultivate a workplace where everyone feels strong, leading to heightened engagement, satisfaction, and productivity.

Use Table 1.1 to conduct a self-evaluation by rating your clarity and understanding of why it is important to be an Inclusive, Empathetic, and Relational Supervisor.

Follow-Up and Action Plan

After completing Table 1.2, you should design and manage your own activities for developing a learning and improvement action plan to enhance your inclusive, empathetic, and relational approach to working with your team. Use the Action Plan for Learning and Improving (APLI) table (Table 1.2) as a tool to manage such actions.

What's Next?

Building on the idea that supervisors are pivotal in positively shaping their teams, the focus is a people-centric approach that fosters an inclusive culture rooted in empathy. Through nurturing empathetic relationships, the essential groundwork is set. Now, the real work begins, and you are ready to go to Chapter 2, "Fundamental Principles for Inclusive, Empathetic, and Relational Supervisor." Chapter 2 lays the foundation for the remaining chapters, including key concepts such as intersectionality, cultural dimensions, generational cohort, critical race theory, gender norms, emotional intelligence, emotional contagion, empathic accuracy, social exchange theory, and social intelligence. But before you move on, don't forget to review the key takeaways and take a moment to reflect on what you learned in this chapter by completing Table 1.3, End of Chapter 1 Discussion Questions and Inquiries.

Key Takeaways

1. The Positive and Influential Supervisor Framework subdivides a supervisor's characteristic to agile supervisor, resilient supervisor, empathetic

Table 1.1   Supervisor's Self-Assessment as to Why the Inclusive, Empathetic, and Relational Supervisor Is Important

Why Inclusive, Empathetic, and Relational Supervisor Is Important Self-Rating							
Day:		Participant:			Team:		
Month:		Supervisor:			Department:		
Directions: Please rate yourself on a scale of 1 to 5, where 1 is "Strongly Disagree" and 5 is "Strongly Agree." Reflect on each statement honestly and provide comments or examples where necessary.							

	Activities	*Description*	*Rating*				
			1	*2*	*3*	*4*	*5*
1		I recognize the value of a diverse team and understand how DEI&B positively influences productivity and innovation.					
2		I ensure that all team members have access to, and are comfortable with, the necessary technologies to perform their jobs.					
3		I am proactive in promoting mental well-being resources and recognizing the potential strains of technological advancements on mental health.					
4		I continuously reflect on and understand my emotions, strengths, and weaknesses, adapting my supervisory style accordingly.					
5		I foster open channels of communication, ensuring that team members feel comfortable sharing their thoughts and concerns.					
6		I strive to build trust with team members, recognizing the challenges and nuances of both remote and on-site work.					
7		I understand the importance of empowering team members, allowing them to take ownership of their tasks and encouraging autonomy.					
8		I prioritize leading alongside my team, focusing on collaboration rather than a top-down approach.					
		Sub-Total (total of each column)					
		Total of above 5 rating scales					
		Average (above total divided by 8)					

Note: Authors' original creation.

Table 1.2 APLI#1-Connected to Table 1.1

Action Plan for Learning and Improving	
Area of Learning and Improving: *Check List for understanding what it means to be an Inclusive, Empathetic & Relational Supervisor*	
Reference: *Table 1.1*	
Three learning and improvement actions for this month that would bring up my three lowest areas of skills self-ratings to enhance my understanding of what it means to be an inclusive, empathetic, and relational supervisor by at least one on the next rating:	
Action 1:	By When:
Action 2:	By When:
Action 3:	By When:

supervisor, organized supervisor, innovative supervisor, engaged supervisor, relational supervisor, ethical supervisor, and inclusive supervisor. The proportional representation of each slice can fluctuate based on environmental (internal and external) conditions, the team, and the supervisor's strengths.

2. An inclusive supervisor ensures that their direct reports are not only treated fairly and respectfully but never made to feel less than anyone else.
3. An empathetic supervisor can recognize their direct reports' needs, ensure clear expectations and behaviors are reinforced positively, and create a positive work environment.
4. A relational supervisor is skilled to effectively listen, provide constructive feedback, and engage in respectful discussions that let employees know how important they are to the organization.

Discussion Questions and Inquiries

Please take a minute and come up with your own answers to these inquiries and questions. After completing the table and answering these questions, discuss your learning with your higher manager. From your viewpoint, briefly express what you have learned about these areas. Your discussion with your manager about your new knowledge and understanding would be a great pathway to your development as a positive and influential supervisor.

Table 1.3   End of Chapter 1 Questions and Inquiries

Your Perspective on What You Learned in Chapter 1	
Area of Inquiry	*What Did You Learn, and How Will You Use Them in Your Position?*
Changing World of Work: remote work	
Changing World of Work: technological advancements	
Changing World of Work: diverse workforce	
Changing World of Work: employee well-being and mental health	
Evolution of the supervisor's role	
People-centered supervisor	
The inclusive supervisor: effectively managing diversity, equity, and belonging	
The empathetic supervisor: managing interpersonal and intrapersonal skills	
The relational supervisor: managing with and through people	

References

Barley, S. R. (2020). *Work and Technological Change*. Oxford, England: Oxford University Press.

Black, J., & La Venture, K. (2017). The human factor to profitability: People-centered cultures as meaningful organizations. *Journal of Organizational Psychology, 17*(2), 24.

Carroll, N., & Conboy, K. (2020). Normalising the "new normal": Changing tech-driven work practices under pandemic time pressure. *International Journal of Information Management, 55*, 102186–102186. https://doi.org/10.1016/j.ijinfomgt.2020.102186

Carson, C. M. (2005). A historical view of Douglas McGregor's theory Y. *Management Decision, 43*(3), 450–460. https://doi.org/10.1108/00251740510589814

Davison, R. M. (2020). The transformative potential of disruptions: A viewpoint. *International Journal of Information Management, 55*, 102149–102149. https://doi.org/10.1016/j.ijinfomgt.2020.102149

Drucker, P. (2012). *The Practice of Management*. New York, NY: Routledge.

Fialho, J. (2022). Benefits and challenges of remote work. In *Digital Technologies and Transformation in Business, Industry and Organizations* (pp. 1–17). New York, NY, Cham: Springer International Publishing.

Flores, M. F. (2019). Understanding the challenges of remote working and it's impact to workers. *International Journal of Business Marketing and Management (IJBMM), 4*(11), 40–44.

Graves, L. M., & Karabayeva, A. (2020). Managing virtual workers—strategies for success. *IEEE Engineering Management Review, 48*(2), 166–172. https://doi.org/10.1109/EMR.2020.2990386

Golhar, D. Y., Deshpande, S. P., & Ahire, S. L. (1997). Supervisors' role in TQM and non-TQM firms. *The International Journal of Quality & Reliability Management, 14*(6), 555–568. https://doi.org/10.1108/02656719710186173

Gong, B., Tobias, P., & Young-Bristol, J. (2023). Leveraging resources to improve supervisors' vision in the remote workplace. *Management Research Review, 46*(6), 777–789.

Hammer, L. B., Allen, S. J., & Dimoff, J. K. (2022). The missing link: The role of the workplace in mental health. *Workplace Health & Safety, 70*(8), 384–384. https://doi.org/10.1177/21650799221105176

Houser, K. A. (2019). Can AI solve the diversity problem in the tech industry? Mitigating noise and bias in employment decision-making. *Stanford Technology Law Review, 22*(1), 290.

Matli, W. (2020). The changing work landscape as a result of the covid-19 pandemic: Insights from remote workers' life situations in South Africa. *International Journal of Sociology and Social Policy, 40*(9/10), 1237–1256. https://doi.org/10.1108/IJSSP-08-2020-0386

McDaniel, B., O'Connor, K., & Drouin, M. (2021). Work-related technoference at home and feelings of work spillover, overload, life satisfaction and job satisfaction. *International Journal of Workplace Health Management, 14*(5), 526–541. https://doi.org/10.1108/ijwhm-11-2020-0197

Mohr, C. D., Hammer, L. B., Brady, J. M., Perry, M. L., & Bodner, T. (2021). Can supervisor support improve daily employee well-being? Evidence of supervisor training effectiveness in a study of veteran employee emotions. *Journal of Occupational and Organizational Psychology, 94*(2), 400–426. https://doi.org/10.1111/joop.12342

Nilles, J. (1975). Telecommunications and organizational decentralization. *IEEE Transactions on Communications, 23*(10), 1142–1147.

Ozimek, A. (2020). *The Future of Remote Work*. Social Science Research Network (SSRN). Rochester, NY: Elsevier.

Ozkazanc-Pan, B. (2021). Diversity and future of work: Inequality abound or opportunities for all? *Management Decision, 59*(11), 2645–2659. https://doi.org/10.1108/MD-02-2019-0244

Popovici, V., & Popovici, A. L. (2020). Remote work revolution: Current opportunities and challenges for organizations. *Ovidius University Annals, Economic Sciences Series, 20*, 468–472.

Rothwell, W. J., Bakhshandeh, B., & Zaballero, A. G. (2023). *Successful Supervisory Leadership; Exerting Positive Influence While Leading People*. New York, NY: Taylor & Francis Group; Routledge.

Sánchez-Hernández, M. I., González-López, Ó. R., Buenadicha-Mateos, M., & Tato-Jiménez, J. L. (2019). Work-life balance in great companies and pending issues for engaging new generations at work. *International Journal of Environmental Research and Public Health, 16*(24), 5122. https://doi.org/10.3390/ijerph16245122

Schwab, K., & Davis, N. (2018). *Shaping the Future of the Fourth Industrial Revolution*. New York, NY: Currency.

Serrat, O. & SpringerLink (Online service). (2017). *Knowledge solutions: Tools, methods, and approaches to drive organizational performance* (1st ed.). Singapore: Springer. https://doi.org/10.1007/978-981-10-0983-9.

Shapiro, J. (2002). How do physicians teach empathy in the primary care setting? *Academic Medicine, 77*(4), 323–328.

Taneja, S., Pryor, M. G., & Toombs, L. A. (2011). Frederick W. Taylor's scientific management principles: Relevance and validity. *Journal of Applied Management and Entrepreneurship, 16*(3), 60–78.

Taylor, F. W. (1911). *The Principles of Scientific Management*. New York and London: Harper & Brothers Publishers (Republished in 1967).

Thomas, J., Barraket, J., Wilson, C. K., Holcombe-James, I., Kennedy, J., & Rennie, E. (2020). *Measuring Australia's digital divide: The Australian digital inclusion index 2020*. Melbourne, Australia: RMIT and Swinburne University of Technology for Telstra.

Yu, J., Park, J., & Hyun, S. S. (2021). Impacts of the COVID-19 pandemic on employees' work stress, well-being, mental health, organizational citizenship behavior, and employee-customer identification. *Journal of Hospitality Marketing & Management, 30*(5), 529–548. https://doi.org/10.1080/19368623.2021.1867283

Chapter 2

Fundamental Principles for the Inclusive, Empathetic, and Relational Supervisor

Introduction

By prioritizing a person-centered approach that makes a concerted effort to value each team member and consistently exhibiting qualities such as respect and empathy, you can have a significant positive impact on the employee experience. This positive outlook not only increases satisfaction in the workplace but also helps reduce stress and improve mental well-being. The result is a work environment that is conducive to employees reaching their highest potential, which in turn strengthens their loyalty to the organization. From an organizational perspective, a lower turnover rate means fewer recruitment and training costs and minimizing productivity expenditure. Beyond monetary concerns, high turnover can dampen morale and reduce commitment to the mission of the company. Therefore, an inclusive, empathetic, and relationship-oriented supervisory approach is crucial to retaining top talent.

Becoming such a leader is not one-dimensional but a holistic transformation based on diverse theoretical insights. A multifaceted endeavor that requires acumen from various models and frameworks and models to develop critical skills. As shown in Figure 2.1 of the *Successful Supervisory Leadership Series Book II Structure*, the bottom frame sets the foundation for the following chapters and provides a comprehensive understanding

DOI: 10.4324/9781003413493-2

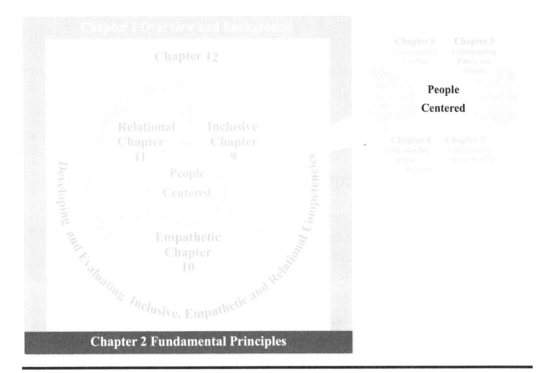

Figure 2.1 *Successful Supervisory Leadership Series Book II Structure.* **Note:** Authors' original creation.

of critical concepts and theories. These include intersectionality, cultural dimensions, generational cohort, critical race theory, gender norms, emotional intelligence, emotional contagion, empathic accuracy, social exchange theory, and social intelligence. When you understand and practice these concepts, it will give you the ability to cultivate an environment that supports inclusivity, empathy, and developing relationships. This will have a positive impact not only on your team but also on the organization as a whole. By increasing communication and cooperation between team members, you can create a more productive and positive working environment.

Key Concepts

This chapter will cover the following key concepts:

- Intersectionality
- Cultural Dimensions
- Generational Cohort
- Critical Race Theory

- Gender Norms
- Emotional Intelligence
- Emotional Contagion
- Empathic Accuracy
- Social Exchange Theory
- Social Intelligence

Managing Diversity, Equity, and Belonging (Inclusive)

As an inclusive supervisor, your responsibility for championing diversity, equity, and belonging (DEB) extends beyond simple acknowledgment. It requires deliberate actions to foster a positive workplace where individuals from diverse backgrounds don't just feel accepted but genuinely valued, respected, and empowered to contribute indisputably. In this environment, individuals from diverse backgrounds feel they are more than just tolerated; they feel valued, respected, and empowered to participate fully. At the core of inclusivity lie the principles of respect and dignity. You treat every employee with the utmost respect, regardless of background, identity, or differences. It's about recognizing and celebrating everyone's unique perspectives, experiences, and contributions to the workplace. Instead of disregarding differences, you embrace them, understanding that variations in background, culture, skills, and experiences are invaluable assets that enrich the organization's collective knowledge and creativity. Equally crucial is ensuring equal opportunities for all employees' growth and advancement. This involves the removal of any barriers hindering career development, providing accessible training and mentoring, and championing fair and unbiased decision-making in promotions and other organizational opportunities (Rothwell et al., 2022, 462023; Zaballero et al., 2012; Herring, 2009; Zaballero, 2009; Cox, 2001; Thomas & Ely, 1996).

Cultivating the skills to be an inclusive supervisor is a complicated process, especially considering the diverse and multifaceted environment in the current workplace. There are many models and theoretical frameworks available that can help explain the complexities of people and the social context we work. First, we will explore Crenshaw's concept of intersectionality, which posits that individuals have multiple, intersecting identities. Subsequently, we'll introduce concepts like cultural dimensions, generational cohort, critical race theory, and gender norms. These are only the beginning points in understanding the complicated elements of diversity, equity, inclusion, and belonging. While you are not expected to be an expert, it's vital to recognize the myriad viewpoints that exist. In order to truly promote an environment in which every team member feels acknowledged, appreciated, and empowered—regardless of background or identity—you must be proactive in understanding those whose viewpoints and experiences differ from your own.

Intersectionality

Intersectionality, a concept introduced by the legal scholar Kimberle Crenshaw, explored the complex ways in which various social identities, such as race and gender, overlap, leading to unique experiences of privilege or discrimination. She critiqued the judicial treatment of a black woman, referencing the case of *DeGraffenreid v General Motors*. In the case, "five black women brought suit against General Motors, alleging that the employer's seniority system perpetuated the effects of past discrimination against Black women" (Crenshaw, 1989, p. 141). Despite the evidence presented, the court dismissed her case, arguing that the company employed both women and black men. This decision overlooked the distinct discrimination black women might experience, separate from black men or white women, underscoring the critical need for an intersectional approach. Crenshaw argued that mainstream feminism often favored the experiences of white women, while anti-racist movements typically focused on black men. However, adopting an intersectional lens suggests that one's societal experience is not just the sum of individual forms of oppression or privilege but also the interconnectedness of these identities. While her early work mainly focused on the interplay between race and gender, the scope of intersectionality has broadened over time, now encompassing identities related to national origin, religion, sexual orientation, gender identity, age, disability, and more (see Figure 2.2).

Understanding and applying the concept of intersectionality can provide you with a broad lens to appreciate the diverse experiences of your team members. Recognizing the multiple identities—be it race, gender, class, sexuality, disability, etc., and the various interconnections—allows you to address potential conflicts and challenges more effectively. As a supervisor, harnessing intersectionality can empower you to craft more inclusive workplace policies, fine-tune mentorship initiatives, and nurture genuine relationships with your team. However, this approach is not without its challenges. Without genuine comprehension, you might inadvertently implement superficial

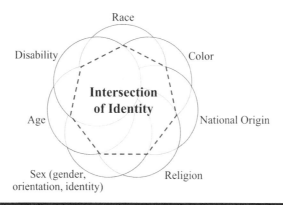

Figure 2.2   Intersection of identity. *Note*: **Authors' original creation.**

changes, reducing "inclusion" to just another corporate catchphrase or flavor of the month. In other instances, organizations prioritize optics over genuine inclusion or tackle isolated incidents of discrimination while ignoring underlying systemic issues that perpetuate inequalities. Remember, this overview merely skims the surface. We encourage you to learn more about the unique characteristics of your team to cultivate an inclusive workspace. It's crucial to grasp that each protected category also has its nuanced frameworks. In this chapter, we'll offer insights into cultural dimensions, generational cohort dynamics, critical race theory, and gender norms. But remember, this is just an introduction. We urge you to delve deeper, understand your team's distinct nuances, and foster an inclusive environment.

Hofstede's Cultural Dimensions

Geert Hofstede, a Dutch social psychologist, developed the cultural dimensions theory after analyzing work values from IBM employees in 40 countries. This framework, rooted in research, has been extensively mentioned in both business and academic circles. It highlights how social culture influences members' values and subsequent behaviors. The key to cross-cultural communication is understanding cultural distinctions. This model helps you understand the importance of cultural variances, which is vital for marketing, negotiations, and team dynamics. Some critics, however, point out its potential for overgeneralization of cultures. Given the data this model is based on originates from the 1970s, it may not be accurate or representative of contemporary cultural changes. This framework offers foundational insights into cultural tendencies. While cultures are continuously evolving, it serves as a valuable starting point. Recognizing that cultures can have profound differences allows you to spark conversations about these variations, fostering open dialogue and enhancing mutual understanding (Hofstede & McCrae, 2004).

Each dimension highlights the differences between cultural groups, including power distance index (PDI), individualism versus collectivism (IDV), masculinity versus femininity (MAS), uncertainty avoidance index (UAI), long-term orientation versus short-term normative orientation (LTO), and indulgence versus restraint (IVR) (Hofstede & McCrae, 2004). Table 2.1 provides a brief description of each dimension and suggested tips.

Generational Cohort

Generational cohort theory has been a topic of interest for researchers, with sociologist Karl Mannheim paving the way in his 1923 essay "The Problem of Generations" (1970). Further advancing this concept, William Strauss and Neil Howe proposed the Strauss-Howe generation theory. They claimed Western societies undergo generational cycles predictably every 80–100 years, a cycle called saeculum. This theory, detailed in its book *Generations: The History of America's Future, 1584 to 2069*, provides a structured framework to chart generations against historical and cultural events. This understanding enables potential foresight into future social trends. Although this offers valuable perspectives, especially for historians or sociologists, it is not without criticism. Some believe the theory is overly deterministic, while others find it too broad in its generalizations. Moreover, its primary focus on Anglo-American history questions its global application.

Understanding the theory of generational cohorts can significantly benefit you as a supervisor. By recognizing the different generational archetypes within your team, you can gain a deeper appreciation for their different values and communication styles. Adapting your communication to these generational nuances can strengthen connections between team members (Strauss & Howe, 1991). Refer to Table 2.2 for a succinct overview of this theory and its relevance to your supervisory role. Although it is a valuable guide, remember not to regard it as an absolute blueprint. Combining personal insights with this generational knowledge can create a more inclusive and harmonious workplace.

Critical Race Theory

With the rise of the Black Lives Matter (BLM) movement, notably following the acquittal of Trayvon Martin's murderer, discussions on systemic racism

Table 2.1 Hofstede's Cultural Dimensions

Cultural Dimensions	Description	Tips for Supervisor
Power distance (PDI)	Refers to how a cultural community views and accepts the unequal distribution of power **High PDI**: Have a greater hierarchy and centralized power. People tend to accept a higher degree of unequal power distribution **Low PDI**: Prefer egalitarianism and are likely to challenge authority	Individuals from high PDI cultures might: • Hesitate to voice concerns or disagreements directly to authority figures • Accept top-down decisions • Motivated by formal recognition from superiors Individuals from low PDI cultures might: • Expect to be consulted and involved in the decision-making process • Prefer more autonomy • Appreciate direct forms of feedback
Individualism vs. collectivism (IDV)	Refers the degree to which a cultural community prefers to function as individuals or as members of group • **Individualism (high IDV):** Value individual achievements, personal rights, and liberties • **Collectivism (low IDV):** Emphasize group harmony, loyalty, and shared interests	Individuals from high IDV cultures might: • Expresses personal opinions • Prefer to be addressed one-on-one • Motivated by formal recognition from superiors Individuals from low IDV cultures might: • Prefer collaborative and group projects • Make decision based on consensus
Masculinity vs. femininity (MAS)	Differentiates cultures based on traditional gender roles • **Masculine (high MAS):** Value assertiveness, competition, and material success • **Feminine (low MAS):** Prioritize relationships, care for others, and quality of life	Individuals from high MAS cultures might: • Prioritize work over personal or family life • Address conflict more directly Individuals from low MAS cultures might: • Have a higher emphasis on a work–life balance • Resolve conflict through dialogue

(Continued)

Table 2.1 (Continued)   Hofstede's Cultural Dimensions

Cultural Dimensions	Description	Tips for Supervisor
Uncertainty avoidance (UAI)	Refers to how comfortable a cultural community is with uncertainty and ambiguity • **High UAI:** Prefer strict behaviors, laws, and policies to mitigate uncertainty • **Low UAI:** Are more accepting of different opinions and adaptable to change	Individuals from High UAI cultures might: • Prefer clear rules, structured situations, and defined protocols • Requires clear reason for change, the benefits, and detailed steps for implementation Individuals from Low UAI cultures might: • Be more open to taking risks and exploring novel solutions • Be more flexible and adaptable to change
Long-term orientation vs. short-term normative orientation (LTO)	Refers to the extent to which a cultural community connects the past with the current and future actions/challenges • **Long-term (high LTO):** Adaptation and practical problem-solving • **Short-term (low LTO):** Prioritize respect for tradition, personal stability, and social obligations	Individuals from high LTO cultures might: • Be more willing to change traditions in the interest of modern demands or future goals • Be more receptive to long-term projects and goals Individuals from Low LTO cultures might: • Have a stronger attachment to current traditions, norms, and practices • Make decisions based on current conditions and immediate results
Indulgence vs. restraint (IVR)	Refers to the degree to which a cultural community allows or regulates gratification of human desires • **Indulgent (high IVR):** Enjoy life and having fun • **Restrained (low IVR):** Control and suppress desires with strict norms	Individuals from High IVR cultures might: • Prioritize work–life balance, personal time, and leisure activities • Value frequent team outings, social events, and celebrations • Be motivated by formal recognition from superiors Individuals from Low IVR cultures might: • Place a strong focus on work, duty, and following established norms • Prefer more formal gatherings with established purpose

Source: Adapted from Hofstede & McCrae (2004).

Table 2.2 Generational Cohort

Generation	Percentage in US Workforce (as of 2023)	Characteristics	Tips for Supervisor
Traditionalists or silent generation (1928–1945)	2%	• **Primary characteristics:** Strong sense of duty, loyalty to institutions, disciplined • **Communication style:** Formal, prefer written communication, face-to-face meetings • **Motivation to work:** Loyalty, job security, and a sense of duty	• Provide opportunities to contribute • Emphasize stability
Baby boomers (1946–1964)	25%	• **Primary characteristics:** Optimistic, competitive, focus on personal accomplishment • **Communication style:** Prefer phone calls and face-to-face meetings, but adaptable to emails • **Motivation to work:** Personal gratification, advancement, and building a legacy	• Provide specific goals and deadlines • Provide opportunities to mentor others • Prefer coaching-style feedback
Generation X (1965–1980)	33%	• **Primary characteristics:** Independent, resourceful, skeptical • **Communication style:** Adaptable to both face-to-face and digital communication. Comfortable with email • **Motivation to work:** Work–life balance, flexibility, job security	• Provide immediate feedback • Offer flexible work arrangements • Emphasize work–life balance • Provide opportunities for personal development

(Continued)

Table 2.2 (Continued)   Generational Cohort

Generation	Percentage in US Workforce (as of 2023)	Characteristics	Tips for Supervisor
Millennials or Generation Y (1981–1996)	35%	• **Primary characteristics:** Confident, civic-oriented, value collaboration • **Communication style:** Predominantly digital-prefer texting, instant messaging, and emails • **Motivation to work:** Purpose-driven, seek personal development, value feedback and recognition	• Build relationship and get to know them personally • Manage by results • Provide flexibility on their schedule and work assignments • Provide immediate feedback
Generation Z (Born after 1997)	5%	• **Primary characteristics:** Tech-savvy, socially aware, values individual expression • **Communication style:** Highly digital-social media, instant messaging, brief and visual content • **Motivation to work:** Desire for financial stability, meaningful work, and a positive social impact	• Offer opportunities to work on multiple projects simultaneously • Provide work–life balance • Encourage self-direction and independence

Source: Adapted from Strauss & Howe (1991) and Purdue Global (n. d.).

intensified, as did debates around critical race theory (CRT). Furthermore, many people began to question the way society is structured and whether it is truly fair and just. As a supervisor, you should be aware of both perspectives. BLM primarily protests and pushes for reforms against manifestations of systemic racism like police violence. In contrast, CRT offers a deep dive into understanding how racism is entrenched in American systems (Lopez & Sleeter, 2023).

Developed in US legal academia during the 1970s and 1980s by scholars including Derrick Bell, Kimberle Crenshaw, and Richard Delgado, CRT posits that racism is more than individual bias—it's embedded within legal systems and societal structures. By exploring systemic racism and its deep-seated influence on structures like legal systems, educational institutions, and workplaces, CRT emphasizes the narratives of marginalized racial and ethnic groups. It challenges conventional ideologies, such as meritocracy and color blindness, which could inadvertently sustain racial disparities (Lopez & Sleeter, 2023; Delgado & Stefancic, 1998).

Unfortunately, critical race theory is often misunderstood, resulting in people having false ideas about what the theory is trying to achieve. Although some may think that CRT leads to more racial division or only sees people as categories based on race, its main purpose is to bring attention to the systemic issues that are entrenched in society and institutions. When you understand that racism is not simply a personal issue with individuals but also entrenched in structures, policies, and even law, you can begin to address the systemic problems causing disparities in the workplace (Lopez & Sleeter, 2023). By understanding CRT and the challenges faced by marginalized individuals, you will be better equipped to be empathetic, more thoughtful, and informed in your interactions. Furthermore, having a foundation in CRT makes you more receptive to facilitating and engaging in conversations about race, even tough ones. These conversations are important to create an inclusive environment where everyone feels respected and are essential to developing mutual trust and understanding within your team.

Gender Norms

Interrelated issues such as gender inequality, sexism, and the emergence of gender-neutral pronouns shape the ongoing dialogue on gender equity and inclusion in the workplace. These factors underscore the deep-seated gender norms and prejudices that have historically been embedded in organizational structures. Workplaces reflect social norms that predominantly favor men, leading to a noticeable gender imbalance in senior roles. This is exemplified by the "Glass Ceiling" phenomenon, where women often find an invisible barrier restricting them from the highest echelons of power. Gender, characterized by social definitions that distinguish between men and women, and the underlying beliefs perpetuating such inequalities, is constantly present in organizational dynamics (Acker, 2009). The persistent "gender pay gap" is a testament to these biases. Even if women have the same roles and qualifications as their male counterparts, they often earn less. As highlighted by the US Bureau of Labor Statistics, Current Population Survey,

> Overall, women are not paid as much as men, even when working full time and year round. On average, women working full time and year round are paid 83.7% of what men are paid. This inequity is even greater for black and Hispanic women.
>
> **(Chun-Hoon, 2023)**

Gender norms that manifested in the workplace often took on insidious forms of sexism. The emergence of the #MeToo movement, originating from a grassroots effort, spotlighted the widespread issue of sexual harassment, particularly in the workplace. It gave victims the platform and courage to share their stories of harassment and assault, illuminating the extent of the problem at different industries and hierarchical levels. The movement underlined that sexual harassment was not only a problem for some but also a systemic problem deeply embedded in workplace cultures worldwide. In response, many companies were forced to reevaluate their internal policies, offer better training, and put measures in place to protect and support victims of harassment. This led to a surge in transparency and accountability, with firms addressing allegations with heightened seriousness and resolution. Moreover, there has been a significant transition toward fostering workplaces where employees can express their concerns freely without fearing retaliation (Atwater et al., 2021; Cheng & Hsiaw, 2022).

However, despite the growing acceptance, not every workplace is fully inclusive of T+ identities. As a supervisor, your role is crucial to ensuring an environment that respects and values non-binary and gender-diverse employees. Begin by deepening your understanding of these diverse gender identities by continuously educating yourself. Prioritize using and respecting individual's preferred pronouns, and perhaps initiate team conversations where members can share their pronouns, such as during introductions. It's essential to cultivate a space where employees can openly discuss their gender identities and related concerns. Remember, your approach sets a precedent. By actively championing and supporting non-binary and gender-diverse team members, you lead by example, setting a standard for the entire team to emulate.

In Chapter 9, we will expand in greater detail on what it means to be an inclusive supervisor. We will further explore the challenges and opportunities of a global market, evolving customer needs, and flexible workplaces. A central theme will be the celebration and management of diversity, underscoring the pivotal role of diversity, equity, inclusion, and belonging (DEI&B) initiatives in contemporary workplaces. We'll elucidate the synergy between

HR and senior management in driving these initiatives. The chapter emphasizes the importance of your role as a supervisor in creating an inclusive environment and motivating your team to participate in DEI&B programs.

Managing Interpersonal and Intrapersonal Skills (Empathetic)

Soft skills, especially empathy, are increasingly important in today's workplaces. Empathy, which goes beyond mere sympathy, focuses on understanding and relating to the emotions and experiences of others. It's about placing yourself in someone else's shoes. According to research by the Center for Creative Leadership, supervisors who demonstrate empathy toward their team members are perceived more positively, reinforcing that a "person-focused" approach significantly impacts performance (Gentry et al., 2007). Moreover, leadership theories consistently highlight empathy as a foundational leadership quality. Beyond emotional understanding, recent studies portray empathy as multidimensional, encompassing both emotional and cognitive aspects (Davis, 1983).

As a supervisor, you constantly navigate complex and diverse environments. In order to be successful, it is crucial that you continuously develop both interpersonal and intrapersonal skills. These skills are indispensable for effective communication and promote both professional growth and personal development. In the following section, we will explore emotional intelligence (EI), emotional contagion, and empathic accuracy. Sharpening your empathetic supervisory competencies is at the heart of a people-centered approach and is a cornerstone of influential leadership. These skills not only enhance the supervisor's effectiveness but also contribute to a positive, collaborative, and productive workplace.

Emotional Intelligence

Emotional intelligence, often termed EI or EQ (emotional quotient), is your ability to identify, comprehend, control, and adjust both your own emotions and those of your team members. This blends intrapersonal skills (pertaining to your inner self) and interpersonal skills (related to interactions with others). As a supervisor, this equips you to steer through social scenarios and manage workplace relationships with greater proficiency.

The term "emotional intelligence" first came about in the mid-1960s, but it was not until Peter Salovey and John Mayer, who significantly advanced the theoretical understanding of the concept in the early 1990s. They defined emotional intelligence as "as the subset of social intelligence that involves the ability to monitor one's own and others' feelings and emotions, to discriminate among them, and to use this information to guide one's thinking and actions" (1990, p. 189). Their work notably influenced researchers like Daniel Goleman, who wrote the book *Emotional Intelligence* in 1995. He argued that emotional intelligence (EI) was responsible for 67% of the skills necessary for top performance from leaders. Furthermore, he posited that EI mattered 2×s more than IQ or technical expertise (Goleman, 2006). He identified five skills (*Harvard Business Review*, 2015, p. 3):

- *Self-Awareness*: knowing one's strengths, weaknesses, drives, values, and impact on others
- *Self-Regulation*: controlling or redirecting disruptive impulses and moods
- *Motivation*: relishing achievement for its own sake
- *Empathy*: understanding other people's emotional makeup
- *Social Skills*: building rapport with others to move them in desired directions

Emotional intelligence (EI) is a dynamic skill that evolves over time based on experiences, reflections, learning, and interactions. The development of EI is an iterative process because our emotions and understanding of ourselves continuously evolve. In addition, our relationships within different social contexts vary significantly. Being able to manage both interpersonal and intrapersonal skills is integral to emotional intelligence.

Intrapersonal Skills

Intrapersonal skills are the abilities and knowledge that enable you to understand and manage your emotions, motivations, beliefs, and goals. These skills involve self-awareness, self-regulation, self-motivation, self-evaluation, internal locus of control, and understanding one's psychological state. Table 2.3 lists the intrapersonal skills with tips for you as a supervisor.

Table 2.3 Intrapersonal Skills

Intrapersonal Skills	Description	Tips for Supervisor
Self-awareness	The ability to recognize and understand one's own emotions, strengths, weaknesses, and triggers	• Regularly set aside time for self-reflection • Journal about your feelings and reactions to different situations • Seek feedback from trusted colleagues or mentors
Self-regulation	The ability to control or redirect disruptive emotions and adapt to changing circumstances	• Practice relaxation techniques, such as deep breathing or meditation • Identify emotional triggers and develop strategies to handle them • Respond rather than react; take a moment before making decisions, especially in high-pressure situations
Self-motivation	The ability to reflect on and assess one's performance, behavior, and emotions	• Set clear personal and professional goals • Find ways to stay inspired, such as reading motivational books or attending workshops • Celebrate small achievements along the way to maintain momentum
Self-evaluation	The ability to reflect on and assess one's performance, behavior, and emotions	• Regularly review your goals and progress • Ask for feedback after projects or interactions • Be open to constructive criticism and use it as a foundation for improvement
Internal locus of control	The belief that one has control over their own actions and can influence outcomes	• Focus on actions you can control, rather than external factors • Challenge negative self-talk that diminishes your sense of control • Celebrate instances where your actions led to positive outcomes

Source: Adapted from Boyatzis et al. (2000) and Gowrisankar (2017).

Interpersonal Skills

Interpersonal skills refer to the skills that enable an individual to interact positively and work effectively with others. These skills include a wide range of skills, including active listening, effective communication, teamwork, conflict resolution, and empathy. Table 2.4 lists the interpersonal skills with tips for you as a supervisor.

Emotional intelligence (EI) is like a muscle that needs consistent training to remain robust and flexible. It's not a one-and-done skill you can acquire and then neglect. As a supervisor, the emotions you encounter from yourself and your team change and mature with the evolving situations and milestones of life. You'll encounter diverse emotional responses and behaviors when you engage with new colleagues or form new connections. Furthermore, as you transition through different phases of life, such as higher education, changing jobs, starting a family, or experiencing personal losses, your emotional needs and the demands on you will shift. Just as a workout does not keep you fit forever, developing high levels of emotional intelligence requires constant care. By refining your EI, you solidify its strength as a crucial asset in your personal and professional competencies.

Emotional Contagion

Hatfield et al. described emotional contagion as "the tendency to automatically mimic and synchronize facial expressions, vocalizations, postures, and movements with those of another person's and, consequently, to converge emotionally" (1994, p. 7). This theory posits that people often subconsciously mirror others' expressions, vocal nuances, and body language during interactions. Intriguingly, by reflecting on these physical cues, one can also experience similar emotional states. For instance, echoing a smile or frown might elicit corresponding feelings of happiness or sadness. This phenomenon makes emotions seemingly "contagious," allowing individuals to inadvertently "catch" the moods of those around them, uplifting or dispiriting (Hatfield et al., 2018).

As a supervisor, you might not always be aware of it, but emotional mimicry and transmission are constantly at play in our interactions. Various factors, including culture, gender, and power dynamics, can shape the degree and nature of this emotional influence. While it's sometimes more noticeable when negative emotions like stress or panic spread, it's essential

Table 2.4 Interpersonal Skills

Interpersonal Skills	Description	Tips for Supervisor
Active listening	The ability to concentrate, understand, and respond to what another person is saying	• Eliminate distractions when conversing • Provide feedback by summarizing or paraphrasing what was said • Avoid interrupting and ensure you understand before responding
Effective communication	The ability to clearly convey thoughts, feelings, and information in both verbal and nonverbal ways	• Practice clarity and conciseness in speech and writing • Be aware of nonverbal cues, like body language and tone • Encourage open dialogue and feedback from others
Empathy	The ability to understand and share the feelings of another	• Practice active listening to truly understand another's perspective • Avoid immediate judgment; strive to understand before forming opinions • Engage in role-reversal exercises to walk in another's shoes
Conflict resolution	The ability to address disagreements or differences, and find a peaceful solution	• Stay calm and objective, focusing on the issue rather than the person • Understand all sides of the disagreement • Find common ground and propose mutually beneficial solutions
Teamwork and collaboration	The ability to work effectively within a group to achieve a common goal	• Value each team member's input and encourage inclusivity • Facilitate open communication within the team • Identify and harness individual strengths for collective benefit
Feedback skills	The ability to give and receive feedback in a constructive manner	• Be specific and objective when providing feedback • Listen actively when receiving feedback, seeking understanding • Focus on behaviors and actions, not on personal attributes
Building relationships	The ability to establish and maintain positive connections with others	• Regularly check-in with team members or peers • Celebrate successes and milestones • Offer support during challenging times

Source: Adapted from Boyatzis et al. (2000) and Gowrisankar (2017).

to recognize that positive feelings, such as joy and enthusiasm, can be just as infectious.

Understanding emotional contagion can be helpful, especially in the workplace. When you understand that the mimicking and converging emotions play a significant role in helping your team bond, empathize, and coordinate more effectively. Additionally, it is essential to remember that not only are emotions "contagious" but behaviors and attitudes can also be contagious. If you want to see change within your team, it starts with you exemplifying the values, emotions, and changes you aspire to see. Your team will take notice and be more likely to adopt similar behaviors and mindsets. When you act as a positive influence, you radiate desired emotions and values throughout your team, setting the tone for a productive and positive work environment.

Empathic Accuracy

As we presented earlier, the workplace brings together individuals from diverse cultural, educational, and personal backgrounds. This can happen both face-to-face and through virtual settings. Navigating this diversity requires understanding and appreciation of social norms and social interactions. Understanding and empathizing with someone's emotions is vital. However, it is important to clarify the terms. The ability to understand and share another person's feelings is known as empathy. The ability to correctly perceive another person's feelings is known as empathic accuracy. Often called "cognitive empathy," empathic accuracy is like "reading" someone's emotions. Studies have shown that some individuals might naturally be better "readers" of emotions. However, as a supervisor, you can sharpen this skill through conscious effort. This ability can contribute to developing more productive and meaningful relationships (Ickes et al., 2000).

Empathic accuracy, crucial to emotional intelligence and emotional contagion, can equip you with the ability to recognize the emotional state of your team and pave the way for effective communication. This insight ensures feedback and directions resonate positively. You can better mediate and resolve conflicts by addressing the underlying disputes. Responding to the emotions of your team, you can create a positive work environment that will lead to increased team cohesion and collaboration by adapting your motivation strategies. Additionally, if you are attuned to your team's emotions, you can spot signs of burnout, stress, or discontent early, enabling timely interventions that prioritize employee well-being. Ultimately, the workplace is imbued with social interactions. By developing the skills to read your team's emotional state, you can substantially bolster team dynamics, enhance productivity, and harmonize the work environment.

Expanding on our introduction to emotional intelligence, Chapter 10 will further explore the attributes of an empathetic supervisor. This will involve refining both your interpersonal and intrapersonal competencies. We'll differentiate between hard and soft skills, provide a deeper understanding of emotional intelligence, and provide further guidance to hone your interpersonal and intrapersonal talents.

Managing with and through People (Relational)

In today's interconnected world, employees want more collaboration and meaningful connections, emphasizing the importance of quality work relationships (Chernyak-Hai & Rabenu, 2018). Focusing on building relationships as a supervisor means deliberately cultivating and nurturing meaningful, trust-based connections with your team. Building on the insights shared earlier, concerted efforts to create an inclusive environment and develop skills to be an empathetic leader are the keys to being a relational supervisor. The last section of this chapter will focus on working with and through people, instead of control over. Rather than adhering strictly to a task-centric focus, the goal is to prioritize trust, recognize contributions, and champion a cooperative work environment. The tasks necessary to do the job become the by-product. In this final section, we will explore Social Exchange Theory and Social Intelligence.

Social Exchange Theory

Social Exchange Theory (SET) suggests that human interactions and relationships hinge on perceived rewards and costs. Essentially, people naturally gravitate toward interactions where they feel the rewards outweigh the costs. Reciprocity drives them, looking for a balance between what they contribute and receive. In the workplace context, the two pivotal relationships you'll encounter are between you and your employees and among the employees themselves. High-quality relationships are usually personal and mutually beneficial, while low-quality relationships tend to be more impersonal, transactional, and one-sided. When employees have a high-quality relationship with you, they value the relationship more and reciprocate by responding positively to demanding work expectations (Kamdar & Van Dyne, 2007). Alternatively, employees with a low-quality or negative relationship with their supervisor express distrust and elicit resistance to any expectations (Peng, 2023). Table 2.5 provides a general summary of employee relationships in the workplace and the associated rewards and costs.

Table 2.5   Employee–Supervisor Relationships: Associated Rewards and Costs

Relationships	*Rewards*	*Costs*
Employee–supervisor	Mentoring/coaching, support, career guidance, skill development, job security, networking, motivation, recognition, promotion *Note:* Positive interactions with supervisors can boost an employee's morale, motivation, and job satisfaction	Time, effort, commitment, adherence to directives, compliance, stress *Note:* A challenging relationship with a supervisor can lead to job dissatisfaction, stress, decreased motivation, and even job turnover
	Trust, respect, feedback, responsibility, autonomy, flexibility, collaboration	
Employee–coworker (Team)	Support, collaboration, social connection, knowledge sharing, networking, emotional support	Conflict, competition, dependency, gossip/ politics, boundaries, work distribution
	Collaboration, work distribution, shared responsibilities, knowledge sharing, team dynamics, group cohesion	
Employee–organization	Compensation, benefits, career advancement, job security, professional development	Time, effort, commitment, adherence to directives, compliance, stress, job demands, organizational politics
	Organizational culture, job responsibility, performance evaluation	

Source: Adapted from Peng et al. (2023), Chernyak-Hai, L., & Rabenu (2018), Mitchell et al. (2012), Kamdar & Van Dyne (2007).

Social Intelligence (SI)

In 1920, the concept of "social intelligence" was introduced by an American psychologist, Edward Thorndike, emphasizing the ability to understand and manage people and act wisely in human relations. In 2007, Daniel Goleman published a book, *Social Intelligence: The New Science of Human Relationships*, which explores how social intelligence shapes our interactions and differentiates emotional intelligence (EI) from SI, stating (p. 83),

> My own model of emotional intelligence folded in social intelligence without making much of that fact, do other theorists in the field. But as I've come to see, simply lumping social intelligence within the emotional sort stunts fresh thinking about the human aptitude for relationships, ignoring what transpires as we interact. This myopia leaves the "social" part out of intelligence.

Although Goleman's book has been praised and criticized, he clearly distinguishes between social and emotional intelligence and identifies two broad categories of social intelligence, social awareness, and social facility.

Social Awareness

Social awareness is the ability to accurately perceive the emotions, feelings, and needs of others and to understand what's going on beneath the surface of interpersonal interactions. It also includes deeply understanding how your words and actions might affect others positively or negatively. It's about being attuned to the moods and emotional currents of those around you, even if they're not explicitly expressed (Goleman, 2006). Table 2.6 lists social awareness skills with tips for you as a supervisor.

Social Facility

Social facility is the ability to act according to one's social awareness. While social awareness is about recognizing and understanding the emotions and feelings of others, social facilities are about effectively managing interactions based on your understanding. It's the skill set that enables smooth, successful, and adept social interactions, relationships, and interventions. Table 2.7 lists social facility skills with tips for you as a supervisor (Goleman, 2006).

Table 2.6 Social Awareness

Social Awareness	Description	Tips for Supervisor
Primal empathy	The ability to feel other's emotions and to sense nonverbal emotional signals	• Be present, minimize distractions, and focus entirely on the individual or group you're engaging with • Pay attention to body language, tone of voice, and facial expression to gain insights into a person's emotional state • Encourage open communication
Attunement	The ability to be in harmony to truly "tune in" to other's emotional state	• Engage when someone is speaking, giving them your undivided attention • Reflect and validate your observation. For example, "It seems you are feeling..."
Empathic accuracy	The ability to accurately perceive and understand the emotions of another person	• Avoid assumptions. If you are unsure, ask • Ensure your team members feel safe to express their thoughts and emotions without judgment
Social cognition	The ability to make sense of the social world	• Stay curious and seek to understand • Educate yourself and continuously learn • Seek diverse perspectives

Source: Adapted from Goleman (2006, pp. 84–91).

In Chapter 11, we explore the role of a relational supervisor in more depth. Here, we introduce the concept of relational intelligence, a term that goes beyond basic interactions. It embodies the art of understanding, nurturing, and maximizing human connections in the workplace. This concluding chapter integrates all elements of a people-centered approach, equipping you to cultivate an inclusive environment anchored in meaningful relationships.

You play a pivotal role in championing inclusivity. A key to this is the principle of treating everyone with respect and dignity, celebrating unique perspectives, and providing equal growth opportunities. This requires drawing from various fundamental concepts. The concept of intersectionality, which recognizes the interplay of multiple identities like race, gender, and class, helps address challenges more effectively. However, a mere superficial understanding can lead to tokenistic inclusion. This chapter introduces concepts like cultural dimensions, generational cohort dynamics, and gender norms, but delving deeper is crucial for genuine inclusivity. The importance

Table 2.7 Social Facility

Social Awareness	Description	Tips for Supervisor
Synchrony	The ability to have a smooth interaction based on nonverbal cues	• Mirror body language without imitating to match the other person to foster a deeper connection • Match tone and pace
Self-presentation	The ability to present yourself effectively and appropriately	• Dress the part, that is appropriate for your role and the culture you are in • Be conscious of your body language, facial expressions, and tone of voice • Ensure that you have a consistent message
Influence	The capacity to influence others and shape outcomes	• Build trust by being transparent, accountable, and consistent • Lead with example and model desired behaviors • Empower others and foster goodwill
Concern	The ability to genuinely care and consider others	• Regularly check-in to ensure everyone has a voice • Offer support and resources to help navigate the situation • Foster an open-door-policy

Source: Adapted from Goleman (2006, pp. 84–91).

of soft skills, particularly empathy, is highlighted, with empathy extending beyond sympathy to genuinely understanding others. Emotional intelligence, emotional contagion, and empathic accuracy are essential competencies for supervisors, facilitating better communication and professional growth. The chapter concluded with Social Exchange Theory and Social Intelligence, emphasizing a people-centered approach.

Use Table 2.8 to conduct a self-evaluation by rating your clarity and understanding of what it means to be an inclusive, empathetic, and relational supervisor.

Follow-Up and Action Plan

After completing Table 2.8, supervisors should design and manage their own activities for developing a learning and improvement action plan to enhance

Table 2.8 Supervisor's Self-Assessment of an Inclusive, Empathetic, and Relational Supervisor

Inclusive, Empathetic, and Relational Supervisor Self-Rating							
Day:		Participant:		Team:			
Month:		Supervisor:		Department:			
Rating Scale: 1 = Poor, 2 = Marginal, 3 = Acceptable, 4 = Good, 5 = Excellent							
Activities		*Description*	*Rating*				
			1	*2*	*3*	*4*	*5*
1	Intersectionality						
2	Cultural dimensions						
3	Generational cohort						
4	Critical race theory						
5	Gender norms						
6	Emotional intelligence						
7	Emotional contagion						
8	Empathetic accuracy						
9	Social exchange theory						
10	Social intelligence						
Sub-Total (total of each column)							
Total of above 5 rating scales							
Average (above total divided by 9)							

Source: Adapted from Schneider (2001) and Luthans, Youssef & Avolio (2007).

their positive and influential relationships with other managers. Use the APLI table (Table 2.9) as a tool to manage such actions.

What's Next?

Becoming an inclusive, empathetic, and relational supervisor takes hard work. Now that you have a basic understanding of key principles, you are ready to go to Chapter 3, Understanding Working with Teams and Groups. Chapter 3 will focus on defining groups, categorizing groups by purpose (formal and informal), examining what groups think, and exploring the importance of

Table 2.9 APLI#1-Connected to Table 2.8

Action Plan for Learning and Improving	
Area of Learning and Improving: *Check List Clarity and Understanding of the Fundamental Principles of Inclusive, Empathetic, and Relational Supervisor*	
Reference: *Table 2.8*	
Three learning and improvement actions for this month that would bring up my three lowest areas of skills self-ratings to enhance an understanding of the fundamental principles of inclusive, empathetic, and relational supervisor by at least one on the next rating:	
Action 1:	By When:
Action 2:	By When:
Action 3:	By When:

groups to you as a supervisor. But before you move on, don't forget to review the key takeaways and take a moment to reflect on what you learned in this chapter by completing Table 2.10, End of Chapter 2 Discussion Questions and Inquiries.

Key Takeaways

1. Being an inclusive supervisor in today's diverse workplace is complex. There are numerous models and theories that help us understand people and workplace dynamics, such as intersectionality, cultural dimensions, generational cohort, critical race theory, and gender norms as tools for understanding diversity.
2. Being an empathetic supervisor requires continuous development of your emotional intelligence (EI), which requires intrapersonal skills (about your inner self) and interpersonal skills (related to interactions with others).
3. Being a relationship supervisor deliberately cultivates and nurtures meaningful, trust-based relationships with your team. This requires the development of social intelligence (SI), the ability to understand and navigate social situations, read and interpret the emotions and behaviors of others, and respond appropriately.

Table 2.10 End of Chapter 2 Questions and Inquiries

Your Perspective on What You Learned in Chapter 2	
Area of Inquiry	*What Did You Learn, and How Are You Going to Use Them in Your Position?*
Intersectionality	
Cultural dimensions	
Generational cohort	
Critical race theory	
Gender norms	
Emotional intelligence	
Emotional contagion	
Empathic accuracy	
Social exchange theory	
Social intelligence	

Discussion Questions and Inquiries

Please take a minute and come up with your own answers to these inquiries and questions on above Table 2.10. After completing the table and answering these questions, discuss your learning with your higher manager. From your viewpoint, briefly express what you have learned about these areas. Your discussion with your manager about your new knowledge and understanding would be a great pathway to your development as an inclusive, empathetic, and relational supervisor.

References

Acker, J. (2009). From glass ceiling to inequality regimes. *Sociologie Du Travail (Paris)*, *51*(2), 199–217. https://doi.org/10.1016/j.soctra.2009.03.004

Atwater, L. E., Sturm, R. E., Taylor, S. N., & Tringale, A. (2021). The era of# MeToo and what managers should do about it. *Business Horizons*, *64*(2), 307–318.

Boyatzis, R. E., Goleman, D., & Rhee, K. (2000). Clustering competence in emotional intelligence: Insights from the Emotional Competence Inventory (ECI). *Handbook of Emotional Intelligence*, *99*(6), 343–362.

Cheng, I., & Hsiaw, A. (2022). Reporting sexual misconduct in the #MeToo era. *American Economic Journal Microeconomics*, *14*(4), 761–803. https://doi.org/10.1257/mic.20200218

Chernyak-Hai, L., & Rabenu, E. (2018). The new era workplace relationships: Is social exchange theory still relevant?. *Industrial and Organizational Psychology*, *11*(3), 456–481.

Chun-Hoon, W. (2023, March 14). 5 fast facts: The gender wage gap. *U.S. Department of Labor Blog*. https://blog.dol.gov/2023/03/14/5-fast-facts-the-gender-wage-gap#:~:text=Stats.,for%20Black%20and%20Hispanic%20women

Cox, T. (2001). *Creating the Multicultural Organization: A Strategy for Capturing the Power of Diversity*. Hoboken, NJ: Jossey-Bass.

Crenshaw, K. (1989). Demarginalizing the intersection of race and sex: A black feminist critique of antidiscrimination doctrine, feminist theory, and antiracist politics. *University of Chicago Legal Forum*, *1*(80), 139–167. http://chicagounbound.uchicago.edu/uclf/vol1989/iss1/8

Davis, M. H. (1983). The effects of dispositional empathy on emotional reactions and helping: A multidimensional approach. *Journal of Personality*, *51*(2), 167–184.

Delgado, R., & Stefancic, J. (1998). Critical race theory: Past, present, and future. *Current Legal Problems*, *51*(1), 467–491. https://doi.org/10.1093/clp/51.1.467

Gentry, W. A., Weber, T. J., & Sadri, G. (2007, April). Empathy in the workplace: A tool for effective leadership. In Annual Conference of the Society of Industrial Organizational Psychology, New York, NY, April.

Goleman, D. (2006). *Emotional Intelligence: Why it Can Matter More than IQ* (Bantam 10th anniversary hardcover ed.). New York, NY: Bantam Books.

Goleman, D. (2006). *Social Intelligence: The New Science of Human Relationships*. New York, NY: Bantam Books.

Goleman, D., & Boyatzis, R. (2008). Social intelligence and the biology of leadership. *Harvard Business Review*, *86*(9), 74–81.

Gowrisankar, M. (2017). Role of locus of control & emotional quotient towards organizational commitment. *International Journal of Management Research and Reviews*, *7*(1), 28.

Harvard Business Review, Goleman, D., Boyatzis, R. E., McKee, A., & Finkelstein, S. (2015). *HBR's 10 Must Reads on Emotional Intelligence (with Featured Article "What Makes a Leader?" by Daniel Goleman) (HBR's 10 Must Reads)*. Boston, MA: Harvard Business Review Press.

Hatfield, E., Cacioppo, J., & Rapson, R. L. (1994). *Emotional Contagion*. New York, NY: Cambridge University Press.

Hatfield, E., Rapson, R. L., & Narine, V. (2018). Emotional contagion in organizations: Cross-cultural perspectives. Individual, relational, and contextual dynamics of emotions. In L. Petitta, C. E. J Hartel, N. M. Ashkanasym, & W. Zerbe (Eds.), *Individual, Relational and Contextual Dynamics of Emotions* (pp. 245–258). Emerald Publishing Limited. https://doi.org/10.1108/S1746 -979120180000014019

Herring, C. (2009). Does diversity pay?: Race, gender, and the business case for diversity. *American Sociological Review*, *74*(2), 208–224. https://doi.org/10.1177 /000312240907400203

Hofstede, G., & McCrae, R. R. (2004). Personality and culture revisited: Linking traits and dimensions of culture. *Cross-Cultural Research*, *38*(1), 52–88. https:// doi.org/10.1177/1069397103259443

Ickes, W., Gesn, P. R., & Graham, T. (2000). Gender differences in empathic accuracy: Differential ability or differential motivation? *Personal Relationships*, *7*(1), 95–109. https://doi.org/10.1111/j.1475-6811.2000.tb00006.x

Kamdar, D., & Van Dyne, L. (2007). The joint effects of personality and workplace social exchange relationships in predicting task performance and citizenship performance. *Journal of Applied Psychology*, *92*(5), 1286–1298. https://doi.org /10.1037/0021-9010.92.5.1286

Lopez, F., & Sleeter, C. E. (2023). *Critical Race Theory and its Critics: Implications for Research and Teaching*. New York, NY: Teachers College Press.

Luthans, F., Youssef, C. M., & Avolio, B. J. (2007). *Psychological capital: Developing the human competitive edge*. Oxford, England: Oxford University Press.

Mannheim, K. (1970). The problem of generations. *The Psychoanalytic Review (1963)*, *57*(3), 378–404.

Mitchell, M. S., Cropanzano, R. S., & Quisenberry, D. M. (2012). Social exchange theory, exchange resources, and interpersonal relationships: A modest resolution of theoretical difficulties. In K. Tornblom & A Kazemi (Eds.), *Handbook of Social Resource Theory: Theoretical Extensions, Empirical Insights, and Social Applications* (pp. 99–118). New York, NY: Springer.

Peng, J., Nie, Q., & Cheng, Y. (2023). Team abusive supervision and team behavioral resistance to change: The roles of distrust in the supervisor and perceived frequency of change. *Journal of Organizational Behavior, 44*(7), 1016–1033. https://doi.org/10.1002/job.2697

Purdue Global (n.d.). *Generational Differences in the Workplace [Infographic].* https://www.purdueglobal.edu/education-partnerships/generational-workforce -differences-infographic/

Rothwell, W. J., Ealy, P. L., & Campbell, J. (Eds.). (2022). *Rethinking Organizational Diversity, Equity, and Inclusion: A Step-by-step Guide for Facilitating Effective Change.* New York, NY: Productivity Press.

Rothwell, W. J., Bakhshandeh, B., & Zaballero, A. G. (2023). *Successful Supervisory Leadership: Exerting Positive Influence While Leading People.* New York, NY: Taylor & Francis Group; Routledge.

Salovey, P., & Mayer, J. D. (1990). Emotional intelligence. *Imagination, Cognition and Personality, 9*(3), 185–211. https://doi.org/10.2190/DUGG-P24E-52WK -6CDG

Schneider, B. (2001). Fits about fit. *Applied Psychology: An International Review, 50*(1), 141–152. https://doi.org/10.1111/1464-0597.00051

Strauss, W., & Howe, N. (1991). *Generations: The History of America's Future, 1584 to 2069.* New York, NY: William Morrow; Quill.

Thomas, D. A., & Ely, R. J. (1996). Making differences matter: A new paradigm for managing diversity. *Harvard Business Review, 74*(5), 79–91.

Zaballero, A. G. (2009). *Diversity Leader: Case Study of a Selected Organization's Transformation* (Master Thesis, University of Nevada, Las Vegas).

Zaballero, A. G., Tsai, H., & Acheampong, P. (2012). Leveraging workforce diversity and team development. In C. Scott & M. Byrd (Eds.), *Handbook of Research on Workforce Diversity in a Global Society: Technologies and Concepts* (pp. 341– 353). IGI Global. https://doi.org/10.4018/978-1-4666-1812-1.ch020

Chapter 3

Understanding Working with Teams and Groups

Introduction

Organizations and businesses are collectively formed by groups, and departments, which manage, operate, and deliver goods and services in their markets. For any manager or supervisor to oversee the operation of their sections of the organization, they need to understand how to work with people in the forms of teams and groups.

A relational supervisor helps their team members and group members focus on the quality of their connections, to increase their capacity for effective influence. Yet, if you want your influence to have a profound and lasting impact on the people you connect with, quality must come before quantity. This does not mean you should abandon the pursuit of quantity completely (Saccone, 2009).

Whether you are a supervisor in a newly formed team or an established one, it is important to establish a fun work environment that values open communication through relationships, fosters inclusion, and has empathy for all teams or group members. Surprisingly, there is a significant distinction between managing a group and managing a team. Despite their apparent similarity, the two have many significant distinctions that can change the way you operate. Understanding the differences between a group and a team and how to promote positive communication patterns in the workplace is crucial to improving your working relationships as a supervisor.

DOI: 10.4324/9781003413493-3

As an inclusive and empathetic supervisor, you need to ensure that your team members feel welcomed in an inclusive culture by keeping the following in mind:

- **Create a Safe Place.** To ensure everyone feels heard and that all ideas, rather than just those of the chosen few, are on the table. Team members should feel free to express their views and opinions.
- **Watch for Group Thinking**. Even though they could have a deep awareness of how one another functions, there's a strong probability that they have adopted the groupthink mindset. As a result, their methods of operation can become routine; they'll view things from the same angle, and their degrees of originality will decrease.
- **Have No Stars but Servants.** It enables a far more collaborative effort toward creating something great as a team, rather than from the person who initially suggested the concept, thus eliminating the competitiveness regarding whose plan it was to begin with.
- **Promote Honesty.** Leaders should routinely reflect on themselves, especially in terms of their interactions with their team. Also, they can ask their staff for input. Only if you pay attention and apply it to change your strategy will you benefit from candid, honest feedback on how you do in relation to some of these indicators.

(Manning, 2021; Kreitner & Kinicki, 2010).

As shown in Figure 3.1 of the *Successful Supervisory Leadership Series Book II Structure*, in this chapter, we attempt to provide an understanding of what a team is and what a group is. We will discuss the fundamental elements of these two critical parts of any organizational operation and what it takes to work with individuals who are the fabric of building a team or group.

Key Concepts

This chapter will cover the following key concepts:

- The Importance of Organizational Structure to Supervisors
- Understanding the Main Differences between Groups and Teams
- Understanding Groups
- Primary Group Characteristics
- Understanding Groupthink

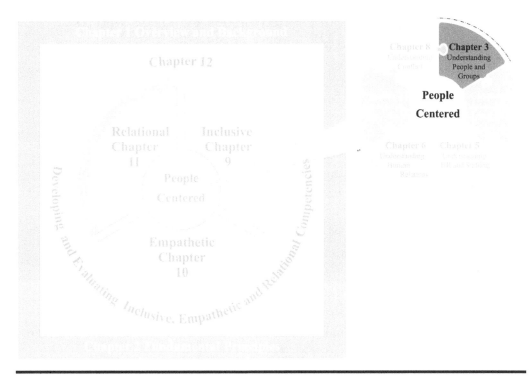

Figure 3.1 *Successful Supervisory Leadership Series Book II Structure. Note:* **Authors' original creation.**

- Understanding Teams, Teamwork, and Team Building
- The Fundamental Factors for Team Building
- Phases of Development in Teams and Groups

Definitions

The following definitions of key terms will help to better understand the main elements of this chapter:

Team

- According to the Merriam-Webster (2022a) dictionary, the team is "a number of persons associated together in work or activity" (n. p.).
- Levi (2017) defined a team as a specific type of unit made up of people who depend on one another to accomplish a common objective. Businesses and organizations employ a number of unique team kinds to accomplish a range of goals.

■ A team of individuals with a variety of jobs and talents who collaborate on a similar project, service, or objective while integrating their roles and providing one another with support. In some cases, or in larger organizations, some teams will assemble a working team (Bakhshandeh, 2002).

Group

■ According to the Merriam-Webster (2022b) dictionary, the group is "a number of individuals assembled together or having some unifying relationship" (n. p.).
■ A group is a collection of interdependent individuals who engage in frequent interaction (Cartwright & Zander, 1968).
■ To qualify as a group, the members of it must define themselves as group members. They must also be defined by others as group members (Rothwell et al., 2016).
■ Working groups are usually made of several teams with specific assignments or tasks (Bakhshandeh, 2002).

The Importance of Organizational Structure to Supervisors

Decisions made about organizational structure affect, and in part determine, methods of interaction among organizational members. They are thus of crucial importance to supervisors, groups, and team members because structure and interaction have at least four key effects.

Who Reports to Whom: This structure, of course, determines who reports to whom. Most supervisors will agree that the background of the manager affects how easily the supervisors can function. When the manager does not have previous experience—or interest—in the supervisor's area of responsibility, the manager may require more information to reach a decision, more detailed explanations regarding supervisory decisions, and may be more or less supportive of the supervisor's efforts than if the manager is thoroughly familiar with them.

Availability of Technical Skills: This structure influences the availability of technical skills. When the organization's structure fosters work specialization, highly specialized skills may be readily available to be tapped in-house for future use.

Availability of Management Skills: This structure also influences the availability of management skills. When past practice fosters decentralized decision-making, more people inside the organization exercise decision-making. The same is not true when, in the fashion of centralized decision-making, decisions are made from the top down and workers only carry them out.

Ease or Difficulty of Exercising Supervisory Duties: Finally, structure influences the ease or difficulty of exercising supervisory duties. Supervisors dealing with broad spans of control and heterogeneous jobs face tougher challenges in people management than when they deal with narrower spans of control or more homogeneous jobs. It is simply tougher to oversee the work of many people performing different work tasks than it is to oversee the work of fewer people or people performing similar tasks.

Supervisors rarely possess the authority of top managers to change organizational structure, as depicted on organization charts. If they detect problems stemming from structure—such as conflicting goals among organizational units, the most they can do is inform middle or top managers. On the other hand, supervisors often influence work allocation and thus organizational design within their own work groups or teams. For that reason, supervisors should be familiar with the key characteristics of teams and work groups.

We are in constant contact with people in personal as well as in professional levels. At work, we are engaged with individuals, teams, and groups at all times; this would make being a relational person mandatory in order to be effective with people (Rothwell et al., 2021). Our life's quality is directly correlated with our relationships. Regrettably, a lot of us frequently put less than our best effort, attention, and intentionality into optimizing how we give, spend, and invest in our relationships. Wouldn't life be different and better if individuals didn't spend years in the same cycles of interpersonal dysfunction—at home, at business, or in their leadership roles? What would alter if people gave more thought to how they donate, invest, and spend in their social or work circles? What if people are continually trying to improve how they connect with others in order to improve their quality of life and increase their influence? (Saccone, 2009).

Understanding the Main Differences between Groups and Teams

Contrary to some myths, groups and teams are two different working concepts in the operations of an organization (Shams & Lane, 2020). A team is a collection of people who work together as a unit, while those in a group coordinate the activities of the team. Although comparable, the two differ when it comes to making decisions and working as a team.

Members of a work group are autonomous and responsible for their own actions. On the other hand, team members collaborate closely to address issues and share mutual responsibilities. These dynamics influence the way tasks are handled, and the overall workings of the team are influenced by these dynamics.

How to Distinguish between Team and Group

The following six factors make it easy to distinguish between groups and teams at work (see Figure 3.2):

1) Each group has just one person in charge. There can be more than one person in charge of a team.
2) Team members are accountable for their actions, not the members of the group.
3) Individual objectives are what the group concentrates on attaining. The team members, on the other hand, concentrate on attaining the team goals.
4) Each member of the group contributes a unique product. Unlike a team that creates things from its combined work.
5) A group's procedure is to debate the issue, decide, and then assign the work to specific group members. On the other hand, a team discusses the issue, chooses a course of action, and then implements it together.
6) Each member of the group is independent. The team members are interdependent, unlike a group.

(Das, 2022; Harmon et al., 2002).

Similarities between Groups and Teams

■ Groups and teams are formed by at least two or more individuals.
■ In both groups and teams, members are in constant interactions.
■ There are in-person and face-to-face relationships between group and team members.
■ In both formats, the main focus is on the achievement of their goals and objectives.
■ Both groups and teams have someone in charge as the leader in different forms and shapes.
■ Both groups and teams share information, data, and resources.

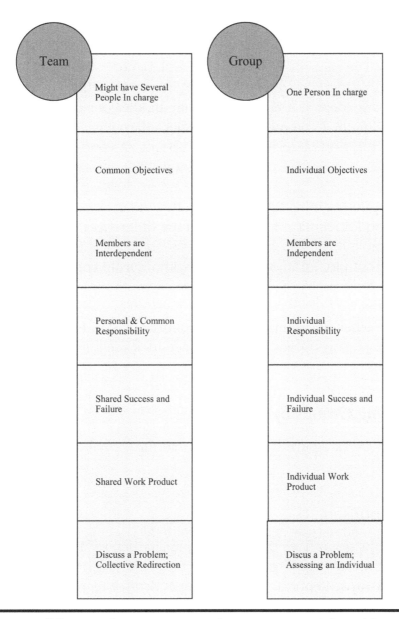

Figure 3.2   Key differences between team and group. Source: Adapted from Das (2022) and Harmons et al. (2002).

Understanding Groups

Groups are the building blocks of organizations. They are the fundamental units from which organizational designs are established. For that reason, supervisors should be familiar with information about how groups function in organizations.

Empathy is one of the most needed competencies in interpersonal relationships when it comes to having a relationship with people, in teams and groups. The capacity to understand and identify with the feelings, experiences, or thoughts of another is known as empathy. Hyper-empathy individuals are adept at seeing things from another person's point of view and responding in a compassionate manner (Manning, 2021). Simply said, empathy in the workplace refers to the capacity of your employees to build genuine, empathic relations with one another that improve interactions and output.

According to Manning (2021), as empathy and sympathy are sometimes misunderstood, it's critical to understand the differences between the two:

- Feelings of pity for another person without truly comprehending what it must be like to be in their shoes are the standard definition of sympathy.
- On the other side, empathy is the aptitude or skill to put oneself in another person's shoes and experience their feelings, thoughts, or opinions.

Categorizing Groups by Purpose

Groups may be categorized by purpose into the formal and informal (Kolb, 2011).

Formal Groups

Formal groups result from the organizational structure. There are two kinds:

Chart Groups. Report to the same supervisor or team leader and take their name from their placement on an organization chart.
Task Groups. Work together to achieve common goals or ends.
   Project teams are task groups assembled from one or many people from different chart groups.

Informal Groups

Informal groups result from individual choice. People are attracted to informal groups by common interests and concerns. There are two kinds:

Shared Interest Groups. These groups are composed of people sharing common interests but not necessarily belonging to the same chart or task group. If, for example, the Vice President of Purchasing and a manufacturing supervisor agree that the company needs to change its shipping policies, they are functioning as a shared interest group.

Friendship Groups. These are comprised of people sharing common values who like to interact socially. Informal groups exert profound influence on organizations because people readily communicate with those sharing common interests and those with whom they socialize.

Categorizing Groups by Function

Groups may also be categorized by what they do (Kolb, 2011; Katz & Kahn, 1978). If viewed in this way, groups may be categorized into four distinctive types as follows:

Production Group

The first of these is called a production or technical group. Members of these groups produce the goods or offer the services that keep an organization in business. Workers in groups of this kind are admired for their ability to produce and for their technical skills and knowledge. Workers on an assembly line belong to a production group, for instance.

Maintenance Group

These groups regulate activities within a firm. Examples include internal auditing and human resources departments.

Adaptive Group

It works to prepare the organization for change and to aid adaptation to conditions outside the firm. Examples include marketing, sales, and purchasing departments.

Management Group

It coordinates operations within the organization. The top management team is the best example of this group.

Primary Group Characteristics

Groups share identifiable characteristics that satisfy member needs. Workplaces can create groups for many purposes, such as to accomplish a task or offer assistance about a certain subject. For instance, a group's goal can be to finish a project. Additional salient characteristics of groups at work include the following (Rothwell et al., 2016; Kolb, 2011; Kerr & Tindale, 2004).

Goals

Most groups are formed by teams, which have objectives that team members must meet. This might be a task, project deliverable, or quota that they must meet. To understand each other's workload, including obstacles and successes, workplaces may form groups with team members with similar aims (Kolb, 2011).

Specialization

Groups are typified by specialization. Each group member is given responsibilities for carrying out specific tasks and activities. Some members are given higher status than others because they enter their jobs with more education, experience, or other qualities commonly admired by their peers. Some members are given higher status than others because they possess unique individual talents (Rothwell et al., 2016).

Structure

The structure of a group establishes the responsibilities of each member. It explains the role each member plays in assisting the organization in achieving its objectives. The members' functions may be related to their jobs. For example, a sales professional may track the total sales made by the group. The positions may also refer to a particular employee's function inside the team, such as helping keep the team upbeat by delivering supportive messages. Each member may have a specific position assigned to them by the leader, or the members may take on their responsibilities on their own as they get to know one another (Rothwell et al., 2016).

Members Count

A group often has more than two members. Depending on the group's goal, they can include a collection of all managers, all employees, or a combination of the two. Although there must always be at least two members in a group, many people may join. Most organizations limit their groups from 15 to 20 people to make them easier for supervisors to manage (Kolb, 2011).

Influence

The ability of the group members to positively affect one another is crucial. While working together on a project or often talking to them to accomplish their objectives, group members may have an impact on one another. Team members may have a beneficial influence on others, but they may also consider how other team members may have an impact on them (Kerr & Tindale, 2004).

Norm

Groups are characterized by the appearance of norms. A norm is an unwritten but widely understood rule in a group that governs behavior, the accepted standards of behavior within a community. They are the standards and guidelines that the group's leaders or participants may encourage everyone to abide by. Norms frequently cover job standards, participation, and communication methods. For instance, a group leader may set the requirement that members check in every morning with an update on the status of their assignment. By establishing norms, groups may maintain clear guidelines that all members can adhere to (Kolb, 2011).

Cohesiveness

Groups also vary by level of cohesiveness, referring to the psychological closeness of group members. Individuals in highly cohesive groups are mutually attracted. They enjoy interaction. Cohesion is increased by similarities in values, backgrounds, education, experience, or other elements that people share. On the other hand, individual differences can decrease cohesiveness. To make groups more cohesive, supervisors should (1) try to get group members to agree on work group or team goals; (2) increase the number of times group members come into contact; (3) select group members sharing similar backgrounds; (4) make the group smaller so that members interact more often; and (5) keep the group to itself (Rothwell et al., 2016).

Interaction

Interacting among members and their team leaders is a crucial component of groups because it enables members to build trusting working relationships. Team members can communicate in various methods, such as instant messaging, video conferencing, or in person. Leaders frequently design team-building exercises that allow team members to communicate, for the sake of group effectiveness, which will be affected by a team's functionality. In order to get assistance with their job or ask a question regarding a task, team members may also contact one another (Kerr & Tindale, 2004).

Use Table 3.1 to conduct a self-evaluation by rating your clarity and understanding of the group's characteristics.

Follow-Up and Action Plan

After completing Table 3.1, supervisors should design and manage their own activities for developing a learning and improvement action plan to enhance their understanding and clarity on the group's characteristics. Use the APLI (Action Plan for Learning and Improving) table (Table 3.2) as a tool to manage such actions.

Understanding Groupthink

According to the Oxford Languages dictionary, groupthink is "the practice of thinking or making decisions as a group in a way that discourages creativity or individual responsibility" (Oxford Languages, 2022).

Highly cohesive groups may become subject to **groupthink**, a condition in which a few vocal members control a group. It is associated with public agreement but private disagreement with group decisions. It occurs when group members prefer to avoid disputes in an effort to appear agreeable. Gantt and Badenoch (2013) identified the common symptoms of groupthink as follows:

■ *Delusions.* Group members think that the group is immune to criticism and that everyone agrees to a course of action or goal.

Table 3.1 Clarity and Understanding of Group's Characteristics by a Supervisor Self-Rating System

Clarity and Understanding of Group's Characteristics by a Supervisor Self-Rating System							
Day:		Supervisor:		Group:			
Month:		Direct Manager:		Department:			
Rating Scale: **1** *= Poor,* **2** *= Marginal,* **3** *= Acceptable,* **4** *= Good,* **5** *= Excellent*							
Characteristics		*Brief Description*	*Rating*				
			1	*2*	*3*	*4*	*5*
1	Goals	Objectives that group members must meet. Such as task, project deliverable, or quota.					
2	Specialization	Each group member is given responsibilities for carrying out specific tasks and activities.					
3	Structure	The structure of a group establishes the responsibilities and roles of each member.					
4	Members count	A group often has more than two members, depending on the goal of the group.					
5	Influence	The ability of the group members to positively affect one another is a crucial component.					
6	Norm	Norm is an unwritten but widely understood rule in a group that governs their behavior.					
7	Cohesiveness	Groups are varied by level of their cohesiveness, referring to closeness of members.					
8	Interaction	Interacting among members and their team leaders builds trusting working relationships.					
Sub-Total (total of each column)							
Total of above 5 rating scales							
Average (above total divided by 8)							

Source: Rothwell et al. (2016), Kolb (2011), and Kerr and Tindale (2004).

Table 3.2   APLI-Connected to Table 3.1

Action Plan for Learning and Improving	
Area of Learning and Improving: *Clarity and Understanding of Group's Characteristics by a Supervisor Self-Rating System*	
Reference: *Table 3.1*	
Three learning and improvement actions for this month that will raise my three lowest areas of clarity in the group's characteristics self-ratings to enhance their understanding and clarity by at least one on the next rating:	
Action 1:	By When:
Action 2:	By When:
Action 3:	By When:

Note: Authors' original creation.

- ■ **Rationalization.** Members prefer to dismiss disagreements as unimportant.
- ■ **Moralization.** Group members are convinced they are morally correct—and others are morally wrong.
- ■ **Stereotyping.** Opponents are stereotyped and lumped into groups rather than viewed as individuals.
- ■ **Compliance with group wishes**. Group members enforce agreement among themselves and create pressures for conformity from those who are otherwise unwilling to go along with group wishes.

To avoid groupthink, Gantt and Badenoch (2013) suggest forming subgroups, inviting outsiders to attend meetings as critics and watchdogs, collecting information from outside sources, and assigning people the role of playing devil's advocate to challenge group assumptions.

Since supervisors work with and through others and most often function in group settings, they should become skilled in managing groups in the following ways:

- ■ Match or stretch their style of supervision to individuals in the group. For instance, supervisors should direct group members who wish to be directed and empowered through increased autonomy to those who wish to receive less direction.

- Work to establish positive group norms. This can be accomplished by establishing rewards for adherence to organizational goals.
- Work to increase group cohesiveness in a way consistent with organizational goals but inconsistent with ways that promote groupthink. This can be accomplished by encouraging and rewarding teamwork while simultaneously using the techniques suggested by Janis to avoid groupthink.

(Harmon et al., 2002).

Understanding Teams, Teamwork, and Team Building

The majority of definitions of collaboration categorize a team as a certain kind of group. Some theorists find it difficult to draw a clear line between groups and teams. Teams are just groupings, in a professional situation (Hackman & Wegman, 2005; Parks & Sanna, 1999). The focus of other theorists is on how team behavior varies from conventional groupings. Teams are organized groups of individuals working together toward clearly defined objectives that require coordinated interactions to complete specific tasks (Hackman & Wegman, 2005; Forsyth, 1999). This definition places emphasis on a crucial aspect of a team: that its members collaborate on a venture for which they are all responsible. To differentiate between groups and teams, however, additional qualifications can be utilized. According to Levi (2017), "One common distinction relates to application. Teams typically engaged in sports or work activities. They have applied functions, and the roles of team members are related to their functions" (p. 5).

Typically, larger firms have groups that are assembled with various teams. Members of these groups possess particular knowledge, talents, and skills relevant to their work. This contrast may be seen in studies on teams and groups. While research on teams is often done in field studies that concentrate on the utilization of teams in the workplace, research on groups is typically done in laboratory settings (Kerr & Tindale, 2004). Katzenbach and Smith (1993) pointed out a distinction between groups and teams from the point of view of performance. Those who define collaboration put a strong emphasis on performance. In addition to sharing a shared goal, a team also has performance goals that are linked to it, and everyone in the team is responsible for achieving them. Additionally, they think a team should only consist of a small number of individuals with complementary abilities who work together. This helps distinction between teams and work groups, whose members share the same duties but don't need integration or collaboration to complete them (Levi, 2017).

Understanding and being able to identify the needs, feelings, and views of others is what it means to be an empathetic leader. This is a vital component if a supervisor plans to manage groups and teams effectively. Every person has unique ideas, social knowledge and understanding, background, and points of view. Leaders may use their aptitude for understanding and empathy while working with this type of team. Managers who demonstrate compassionate leadership toward their direct reports are seen by their superiors as having greater job performance. In the hands of a likable and respected boss, empathy is a useful leadership tool (Kreitner & Kinicki, 2010).

Likewise, a relational supervisor is considerate and extends support before being requested. You gain a reputation as a key team member when people realize they can count on you. Every profession recognizes the value of reliability as a relational skill (Duck & McMahan, 2012). Being empathetic and rational is only possible in a diverse and inclusive environment. A diverse and inclusive workplace is one where everyone feels supported and included in all aspects of the workplace, regardless of what they do for the organization or who they are (Mastropier & Scruggs, 2010).

Team Types

Six types of work teams have been identified through research based on the tasks they complete (Levi, 2017; Lecioni, 2016; Sundstrom, 1999).

Production Teams

Teams in factories, for example, those who produce or put items together repeatedly.

Service Teams

Customers often transact with service providers such as food delivery services and maintenance personnel.

Management Teams

These consist of managers, who collaborate to plan, create policies, or administer an organization's operations.

Project Teams

Teams of professionals, such as those in engineering and research, are assembled to complete a certain task within a predetermined timeframe.

Performing Teams

Sports teams, theatrical troupes, and surgical teams all conduct brief routines performed under many circumstances and call for specific knowledge and substantial practice.

Parallel Teams

Employee engagement groups and advisory boards are examples of temporary teams that function outside of regular work and offer suggestions or recommendations for transforming a business.

What Is Teamwork?

Having a team is one thing, but teamwork is quite another. A successful team may achieve success and provide outstanding outcomes. Without collaboration, teams don't function well! Every business needs teamwork to be successful (Maxwell, 2003). Working effectively with others is essential for a fulfilling and long-lasting career. This is why collaboration is so valued in the workplace. The following elements are generated by team members who work as a team for accomplishing their common goals (YTI, 2022).

Brings Forth New Ideas

In today's cutthroat business environment and tough market, companies need innovative, new ideas to flourish. You can bring to the table a special viewpoint that will be advantageous to the company as a whole. Businesses succeed when they have a diversified crew that can each provide unique ideas (YTI, 2022).

Assists in Solving Problems

Group cooperation can help resolve challenging issues. The team may share ideas and come up with innovative solutions during brainstorming sessions. Teams can identify the greatest solutions by cooperating (YTI, 2022).

Provides a Supportive Environment

Working together develops a method to ensure that deadlines are fulfilled and that the work is of a high standard. There is always someone else on the squad to pick up the slack when one member falters. Work is done more quickly when it is distributed across team members, which improves the effectiveness of the entire enterprise. As you work together to achieve a common objective, your team will become closer (YTI, 2022).

Develops Morale

When you contribute to anything that yields results, you will feel your labor is respected. Confidence and trust are increased within the team if you present a suggestion that boosts productivity, like a new file system. Every team member brings a unique skill set to the table. Members of a team develop a powerful impression of belonging and a sincere commitment to one another and the overall objective through working together (YTI, 2022).

The Fundamental Factors for Team Building

Expertise and abilities are crucial for a successful team-building process, and any business or organization may benefit from its effective planning, competent execution, and skilled management (Donahue, 2022). Consider incorporating these concepts into your work teams as you construct and improve them:

Purpose

Work teams are contingent on leadership having a clear goal in mind. They are well aware of the goals the team is supposed to accomplish with the right tools. Teams will struggle and grow irritated trying to figure out how to work and grow without a compelling and clear leadership (Rothwell et al., 2021).

People

Roles and duties are clearly defined inside and within work teams, making collaboration easier while maximizing team members' knowledge, talents, and skills. Teams with defined roles and duties will struggle to know who is responsible for what. Teams may work hard, but they won't perform well if they lack the necessary knowledge and expertise (Rothwell & Bakhshandeh, 2022).

Design

The team must be certain about its organizational structure. The execution of practical team designs depends on factors including structure, management ladder, task distribution, available resources, and productivity flow (Levi, 2017).

Rituals

Operating practices successfully direct how a team collaborates with other teams. Consider how the team communicates, uses technology, resolves disagreements, makes decisions, and completes the task. High-performing teams are always assessing and enhancing their teamwork. Teams will undoubtedly be useless and inefficient without well-designed operational practices (Rothwell & Bakhshandeh, 2022).

Relationships

Working together builds and develops trust among individuals. The actions that can foster trust and erode it are recognized by and agreed upon by highly productive teams. Team members get to know each other outside of work, form relationships that often endure far longer than the team itself, and show concern for one another. They become conscious of and sensitive to one another's preferred method(s) of interaction, decision-making, and conflict resolution. They provide a secure environment for each individual to develop. In other words, the team members are brought together by their personal connections and are motivated to work together toward the team's specific goal (Rothwell et al., 2021).

Resources

A thorough model of resource management that supports the availability of resources, such as administrative, technical, and financial assistance, which are essential to the team's productivity and performance, should underpin the team's activities and functions (Levi, 2017).

KPIs

Key performance indicators are an assessment mechanism to measure the team's effectiveness, which must be agreed upon by the organization, the team, and the team members (Rothwell & Bakhshandeh, 2022).

Phases of Development in Teams and Groups

The terms we use to describe the stages of team development were created by educational psychologist Bruce Tuckman, who presented his research in the 1965 paper "Developmental Sequence in Small Groups." His team development and team dynamics studies were the foundation for his theory, known as Tuckman's Stages. His widely held opinion on team development is that all stages are required for a group to collaborate as successfully as possible in order to achieve success. The fifth step, adjourning, was introduced in 1977 by Tuckman and his doctorate student Mary Ann Jensen to his work, which included just the first four stages initially. This stage is used to denote when a team has finished a project. Each of these five stages distinctly depicts a stage that teams go through when working on a project as they fulfill all required duties and processes to be successful (Rothwell et al., 2023).

Let's go down each stage's specifics (see Figure 3.3) and what you can anticipate from your team in each one now that we understand the stages' origin.

Forming

When the team members first get together to meet, it is called the formation stage. It might be said that everyone is settling in and getting to know

Figure 3.3 Bruce Tuckman's five stages of group and team development. Source: Tuckman (1965).

each other throughout this orientation session. Consider the forming phase like the opening day of school or starting a new job. Everyone is eager to get into action and begin the job, and there is enthusiasm in the air. When roles and group dynamics are still being formed, a team leader usually steps forward to take leadership and guide the individual members. In this stage, team members talk about elements such as goals, roles, team strategies, and ground rules (Rothwell et al., 2023).

Storming

Storming follows. The second stage is considered not only the most important but also the most challenging. Due to the clashing of work styles and personalities within the team, it may be rife with conflict. It's also typical for team performance to suffer a little during the storming stage, since members might occasionally differ on objectives, tactics, roles, and duties. Additionally, be aware of cliques or subgroups that may start to emerge at this time. In this phase, members must cooperate and play to each other's strengths in order to overcome barriers and maintain momentum throughout the storming stage so as to avoid becoming slowed down. Additionally, spend effort early on resolving issues to prevent them from continuing to be a problem during the subsequent stages (Rothwell et al., 2023).

Norming

Your team can begin norming once you've weathered the storm, if you catch my drift. There is no longer internal rivalry or conflict because the team members have found out how to operate together. Everyone is united, and an understanding of who the leaders are, what each person's job is, and what will happen next emerges. The team has a stronger feeling of unity and is getting to know each other's personalities and sense of humor better. When providing helpful feedback via online forms or seeking assistance as you do various chores, you should feel at ease during the norming stage (Rothwell et al., 2023).

Performing

The performing stage is next, which often has the most harmonious workplace where individuals are the happiest and most enthusiastic and where team performance is high. Everyone in the organization is totally dedicated to attaining the established goals, and there is a clear and solid framework in place. Everyone on the team, regardless of their function, feels focused, aligned, and with a sense of purpose when performing. No matter what difficulties and conflicts may still arise, they are managed and handled in an honest and productive manner. Additionally, if a disagreement arises, it is simpler and quicker to resolve because the team members have already formed a link and a relationship (Rothwell et al., 2023).

Adjourning

The adjourning step is the last but not the least. Most, if not all, of the team's objectives have been realized at this phase, which is sometimes referred to as termination, grieving, or ending. Final tasks and paperwork are finished, and the project is now complete. Team members frequently are removed from their job and sent to a different project as the workload decreases. Additionally, the team members often have a debriefing where they analyze what went well and what may be improved for next projects (Rothwell et al., 2023).

What's Next?

The next chapter, "Understanding Communication," acknowledges the important role of communication in developing an inclusive, empathetic, and relational supervisor. Therefore, Chapter 4 will focus on effective communication, including interpersonal communication as well as organizational communication and all the potential barriers to communication. In addition, it will examine the main supervisory responsibilities for communicating. Don't forget to review the key takeaways and take a moment to reflect on what you learned in this chapter by completing Table 3.3, End of Chapter 3 Discussion Questions and Inquiries.

Key Takeaways

1. Decisions made about organizational structure affect, and in part determine, the methods of interaction among organizational members. They are thus of crucial importance to supervisors, groups, and team members because structure and interaction have at least four key effects, (1)

Table 3.3   End of Chapter 3 Questions and Inquiries. Your Perspective on What You Learned in Chapter 3

Your Perspective on What You Learned in Chapter 3	
Area of Inquiry	*What Did You Learn, and How Are You Going to Implement It in Your Position?*
The importance of organizational structure to supervisors	
Understanding the main differences between groups and teams	
Categorizing groups by purpose	
Primary group characteristics	
Understanding teams, teamwork, and team building	
The fundamental factors for team building	
Phases of development in teams and groups	

who reports to whom, (2) availability of technical skills, (3) availability of management skills, and (4) ease or difficulty of exercising supervisory duties.

2. Contrary to some myths, groups and teams are two different working concepts in the operations of an organization. A team is a collection of people who work together as a unit, whereas a group coordinates their activities. Although comparable, the two differ when it comes to making decisions and working as a team.

3. Groups are the building blocks of organizations. They are the fundamental units from which organizational designs are established. For that reason, supervisors should be familiar with information about how groups function in organizations.

4. Teams are described as organized groups of individuals working together toward clearly defined objectives that call for coordinated interactions to complete specific tasks (Forsyth, 1999).

5. Highly cohesive groups may become subject to *groupthink*, a condition in which a few vocal members control a group. It is associated with public agreement but private disagreement with group decisions. It occurs when group members prefer to avoid disputes in an effort to appear agreeable.

Discussion Questions and Inquiries

Please take a minute to answer the following inquiries and questions in Table 3.3. From your point of view, what have you learned about the following areas?

References

Bakhshandeh, B. (2002). *Business Coaching and Managers Training*. Unpublished workshop on coaching businesses and training managers. San Diego, CA: Primeco Education, Inc.

Cartwright, D., & Zander, A. (1968). *Group Dynamics*. New York, NY: Harper & Row.

Das, M. (2022). *Differences Between Group and Team*. Organizational Behavior; Group and Team. Retrieved December 28, 2022, from https://www.linkedin.com/pulse/differences-between-group-team-maheshwar-das/

Donahue, W. E. (2022). *Resolving Team Issues and Challenges*. State College, PA: Centerstar Learning.

Duck, S., & McMahan, D. T. (2012). *The Basic of Communication; A Relational Perspective* (2nd ed.). Los Angeles, CA: SAGE Publication, Inc.

Forsyth, D. (1999). *Group Dynamics* (3rd ed.). Belmont, CA: Thompson.

Gantt, S. P., & Badenoch, B. (2013) (Eds.), *The Interpersonal Neurobiology of Group Psychotherapy and Group Process* (1st ed.). London: Karnac Books.

Hackman, J. R., & Wageman, R. (2005). A theory of team coaching. *Academy of Management Review, 30*(2), 269–287. https://doi.org/10.5465/amr.2005.16387885

Harmon, S. K., Brallier, S. A., & Brown, G. F. (2002). Organizational and team context. In G. D. Heinemann & A. M. Zeiss (Eds.), *Team Performance in Health Care. Issues in the Practice of Psychology*. Boston, MA: Springer. https://doi.org/10.1007/978-1-4615-0581-5_5

Katz, D., & Kahn, R. L. (1978). *The Social Psychology of Organizations* (2nd ed.). Hoboken, NJ: John Wiley & Sons.

Katzenbach, J., & Smith, D. (1993). *The Wisdom of Teams*. Cambridge, MN: Harvard Business School Press.

Kerr, N., & Tindale, R. (2004). Group performance and decision making. *Annual of Psychology, 55*(1), 623–655. https://doi.org/10.1146/annurev.psych.55.090902.142009

Kolb, J. A. (2011). *Small Group Facilitation; Improving Process and Performance in Group and Teams*. Amherst, MA: HRD Press, Inc.

Kreitner, R., & Kinicki, A. (2010). *Organizational Behavior* (9th ed.). New York, NY: McGraw-Hill Irwin.

Lencioni, P. (2016). *The Ideal Team Player*. Hoboken, NJ: Jossey-Bass. A Wiley Brand.

Levi, D. (2017). *Group Dynamics for Teams* (5th ed.). Los Angeles, CA: Sage Publications.

Manning, K. (2021). *The Empathetic Workplace*. New York, NY: Harper Collins Leadership.

Mastropier, M. A., & Scruggs, T. E. (2010). *The Inclusive Classroom; Strategies for Effective Differentiation Instruction* (4th ed.). Upper Saddle River, NJ: Pearson.

Maxwell, J. C. (2003). *The 17 Indisputable Laws of Teamwork*. Nashville, TN: Thomas Nelson, Inc.

Merriam-Webster Dictionary. (2022a). *Team*. Retrieved December 23, 2022, from https://www.merriam-webster.com/dictionary/team

Merriam-Webster Dictionary. (2022b). *Group*. Retrieved December 23, 2022, from https://www.merriam-webster.com/dictionary/group

Oxford Languages. (2022). *Groupthink*. Retrieved December 23, 2022, from https://www.google.com/search?q=definition+of+groupthink

Parks, C., & Sanna, L. (1999). *Group Performance and Interaction*. Boulder, CO: Westview.

Rothwell, W. J., & Bakhshandeh, B. (2022). *High-Performance Coaching for Managers*. New York, NY: Taylor & Francis Group; CRC Press.

Rothwell, W. J., Bakhshandeh, B., & Zaballero, A. G. (2023). *Successful Supervisory Leadership; Exerting Positive Influence While Leading People*. New York, NY: Taylor & Francis Group; Routledge.

Rothwell, W. J., Imroz, S. M., & Bakhshandeh, B. (2021). *Organization Development Interventions, Executing Effective Organizational Change*. New York, NY: Taylor & Francis Group; Routledge.

Rothwell, W. J., Stavros, J. M., & Sullivan, R. L. (2016). *Practicing Organization Development: Leading Transformation and Change* (4th ed.). Hoboken, NJ: John Wiley & Sons, Inc.

Saccone, S. (2009). *Relational Intelligence*. San Francisco, CA: Jossey-Bass. A Wiley Imprint.

Shams, M., & Lane, D. A. (2020). Team coaching and family business. *Coaching Psychologist*, *16*(1), 25. https://web-s-ebscohost-com.ezaccess.libraries.psu.edu /plink?key=100.69.46.110_8000_1212876778&site=ehost&scope=site&db=s3h &AN=144722706&crl=f

Sundstrom, E. (1999). The challenges of supporting work team effectiveness. In E. Sundstrom (Ed.), *Supporting Work Team Effectiveness* (pp. 2–23). San Francisco, CA: Jossey-Bass.

Tuckman, B. W. (1965). Developmental sequence in small groups. *Psychological Bulletin*, *63*(6), 384–399. https://doi.org/10.1037/h0022100

YTI Career Institute. (2022). Reasons teamwork is important in the workplace. Retrieved December 23, 2022, from https://yti.edu/blog/reasons-teamwork-is -important-in-the-workplace

Chapter 4

Understanding Communication

Introduction

The majority of people are keen to get along well with their loved ones, friends, and coworkers at work, especially their managers or supervisors. Everyone will eventually find out the hard way that efficient communication and attentive listening form the basis of excellent relationships. Communicating is a process of exchanging information (the content) and/or feelings (how people feel about each other and the content) between people. It is a series of actions intended to achieve a desired result. Effective communication is a crucial component of developing and maintaining healthy relationships on both a personal and professional level.

Understanding the value of communication and how it plays a part in building a functioning connection is one thing; however, mastering effective communication techniques and conveying your message without the other person misinterpreting it is quite another! You probably witnessed or experienced situations when the lack of excellent communication skills has resulted in conflicts with friends, coworkers, or even acts of contempt. This fact alone provides strong support for the value of effective communication and active listening abilities.

The primary problem in inner-personal interactions, according to the Project Management Institute (PMI), is a lack of communication between individuals. Communication misunderstanding is the top problem in

DOI: 10.4324/9781003413493-4

businesses, and it affects people, teams, and departments. Three categories of communication exist: (a) Written, (b) Verbal, and (c) Non-Verbal, which includes attitude, body language, and facial expressions. Over 55% of communication transmitted or received is of this last sort (PMI, 2013; Bakhshandeh, 2004).

As an effective and empathetic supervisor, in order to encourage and assist employees, empathic communication requires embracing and tolerating their diverse viewpoints and feelings, as well as sharing yours with them. Also, it involves carefully listening in an effort to comprehend the feelings of the person with whom you are speaking (Andersson, 2016).

The closeness and dominance relational communication signals were utilized to forecast the task and association leadership fashion in supervisors. According to Mikkelson, Sloan, and Hesse (2019), 307 participants worked in different sectors and completed the study's relational communication and leadership styles questionnaires regarding their immediate supervisor. As expected, messages about closeness and dominance were strongly correlated with task-oriented leadership styles and relationships, respectively. Moreover, dominance communications were connected to a relationship-oriented style, whereas intimacy messages were connected to a task-oriented approach.

According to regression analysis, influence was the strongest predictor of a task-oriented style, whereas receptivity and trust were the best forecasters of a relationship-oriented style. The results generally show that signals about closeness and authority are necessary for all leadership philosophies (Mikkelson et al., 2019).

As shown in Figure 4.1 of the *Successful Supervisory Leadership Series Book II Structure*, we will work in this chapter on some aspects of communication relevant to supervisory positions.

Key Concepts

This chapter will cover the following key concepts:

- Effective Communication
- Communicating Models Used at Workplace
- Interpersonal Communication
- Organizational Communication
- Types of Effective Listening

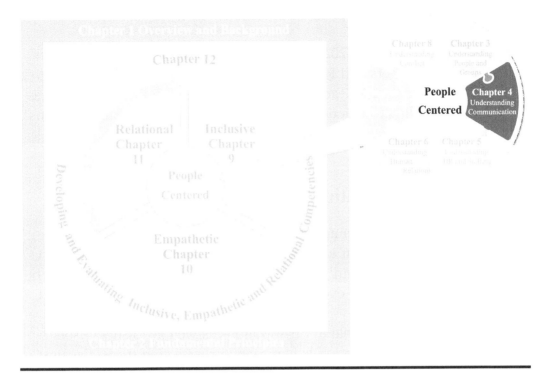

Figure 4.1 *Successful Supervisory Leadership Series Book II Structure.* **Note: Authors' original creation.**

- Active Listening
- Supervisory Responsibilities for Communicating

Definitions

The following definitions of key terms will help to better understand the main elements of this chapter:

Communication

- According to Weekley (1967), the Latin term *communicare*, which means to share or make common, is the origin of the English word *communication.*
- Merriam-Webster (2023) dictionary defined communication as "a process by which information is exchanged between individuals through a common system of symbols, signs, or behavior."
- Pearson and Nelson (2000) explain communication as the process of comprehending and exchanging meaning.

Active Listening

■ According to Leonard (2020), the definition of active listening was created by Carl Rogers and Richard Evans Farson and is characterized as "a skill that requires a few actions: listening for the full meaning of a message, responding to emotions, and noticing nonverbal communications" (p. 5).

Effective Communication

Effective and efficient communication is essential to team productivity and team spirit. Without it, team members will not understand each other, will be unable to gain team acceptance for their ideas, and will be unable to influence others even when their ideas are well-founded and compelling.

Communication is essential to organizations as well as to supervisors and team members. Information is important for achieving success against competitors and for coordinating an organization's internal activities. Yet substantial evidence exists to demonstrate that communication is frequently a problem in organizations. Ineffective communication with employees has been cited as a cause contributing to 10% of business failures each year (Jiang & Men, 2017; Bakhshandeh, 2004).

Many common communication problems between supervisors or managers with their teams include the following:

1. Employees receive insufficient information about their jobs and organizations.
2. Management does not follow-up on employee messages.
3. Messages are sent too early or too late to be of use.
4. The grapevine supplants the void filled by the lack of openness, candor, and visibility of management.
5. Impersonal channels substitute face-to-face contact.
6. Lack of employee input into decisions that affect them is common.

(Bakhshandeh, 2018; Roberts, 2005).

For all these reasons, communicating is an important issue for supervisors and for team members.

A study was conducted by Ramos-Maçães and Román-Portas (2022) about the relevancy of communication and effectiveness of organizational leadership. This study's objective was to conduct an empirical analysis of the interactions between employee commitment, organizational communication, and leadership in the context of organizational transformation. To clarify the relationships between the components and investigate the mediating roles of leadership and employee commitment in the connection between organizational transformation and effective communication, a structural model was created.

An online survey in the quantitative model was carried out using a sample of 335 hotel industry workers. The results showed that organizational communication had a favorable relationship with organizational transformation and had a good and significant impact on leadership and employee commitment. This study also makes the case that employee dedication, effective leadership, and communication are crucial factors in the accomplishment of organizational transformation. By classifying the prognosticators of organizational change and examining how certain antecedents impact the effectiveness of organizational change, the findings can provide academics and managers a useful and much-needed method to managing change (Ramos-Maçães & Román-Portas, 2022).

Communicating Models Used at the Workplace

A model is a simple representation of something more complex. It helps us understand an otherwise complicated process or procedure. For example, taking apart a model airplane to see how it works is easier than taking apart a real airplane.

Interpersonal Communication and Organizational Communication are two models that are useful in understanding communication while working with people in organizations (Rothwell, 2015).

Interpersonal Communication

Simply defined, interpersonal communication is the transmission of meanings between two or more people. Shannon and Weaver (1949) developed a classic model of interpersonal communication—what they called a mathematical model that is still widely used today. See Figure 4.2.

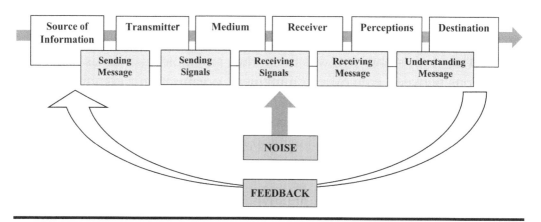

Figure 4.2 Model of interpersonal communication. Source: Adapted from Bakhshandeh, Rothwell, and Imroz (2023), Bakhshandeh (2018), and Shannon and Weaver (1949).

The following elements are key components of this model:

■ **Source of information** is the origin of this information and the purpose of delivery.
■ **The transmitter** is the one who sends a message that is encoded into language.
■ **The receiver** is the one who receives a message and decodes (interprets) it.
■ **The message** is the ideas encoded into symbolic language (words and numbers are symbolic language).
■ **The medium** is the means by which a message is conveyed. The most common media include spoken word, written word, nonverbal (body language), or some combination.
■ **Noise** is that which distorts a message much as static interferes with radio or television reception, or others' input, such as biases, judgments, and stereotyping.
■ **Feedback** is the acknowledgment by a receiver that a message is being received.
■ **Perception** is the way people interpret the meaning of the message, the sender's intent, and the world around them.

(Bakhshandeh et al., 2023; McLean, 2005; Shannon & Weaver, 1949).

Nearly 92% of a project manager's time consists of communication. Only 8% of the communication process involves actual spoken words. Over 55% of the communication process consists of such nonverbal elements as body language, vocal intonation, silence, physical surroundings, and how closely the speaker stands in proximity to the listener (PMI, 2013).

A simple example should help illustrate how the model works. Suppose a supervisor wants to give an order to an employee. The supervisor in this example is the transmitter. The employee is the receiver. The order is a message that has been encoded into specific words by the supervisor. Most orders are given by spoken word, which is the medium (synonymous with the channel). If the employee is working on a loud piece of equipment, the supervisor may have to shout to give the order. The equipment creates noise that interferes with transmission and message reception. If the employee is unable to make out the message over the sound of machinery, the employee may cup a hand to one ear and shout, "What?" That is feedback, an indication from the receiver that the message was heard and may need to be repeated or understood. If the employee questions the order because of suspicion or distrust of the supervisor—perhaps they have quarreled in the past and the employee suspects the supervisor is out to get him—then the way the message is received is affected by perception.

This model is useful for supervisors because it helps them analyze communication between themselves and others. Supervisors deal with transmitters like supervisors, peers, employees, and customers. Supervisors also deal with the same people as receivers. Messages include orders, complaints, compliments, gossip, or small talk about matters distinct from the work setting. Media include spoken, written, and body language. Noise is any distraction which includes assumptions made by the transmitter about what the receiver knows, distractions while putting a message into words, distractions stemming from the words themselves, or inattention by receivers (Montague et al., 2013).

Barriers to Interpersonal Communication

Barriers to effective communication can stem from any of the following sources (see Table 4.1):

As the sender of messages, you need to pay attention to the following aspects of the forms of communication which might impact the effectiveness of your communication:

■ Carefully encrypt your message, specify your preferred means of transmission, and make sure it is simple to interpret.

Table 4.1 Barriers to Interpersonal Communication

Barriers to Interpersonal Communication	
Areas of Communication	*Barriers*
Difficulties of subject matter	• Unfamiliar subject • Technical data
Deficiencies in the communicator	• Doesn't understand subject • Understands the subject but cannot explain it • Lacks speaking, writing, or listening skills • Lacks motivation to communicate clearly • Is in too big a hurry • Has a negative attitude toward the receiver
Obstacles inherent in the medium	• Limitations of letter, memo, report, speech • Limitations of language
Problems with channels	• Communication fails to arrive at the right destination
Deficiencies in the receiver	• Does not have assumed knowledge of the subject • Does not understand the language of the writer or speaker • Lacks reading or listening skills • Lacks motivation to receive message • Is in too big a hurry • Has a negative attitude toward the writer or speaker

Note: Authors' original creation.

■ The following are some characteristics of the recipient that you should be mindful of before sending your message:
  – **Nonverbal.** Nonverbal communication, which is based on your body language, facial expressions, and habits, is a significant aspect of one-on-one or in-person communication.
  – **Paralingual.** Your voice's tone and pitch are quite effective in getting your point through.
  – **Words.** Important components of your message are the words you use and how you use them.
  – **Meanings.** Even in written communication, the interpretations that the recipients ascribe to your communications vary based on the words, nonverbal cues, and paralinguistic elements that were used.

■ In order to verify the correctness of the communications and the extent to which the receivers understand the messages, it is helpful to solicit the comments or feedback from the recipients.

- If you leave any questions at the conclusion of the message you can get feedback.
- In the end, it is up to the recipients to confirm that they received the communications and that they comprehended their purposes and contents.

(Bakhshandeh et al., 2023; Bakhshandeh, 2018; Levi, 2017; Kold, 2011).

As the sender of the message you need to pay attention to the following interfering elements in an effective communication:

- Noise of any kind
- Distance, physical and temporal
- Ineffective coding of message
- Improper encoding of message
- Opinion, bias, and stereotyping
- Attitude and hostility
- Language differences
- Cultural differences

(Bakhshandeh et al., 2023; Bakhshandeh, 2018; Levi, 2017; Kold, 2011).

Overcoming barriers to communication is an important part of the supervisor's job (see Table 4.2). It is also essential to effective teamwork.

One of the ways to be effective in removing barriers to communication is to be empathetic about cultural inclusiveness. By the use of culturally inclusive communication, we are able to harness one aspect of the working environment—communication—to foster inclusion. This indicates that we are utilizing communication—a means of communicating information—in a way that makes everyone feel as though they belong, regardless of their background (Hassan & Connaughton, 2022). Being adaptable, considering how others are replying, and making changes are all part of communicating in a way that is culturally inclusive. Please keep in mind that we want to establish a place where everyone feels welcome, thus the rules below may not always apply (Duck & McMahan, 2012).

Organizational Communication

Many people work in organizations for their living, and the numbers continue growing, which makes the effective communication in organizations essential to their performance and productivity. The context of organizational communication is not a new thing, as Lewis (1975) defined it as

Table 4.2 Methods for Overcoming Communication Barriers

Methods for Overcoming Communication Barriers	
Barriers	*Methods*
Difficulties of subject matter	• Simplify presentation, gearing it to the receiver's level of understanding
Deficiencies in the communicator	• Teach the receiver about the communication • Structure the presentation, beginning with simple information and building gradually on it • Train the communicator in speaking or writing • Heighten the motivation of the communicator by linking rewards to improved communication • Slow down the communicator so the receiver has time to decipher the message • Work on building trust between communicator and receiver
Obstacles inherent in the medium	• Use multiple media to reinforce content • Build in reinsertion of information
Problems with channels	• Follow-up on messages by requesting feedback
Deficiencies in the receiver	• Encourage questions • Improve reading and writing skills

Note: Authors' original creation.

"the sending and receiving of information within a complex organization, exchanging information and transmitting meaning within an organization, and coordinating a number of people who are interdependently related" (pp. 4–5). As Lewis notes, "Communication is the essence of managerial procedure. It is the focal point of executive action, which is central to the control and survival of organizations and is a requisite to effective management" (Lewis, 1975, p. 4). Another useful model for understanding communication is the organizational model (see Figure 4.3). It differs from the model of interpersonal communication described in the previous section. The organizational model has two components: formal and informal.

Formal Model

This model is based on the organization's command structure. Any message in this model is said to have direction, meaning it flows from one point to

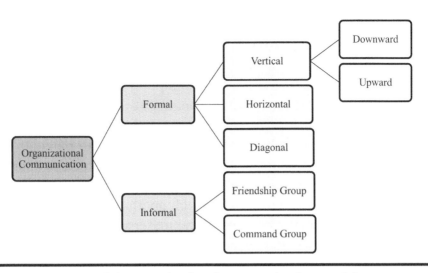

Figure 4.3 **Directions of the organizational communication model. Source: Authors'
original creation.**

another in the command structure. This model practices three directions:
(a) vertical message, (b) horizontal message, and (c) diagonal message (see
Figure 4.4) (Hassan & Connaughton, 2022; Pearson & Nelson, 2000):

Vertical Message. Supervisors in traditional organizations focus much
of their attention on downward communication. It is frequently associated with orders about handling tasks, explanations about the reasoning behind decisions made, and directives about handling procedures

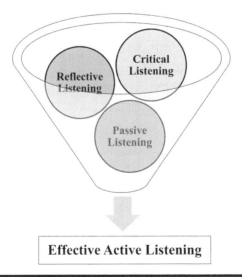

Figure 4.4 **Effective active listening. Source: Adapted from Bakhshandeh, Rothwell,
and Imroz (2023).**

or about policies, feedback about employee performance, and indoctrination intended to persuade, cajole, motivate, or instruct employees. Too many supervisors assume any message that is clear will also be accepted and understood. This assumption is a myth (Hassan & Connaughton, 2022; Pearson & Nelson, 2000).

Downward Communication. This type is subject to faulty transmission. That is especially true when a message is expected to make its way from top managers to hourly employees through numerous management levels. "If top management represents 100 percent understanding, by the time the message travels through another five levels, only 20 percent of the original message will be understood" (Lewis, 1975, p. 71). As the message flows downward from managers through the chain of command, some ideas are not transmitted because they are forgotten or are considered unimportant, a phenomenon known as **filtering**. Other ideas creep into the message as each receiver translates ideas into familiar terms and places interpretations on them, a phenomenon known as **distortion**. In some cases, distortion is deliberately engineered to make one group look good at the expense of others. Filtering and distortion occur as a message is transmitted down the chain of command (Hassan & Connaughton, 2022; Pearson & Nelson, 2000).

Top management's understanding of its message is 100%, although the following distortions and filtering result in those down the chain of command to receive only 20% of the actual intent of the message:

■ Deliberate suppression of information
■ Simplifications of message
■ Ambiguity (double meanings)
■ Misunderstandings
■ Hourly workers

Upward Communication. This deserves greater attention than it typically receives. It is commonly associated with questions and suggestions about handling tasks, information about problems experienced by employees while carrying out work, facts about results, feedback on how well company policies or procedures are working; and indoctrination intended to persuade, cajole, or flatter supervisors or employees. In too many traditional organizations, supervisors assume that employees are completely willing to pose questions, ask for help when needed, provide information about problems experienced as they do their jobs, relay facts about work, or furnish feedback on how well company policies or procedures are working. That is simply not the case (Ramos-Maçães & Román-Portas, 2022). The reason is that people are motivated to communicate only when it will better their situations. Employees are not inclined to communicate anything that makes them look bad, appear incompetent, or seem unable to carry out duties. They are sometimes self-interested enough to conceal or filter information that will improve the situation of those they dislike or distrust or that will worsen their own standing (Hassan & Connaughton, 2022; Pearson & Nelson, 2000).

In team-based organizations, upward communication is critically important.

Team members must be able to communicate upward as the need arises and receive prompt and specific feedback on suggestions they offer or requests for help they make. A common reason for team failure is the inability or unwillingness of middle and top managers to provide prompt, specific feedback to teams.

Horizontal Communication. This method is increasing in importance because many problems in today's complex organizations require deliberation across many functions or occupational specialties. That creates problems in traditional organizations because classical management theory suggests that communication across lines of authority should be handled by the chief decision-makers of those functions. If problems in one work group affect another, employees should inform their supervisors and let them solve the problems and communicate with supervisors in other work groups (Hassan & Connaughton, 2022; Pearson & Nelson, 2000).

Of course, that is not always practical, necessary, or even desirable. Chief decision-makers may lack time or sufficient technical expertise to deal with some problems. Early in this century Henri Fayol suggested that supervisors should be able to talk over some matters among themselves (Andersson, 2016). Communication could thus cross lines of authority under certain conditions, provided managers were informed and consented to such arrangements. Fayol believed this was necessary to increase the speed of problem-solving and avoid overloading managers with trivial problems. Team-based organizations are better structured to handle fast, technically oriented problem-solving. That is one of their key advantages. Indeed, cross-functional teams may be formed that cut across standing teams, and they can effectively tackle problems overlapping the responsibilities of standing teams (Levi, 2017).

Diagonal Communication. Diagonal Communication is also increasing in importance for the same reason that horizontal communication is—that is, reduced elapsed time in decision-making. The supervisor or team members who go directly to a computer programmer for help, without stopping first to talk with the programmer's supervisor, make use of diagonal communication. Appeals for specialized staff or technical support often flow diagonally. Special projects—like new product start-ups or new ventures of any kind—often require collaboration across many functions and between hierarchical levels. In these cases diagonal communication is usually a necessity (Hassan & Connaughton, 2022; Pearson & Nelson, 2000).

Barriers to Formal Model of Organizational Communication. Barriers to communication in this model stem from many causes as messages are directed upward, downward, horizontally, or diagonally. Supervisors or team members must cope with these barriers on a daily basis. They should thus reflect on methods of solving problems created by these barriers. Information does not reach appropriate people in organizations for any or all of the following reasons:

- ■ ***Status differences.*** It is difficult for low-status people to reach high-status individuals in an organization.
- ■ ***Trust issues.*** People do not communicate if they distrust others or do not know their likely reaction to news.
- ■ ***Lack of awareness.*** Who should receive information? Is it important?
- ■ ***Lack of skills.*** Can the communicator read or speak effectively?
- ■ ***Lack of time.*** Do people have time to receive information?

(Leonardo, 2020)

Informal Model

The second component of the organizational model is the informal model. Unlike the formal component that flows through the chain of command, the informal component flows through friendship groups. A **friendship group** is any collection of people who share interests. Friendship groups may fall outside a **command group** consisting of people reporting to the same supervisor or working in the same standing team. Informal communication is associated with the grapevine because, like a grapevine, it wanders all over (Hassan & Connaughton, 2022; Pearson & Nelson, 2000).

More than one supervisor and chief executive has railed bitterly about the **grapevine.** It is frequently cited as a cause of low morale, a source of misleading information, and evidence that employees do not have enough work to keep them busy.

The flow of information through the grapevine is unpredictable, though speedy. (The more controversial the information, the faster it is likely to spread.) There are four ways rumors spread:

1. *Individual-by-individual.* Transmission of messages passes from one person to another much like a chain.
2. *Individual-to-group.* One person tells many others.
3. *Individual-to-others.* One person tells two or three others, who in turn relate the rumor to two or three others, and so on.
4. *Individual-cluster.* One person tells others, only some of whom spread the rumor. Others conceal it, either intentionally or unintentionally.

The grapevine has both advantages and disadvantages. Among its advantages is that it gives supervisors an indication of what concerns and interests employees, provides an outlet for emotions, serving much like a safety valve, and speeds the flow of important information. Disadvantages include its tendency to build apprehension among employees because the grapevine often carries more negative than positive information. It has the potential for eliciting undesirable behavior, such as prompting employees to seek work elsewhere as soon as they get unreliable word about a pending layoff or plant shutdown, or its potential for being used, even manipulated, by unscrupulous people for self-seeking ends (Greer, 2000).

Effective supervisors know how to manage the grapevine so that its advantages are used to deliver the desired message, and its disadvantages are minimized. In team-based organizations, team members manage the grapevine by exercising openness and honesty among themselves and demanding it from those to whom they report.

To manage the grapevine, supervisors should keep the following tips in mind:

■ Listen to informal (grapevine) communication to keep up-to-date on employee concerns and problems.
■ Provide facts when the grapevine is carrying false information.

- Confront individuals who are maliciously spreading information about other people.
- Realize why the grapevine exists; it is faster than formal channels and gives people information when not available from other sources.

Types of Effective Listening

Carl Rogers and Richard Evans Farson, two psychologists, first introduced the idea of active listening in 1957 while working on a journal paper. They defined the term as "a skill that requires a few actions: listening for the full meaning of a message, responding to emotions, and noticing nonverbal communications" (Leonard, 2020, p. 5). Many individuals mistakenly believe that since they can simply hear someone else talking, they have already paid attention to them, comprehended what they were saying, and grasped what the speaker was trying to convey. As you may remember, we discussed the influence of our inner chatter on our objectives and the manner we listen to communication in the session on it mentioned above.

During conversation, there are several ways to listen; some of the more well-researched methods are (a) critical listening, (b) reflective listening, and (c) passive listening (Leonardo, 2020). In this section, we examine several listening strategies and examine how they connect to the idea of active listening as a whole.

Critical Listening

The listeners must put in the most thought and effort while engaging in critical listening. While digesting the communication and separating views, perceptions, and prejudice from the facts in the message, the listeners maintain their attention on the message. This method is helpful when we need to evaluate the information we are getting, such as when we are reading the news or listening to someone analyze a problem or an incident (Leonardo, 2020; Goulston, 2010; Roberts, 2005).

Reflective Listening

When we are reflecting back on what the speakers have said and what we have heard in the message, we communicate by using our own words. By using this strategy, we may tell the speakers and let them know that we have heard and comprehended their message without having to analyze, criticize, or condemn it (Leonardo, 2020; Goulston, 2010; Roberts, 2005).

Passive Listening

The speakers are the main focus of passive listening. The listeners should refrain from interjecting or interrupting the speaker while they convey the topic and terms they choose to employ. Unfortunately, this sort of listening is the most prevalent. Most individuals simply wait for their chance to speak while they listen quietly. The listeners are not focused on the speakers' message or substance when using this listening technique (Leonardo, 2020; Goulston, 2010; Roberts, 2005).

Active Listening

All of the listening techniques mentioned above are present in healthy amounts during a successful, active listening (see Figure 4.4). Effective active listeners use reflective listening to ensure the speakers feel heard, critical listening to comprehend the message in order to establish their opinions on the speakers' nonverbal signs and the emotions that go along with it, and passive listening to remain silent while the speakers are delivering their messages (Leonardo, 2020; Goulston, 2010; Roberts, 2005).

Elements of Active Listening for Supervisors. The strategies outlined below (see Table 4.3) may be helpful if you're looking to improve your capacity for active listening. They stem from the idea that active listening is a skill that is constantly up for development.

Follow-Up and Action Plan

After completing Table 4.3, supervisors should design and manage their own activities for developing a learning and improvement action plan to enhance their understanding and clarity on the group's characteristics. Use the following Action Plan for Learning and Improving (APLI) table (Table 4.4) as a tool to manage such actions.

Supervisory Responsibilities for Communicating

Given the nature of supervisory positions, supervisors are in communication with different levels of organization employees and have a level of responsibilities to such people, as follows.

Table 4.3 Supervisor's Elements of Active Listening Self-Rating Sheet

Supervisor's Elements of Active Listening Self-Rating Sheet							
Supervisor's Name		Date	Supervisor's Manager	Department			
Rating Scale: 1 = Poor, 2 = Marginal, 3 = Acceptable, 4 = Good, 5 = Excellent							
	Methods	*Descriptions*	*1*	*2*	*3*	*4*	*5*
1	*Concentrating on the purpose*	In order to genuinely comprehend and sympathize with the others, active listening starts with the intention to be aware of and sensitive to them, as well as the objective and purpose of the conversation.					
2	*Being respectful*	Being mindful of the current moment is the first step toward being courteous. There should be no daydreaming, interrupting, or planning your response. Instead, focus on the meaning and purpose behind their words and actions.					
3	*Paying attention to body language*	The conscious and unconscious motions and movements that indicate or convey information are referred to as body language. It may involve touch, eye contact or movement, posture, hand gestures, and facial emotions. Consider what your body language conveys when listening to others.					
4	*Giving reassuring verbal cues*	Verbal cues are indications that a listener has understood what has been spoken. When the speakers want the listeners to pay close attention, they may use linguistic signals such as speaking more slowly or loudly to stress a point.					
5	*Clarify information*	Occasionally, maintaining eye contact and nodding throughout a discussion is insufficient. You could question if your mind fully processed the scene. You can both fill up any knowledge gaps by asking the speaker for clarification and providing a paraphrase in return.					

(Continued)

Table 4.3 (Continued) Supervisor's Elements of Active Listening Self-Rating Sheet

Supervisor's Elements of Active Listening Self-Rating Sheet							
Supervisor's Name	Date		Supervisor's Manager	Department			
Rating Scale: 1 = Poor, 2 = Marginal, 3 = Acceptable, 4 = Good, 5 = Excellent							
	Methods	*Descriptions*	*1*	*2*	*3*	*4*	*5*
6	*Asking questions*	Confusion may be removed by asking questions. Despite your belief that you have understood the most of what they stated, you still have questions. You may make sure you have received the proper information by asking clarifying questions.					
7	*Listening attentively*	You may also show interest by posing inquiries. An open-ended query might urge the speaker to expand on a significant or intriguing point. Additionally, it demonstrates that you have been paying close attention and that you are eager to learn more.					
8	*Avoiding judgment*	It's critical to maintain an impartial, open, and nonjudgmental attitude. Making the effort to improve your listening skills allows you to interact with concepts, viewpoints, and chances that you might not have had access to in the past.					
9	*Summarizing*	Make sure to leave the conversation on a positive tone as it nears its conclusion. Share a brief summary of the speaker's remarks or some brief notes. When prompted, express your views and opinions in a way that shows you have carefully considered the material.					

(Continued)

Table 4.3 (Continued) Supervisor's Elements of Active Listening Self-Rating Sheet

Supervisor's Elements of Active Listening Self-Rating Sheet							
Supervisor's Name		Date	Supervisor's Manager		Department		
Rating Scale: 1 = Poor, 2 = Marginal, 3 = Acceptable, 4 = Good, 5 = Excellent							
	Methods	*Descriptions*	*1*	*2*	*3*	*4*	*5*
10	*Reflecting*	Consider what you learned in the aftermath of the interaction. You could have had intense emotions or thoughts that needed to be processed or recorded, regardless of whether it was a lecture, an interview, or a discussion with an old friend.					
		Individual Columns' Totals					
		Total of above Individual Columns					
		Final Average (above total divided by 10)					

Source: Adapted from Bakhshandeh et al. (2023), Rothwell et al. (2021), and Rogers and Farson (1957).

Table 4.4 APLI-Connected to Table 4.3

Action Plan for Learning and Improving	
Area of Learning and Improving: *Supervisor's Elements of Active Listening Methods Self-Rating Sheet*	
Reference: *Table 4.3*	
Three learning and improvement actions for this month that will raise my three lowest areas of the Supervisor's Elements of Active Listening Methods Self-Rating Sheet to enhance my understanding and clarity by at least one on the next rating:	
Action 1:	By When:
Action 2:	By When:
Action 3:	By When:

Note: Authors' original creation.

Supervisory Responsibilities in Communicating with Employees

Supervisors should communicate with employees about job standards and supervisory expectations, organizational policies, and procedures affecting employees' jobs, the distribution of work and rewards, organizational plans affecting employees, and possible changes before they take effect. In team-based organizations, team members owe each other honest feedback, particularly when one team member's performance is impeding other team members or the entire team. A good approach for a team is to devise "communication rules" that set forth in writing the rules that team members will observe when communicating with each other. Openness and honesty should be at the top of that list of rules.

Supervisory Responsibilities in Communicating with Coworkers

Supervisors should communicate with their peers (other supervisors) about joint problems faced by their respective work groups, the effects of one supervisor's actions or policies on employees of another supervisor, and their mutual interpretations of policies and procedures. Above all, supervisors should lend their support to other supervisors who are part of the same management team as themselves—and should make it a rule never to speak ill of another supervisor because that can impact his or her ability to perform.

Supervisory Responsibilities in Communicating with Staff Departments

Supervisors should communicate with staff departments such as accounting and human resources and management information systems about technical matters falling into the specialized areas of these staff specialists. Staff functions exist to support the line, such as operating supervisors and their employees. Team members should also feel free to request assistance from staff experts as the need arises.

Caveats for Effective Communication by Supervisors

To maintain good communication with others, supervisors and team members should follow several guidelines for effective communication (Bakhshandeh, 2018; Rothwell, 2015; McLean, 2005):

1. They should think of the receiver's viewpoint while preparing messages and communicating with others. The big problem in communicating is to consider the possible reactions of listeners to a message based on the receiver's perspective and concerns. As the old saying goes, "what you hear depends on where you sit in the organization."

2. Be positive and convey this positivity in your message and toward the receiver. Nothing undercuts communication so much as a lack of confidence—or negative attitudes.

3. Make it a point to dwell on solutions to problems, not just on problems. It is easy to criticize and find fault. But solving problems or offering solutions is usually far more difficult.

4. Remember that most communication problems are caused by getting information to the right people, those who need it for their own decision-making or action-taking. Managers, supervisors, and team members do not spend enough time identifying precisely **who** should receive information because it is necessary for their work. Avoid being on the receiving end of comments like, "Why didn't you tell me that?"

5. Remember that psychological rather than logical forces drive communication. People will communicate with those whom they perceive as capable of helping them achieve their personal and professional goals. They will not communicate with those whom they perceive as incapable of helping them achieve their goals or delaying or sabotaging their efforts. That means supervisors perceived as threatening will be less likely to receive questions or suggestions from employees than supervisors perceived to be approachable or open-minded.

6. Communication is a function of experience. People are more likely to communicate with those with whom they have had previous dealings. They are less likely to approach those they do not know or do not feel comfortable with.

7. Communication is greatly influenced by trust. If employees trust their supervisors or team members, they are more comfortable and morale is high. They believe what they are told. But if trust is low, great difficulty exists in communicating.

8. Trust is hard to build but is easy to lose. To lose it, supervisors need only be perceived as concealing what they know from their employees or deliberately telling untruths. To lose the trust of teammates, team members need only be perceived as a "loose cannon," a "spy of

management," or "someone who is out for what they can gain for themselves only."

What's Next?

The next chapter, "Understanding Human Resources and Staffing," acknowledges the important role human resources play in staffing, orienting, training, developing employees, and establishing an empowering environment for diversity, equity, inclusion, and belonging. Before you move on, don't forget to review the key takeaways and take a moment to reflect on what you learned in this chapter by completing Table 4.5, End of Chapter 4 Discussion Questions and Inquiries.

Key Takeaways

1. Categories of communication are (a) written, (b) verbal, and (c) nonverbal, including attitude, body language, and facial expressions. Over 55% of communication transmitted or received is of this last sort (PMI, 2013; Bakhshandeh, 2004).
2. Effective and efficient communication is essential to team productivity and team spirit. Without it, team members will not understand each other, will be unable to gain team acceptance for their ideas, and will be unable to influence others even when their ideas are well-founded and compelling.
3. Simply defined, interpersonal communication is the transmission of meanings between two or more people.
4. Near 92% of a project manager's time consists of communication. Only 8% of the communication process involves actual spoken words. Over 55% of the communication process consists of such nonverbal elements as body language, vocal intonation, silence, physical surroundings, and how closely the speaker stands in proximity to the listener (PMI, 2013).
5. Many people work in organizations for their living, and the numbers continue growing, which makes the effective communication in organizations essential to their performance and productivity.
6. Many individuals mistakenly believe that simply since they can hear someone else talking, they have already paid attention to them,

Table 4.5   End of Chapter 4 Questions and Inquiries. Your Perspective on What You Learned in Chapter 4

Your Perspective on What You Learned in Chapter 4	
Area of Inquiry	*What Did You Learn, and How Are You Going to Implement It in Your Position?*
Effective communication	
Communicating models used at workplace	
Interpersonal communication	
Organizational communication	
Types of effective listening	
Active listening	
Supervisory responsibilities for communicating	

comprehended what they were saying, and grasped what the speaker was trying to convey.

Discussion Questions and Inquiries

Please take a minute to answer the following inquiries and questions in Table 4.5. From your point of view, what have you learned about the following areas?

References

Andersson, A. (2016). Communication barriers in an interorganizational ERP-project. *International Journal of Managing Projects in Business*, 9(1), 214–233. https://doi.org/10.1108/IJMPB-06-2015-0047

Bakhshandeh, B. (2004). *Effective Communication: Getting Present.* 2-Sets CD. San Diego, CA: Primeco Education, Inc.

Bakhshandeh, B. (2018). *Team Building & Problem Solving.* Unpublished two-days' workshop on resolving team conflict and building a strong relationship among team members. Carbondale, PA: Primeco Education, Inc.

Bakhshandeh, B., Rothwell, W. J., & Imroz, S. M. (2023). *Transformational Coaching for Effective Leadership. Creating Sustainable Change Through Shifting Paradigms.* New York, NY: Taylor & Francis Group; Routledge.

Duck, S., & McMahan, D. T. (2012). *The Basic of Communication; A Relational Perspective* (2nd ed.). Los Angeles, CA: SAGE Publication, Inc.

Goulston, M. (2010). *Just Listen: Discover the Secret to Getting Through to Absolutely Anyone.* New York, NY: AMACOM.

Greer, F. C. (2000). Grapvine. *The Jerusalem Post (1950–2008).* Retrieved January 24, 2023, from https://ezaccess.libraries.psu.edu/login?qurl=https%3A%2F%2Fwww.proquest.com%2Fhistorical-newspapers%2Fgrapvine%2Fdocview%2F1443873999%2Fse-2%3Faccountid%3D13158

Hassan, A. B., & Connaughton, S. L. (2022). Ethical leadership, perceived leader–member ethical communication and organizational citizenship behavior: Development and validation of a multilevel model. *Leadership & Organization Development Journal*, 43(1), 96–110. https://doi.org/10.1108/LODJ-07-2021-0356

Jiang, H., & Men, R. L. (2017). Creating an engaged workforce: The impact of authentic leadership, transparent organizational communication, and work-life enrichment. *Communication Research*, 44(2), 225–243. https://doi.org/10.1177/0093650215613137

Kold, J. A. (2011). *Small Group Facilitation: Improving Process and Performance in Groups and Teams.* Amherst, MO: HRD Press.

Leonardo, N. (2020). *Active Listening Techniques.* Emeryville, CA: Rockridge Press.

Levi, D. (2017). *Group Dynamics for Teams* (5th ed.). Thousand Oaks, CA: Sage Publications, Inc.

Lewis, D. (1975). Languages and language. *The Journal of Philosophy, 74*(2), 129–139. https://doi.org/10.2307/2025576

McLean, S. (2005). *The Basics of Interpersonal Communication* (p. 10). Boston, MA: Allyn & Bacon.

Merriam-Webster. (2023). *Communication*. Retrieved January 17, 2023, from https://www.merriam webster.com/dictionary/communication

Mikkelson, A. C., Sloan, D., & Hesse, C. (2019). Relational communication messages and leadership styles in Supervisor/Employee relationships. *International Journal of Business Communication, 56*(4), 586–604. https://doi.org/10.1177/2329488416687267

Montague, E., Xu, J., Chen, P.-Y., Chewning, B., & Barrett, B. (2013). Nonverbal interpersonal interactions in clinical encounters and patient perceptions of empathy. *Journal of Participatory Medicine, 5*, 33. Retrieved January 21, 2023, from https://participatorymedicine.org/journal/evidence/research/20i3/o8/14/nonverbal-interpersonal-interactions-in-clinical-encounters-and-patient-percep-tions-of-empathy/

Pearson, J., & Nelson, P. (2000). *An Introduction to Human Communication: Understanding and Sharing*. Boston, MA: McGraw-Hill.

PMI (Project Management Institute, Inc.). (2013). *A Guide to the Project Management Body of Knowledge* (PMBOK guide-5th ed.). Newtown, PA: PMI, Global Standard.

Ramos-Maçães, M., & Román-Portas, M. (2022). The effects of organizational communication, leadership, and employee commitment in organizational change in the hospitality sector. *Communication & Society, 35*(2), 89–106. https://doi.org/10.15581/003.35.2.89-106

Roberts, D. (2005). *Everyday Communication Techniques for the Workplace*. Chicago, IL: Ragan's Management Resources.

Rogers, C. R., & Evans Farson, R. (1957). *Active Listening*. Mansfield Centre, CT: Martino Publishing.

Rothwell, W. J. (2015). *Beyond Training & Development. Enhancing Human Performance Through a Measurable Focus on Business Impact* (3rd ed.). Amherst, MA: HRD Press, Inc.

Rothwell, W. J., Imroz, S. M., & Bakhshandeh, B. (2021). *Organization Development Interventions, Executing Effective Organizational Change*. New York, NY: Taylor & Francis Group; Routledge.

Shannon, C. E., & Weaver, W. (1949). *The Mathematical Theory of Communication*. Champaign, IL: University of Illinois Press.

Weekley, E. (1967). *An Etymological Dictionary of Modern English* (Vol. 1). New York, NY: Dover Publications.

Chapter 5

Understanding Human Resources and Staffing

Introduction

A fully inclusive company fosters a feeling of community and worth among its members, helping them understand how important their contributions are to the organization's success. To build ecosystems based on diversity and equity, discriminatory structures and policies must be acknowledged and then dismantled. Leadership in this process must be purposeful, accountable, and able to move quickly. A crucial component of maintaining inclusion is corporate responsibility, which involves monitoring performance indicators, analyzing employee happiness and engagement, and regularly reviewing specified goals and objectives (Adjo et al., 2021).

The advantages of investing in human resource practices have been supported by a number of strategic HR management investigations conducted over the past three decades. Studies have shown a favorable relationship between organizational performance and HR approaches aimed at enhancing employee proficiency, motivation, and the opportunity to succeed (Jiang et al., 2017).

Human resources may be categorized into two categories: (1) A human resource is first and foremost a person! Employees inside an organization are referred to as human resources. You are a human resource if you are currently employed! The emphasis on the employees' importance as a resource and the need for successful management is highlighted by this description of them. (2) The department or function inside a business that manages the workers is known as human resources, but this lesson's main focus isn't just another word for employees (French, 2007).

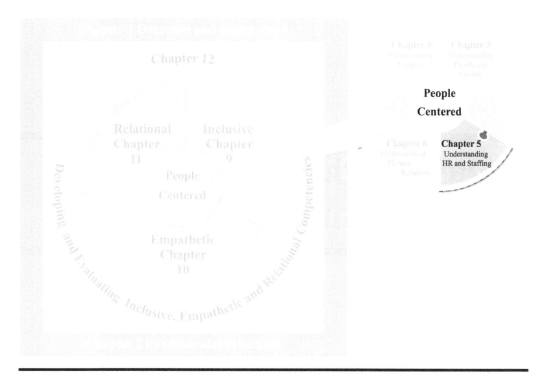

Figure 5.1 *Successful Supervisory Leadership Series Book II Structure. Note:* **Authors' original creation.**

The role of the supervisor or team member may vary in staffing from making decisions to advising department managers or others on what decisions they should make. In self-directed teams, team members typically assume responsibility for all staffing after receiving appropriate training. The team facilitator, who serves as a coach, often assists them in their roles.

As shown in Figure 5.1 of the *Successful Supervisory Leadership Series Book II Structure*, we look at the relationship between human resources and staffing in this chapter, and as a supervisor, you are involved in both definitions. This means you play an important role in deciding how many staff are needed to complete a task as well as what skills and experience they require.

Key Concepts

This chapter will cover the following key concepts:

■ Understanding Human Resources
■ Major Roles of Human Resources Department

- Diversity, Equity, Inclusion, and Belonging
- Understanding Staffing
- Recruiting and Selecting People
- Analyzing and Describing the Work
- Orienting and Training

Definitions

The following definitions of key terms will help to better understand the main elements of this chapter:

Human Resources

Oxford Language (2023) defines Human Resources as

- "the personnel of a business or organization, especially when regarded as a significant asset,"
- "the department of a business or organization that deals with the hiring, administration, and training of personnel."

Staffing

- Staffing is the process of recruiting, selecting, hiring, orienting, and training people for work in an organization (Rothwell & Kazanas, 2003).
- Staffing is the process of finding, choosing, analyzing, and establishing a working rapport with present or potential workers. Finding qualified applicants to fill the various positions inside the firm is the major objective of staffing (Sharma & Sharma, 2018).

Recruiting

- Finding, evaluating, and employing the finest individuals for available jobs in your firm is the task and process of recruitment. Depending on how your firm organizes and conducts recruiting, the hiring process might be drawn out and involve several processes and stakeholders (Rothwell & Kazanas, 2003).
- Finding, vetting, recruiting, and finally onboarding qualified job prospects is a firm's process of recruitment (Carasco & Rothwell, 2020).

Orienting

According to Vocabulary (2023), orienting means:

■ "Positioning with respect to a reference system or determining your bearings physically or intellectually."

Understanding Human Resources

The phrase "human resource" was originally used by American institutional economist John R. Commons in his 1893 book *The Distribution of Wealth*. However, it wasn't until the 20th century that HR divisions were legally established and given the responsibility to resolve disputes between workers and their employers (Bundy, 1997).

Human Resources or HR is the department of a company tasked with discovering, vetting, hiring, and training job candidates. Additionally, it manages benefit plans for employees. In the 21st century, HR is critical to helping businesses adapt to a business climate that changes quickly, and to the increased need for qualified workers.

Major Roles of the Human Resources Department

By managing your company's most precious asset, its personnel, a competent human resources (HR) management department may assist offer organizational structure and the capacity to satisfy business demands. The HR department is made up of several disciplines, and human resources managers who are employed by smaller businesses might handle more than one of the five primary responsibilities of talent management, employee compensation and benefits, training and development, compliance, and workplace safety (see Figure 5.2) (Carasco & Rothwell, 2020; Collings et al., 2019; French, 2007).

Talent Management

The HR department's talent management staff has a wide range of responsibilities. Previously, separate divisions of the department have been consolidated under a single heading. The team in charge of talent management oversees hiring, developing, and keeping personnel.

Figure 5.2 Major Roles of the Human Resources Department. *Source*: Adapted from Carasco and Rothwell (2020), Collings et al. (2019), and French (2007).

Recruitment. The entire hiring process is under the supervision of recruiters, including posting job openings on job boards, finding candidates at job fairs and through social media, acting as the first point of contact for background checks to screen applicants, holding preliminary interviews, and synchronizing with the hiring manager responsible for making the final decision.

Employee Relations. The part of the talent management unit that is focused on fostering the employer–employee connection is known as employee support. Managers of human resources in this position research corporate culture, dispute resolution in the workplace, encourage employee engagement, and strive for job satisfaction.

Labor Relations. This team will similarly involve itself with the labor relations if the company's workforce is unionized. This includes drafting collective bargaining agreements, developing managerial answers to union organizing drives, and deciphering labor union contract inquiries (French, 2007).

Compensation and Benefits

One or two human resources specialists can frequently supervise the salary and benefits positions in smaller businesses, but in organizations with a bigger workforce, the responsibilities are generally divided up. HR's role in compensation includes assessing the pay practices of rival companies, creating the compensation structure, and handling tasks like communicating with the company's 401(k) administrator or negotiating group health insurance costs with insurance carriers (Carasco & Rothwell, 2020).

Training and Development

Every business wants to see its workers flourish, so it must provide them with all the resources they need. These tools can include (a) new employee orientation, (b) leadership training programs, (c) personal and professional development, and (d) management training; they don't always have to be tangible, like computers, work-related software, or instruments for a certain trade. The HR team includes training and development, sometimes known as learning and development (Collings et al., 2019).

HR Compliance

Compliance with laws and regulations is an essential feature of every HR function. Keeping businesses out of trouble with local, state and federal regulations requires a staff dedicated to monitoring the complicated and always changing employment and labor rules. When a company violates the law, applicants or workers may file lawsuits alleging unfair hiring and employment methods and procedures or dangerous working conditions (Collings et al., 2019).

Workplace Safety

OSHA (The Occupational Safety and Health Act of 1970) truly requires firms to create a safe working environment for their employees, despite the fact that every business desires to offer a secure workplace for its workers. HR places a lot of emphasis on creating and promoting safety training and keeping the legally required logs in the case of workplace accidents or deaths (Carasco & Rothwell, 2020).

Staffing and Training Responsibilities

One crucial aspect of HR's staffing duties is finding candidates with the appropriate qualifications. But before you can identify the recruiting requirements and carry out a job analysis to determine what skills are required to complete the job, you must assess the hiring need. Consider this: How could you interview for a new position if you don't know what it entails? (Bundy, 1997).

After doing a thorough job analysis and selecting the ideal applicant, you will need to train them so they can start out on the right foot. Although training may start with orientation, it is a continuous process that must adapt to the organization's shifting demands. HR is responsible for ensuring that workers receive the right training when they are employed. They may also be engaged in creating the training materials, since they maintain track of continuing training requirements (Collings et al., 2019).

Diversity, Equity, Inclusion, and Belonging (DEI&B)

Another responsibility of the Human Resources department is to implement and manage the application of all aspects of DEI&B in their organization. If you recall, in Chapter 1, we delved into the changing dynamics of the workplace, highlighting significant demographic transitions. These shifts usher in both unique opportunities and challenges for organizations. HR is central in acknowledging the advantages of having a workforce that is diverse in race, ethnicity, gender, sexual orientation, and other factors, placing more emphasis on diversity and inclusion. However, DEI&B is a very large concept with many related elements that would not fit in the focus of this chapter. However, in this section we briefly explain the DEI&B and the role of human resources related to it. (We will discuss the supervisory responsibilities on diversity, equity, inclusion, and belonging further in Chapter 9.)

The DEI&B (diversity, equity, inclusion, and belonging) function is concerned with the traits, experiences, and working methods that distinguish individuals from one another, as well as how organizations might use these traits to further their own goals. Additionally, it covers topics that focus on communications, legal and regulatory challenges, technology, analytics, outsourcing, efficient diversity strategies, and international diversity issues. Equal employment opportunity (EEO) legislation at the federal, state, and municipal levels are mentioned, although they are not its main focus. Both the personnel management role and the employee relations role are under the umbrella of the EEO subject (Foy, 2021; Adjo et al., 2021).

Experiencing DEI&B in Organization. DEI&B does more than only hire a variety of workers. A sense of organizational justice and belonging is fostered by DEI&B, which also gives employees the guarantee of fair and decent treatment and opportunity in all facets of employment. Because of the complexity of today's workplaces, inclusion is essential for fostering

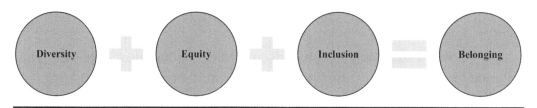

Figure 5.3   Relationship between the elements of DEI&B. *Note:* **Authors' original creation.**

creativity and team cohesiveness as well as enabling employees to easily contribute to company projects and outcomes (O'Connor, 2021; Foy, 2021).

When an employee can confidently represent their true selves, it improves their well-being, boosts their confidence, and deepens their dedication to the company. Conversely, a worker's perception of psychological safety at work may be impacted by a failure to implement successful DEI&B activities. When underrepresented groups' voices are heard, and their ideas are valued and developed, they become more confident. Both organizational effectiveness and employee morale are enhanced (see Figure 5.3) (O'Connor, 2021; Foy, 2021).

What Is the Role of Human Resource in DEI&B? The role of Human Resources management is to promote inclusive workplace cultures that offer opportunities to all employees, while also coming up with creative solutions to overcome workplace prejudice. Workplace DEI&B is complicated, and the goal is not just to have a diverse workforce (Rothwell et al., 2022).

The Elements of DEI&B. Let's look at the four elements of DEI&B individually and get related to what they mean and what areas of human resources and employment they are covering:

Diversity

There are various ways to define diversity. Organizations routinely modify the term to fit their unique setting. Diversity, in general, refers to the similarities and contrasts that exist among people, taking into consideration every facet of each person's personality and sense of self. The following list of diversity's common dimensions includes the following (Chiou et al., 2022; Rothwell et al., 2022):

- Age
- Ethnicity or national origin
- Race and color

- Family status
- Gender identity
- Sexual orientation
- Language
- Disability
- Physical characteristics
- Religion and spirituality
- Veteran status

Equity

In the workplace, equity refers to treating everyone equally in terms of access, opportunity, and progress. This activity includes locating and attempting to remove obstacles to disadvantaged groups receiving equitable treatment, from the team level to systemic changes in businesses and industries. Understanding that the social institutions in which we now operate are not equitable and that these injustices are mirrored in our organizations is typically necessary to enact change through the lens of equity (Chiou et al., 2022; Rothwell et al., 2022).

Inclusion

The term "inclusion" refers to the degree to which each individual feels supported, appreciated, and valued as a member of a group or team. Each person has a responsibility to both request and recognize inclusion from other people. Every individual tends to feel more involved and is more willing to contribute to the business outcomes of the firm in such a setting. People from different backgrounds must communicate, collaborate, and comprehend one another's needs and viewpoints in this sort of environment—in other words, they must show cultural competency (Chiou et al., 2022; Rothwell et al., 2022).

Belonging

The concept of belonging is centered on how employees feel about being welcomed at work. Each team member should believe that their viewpoint is respected and contributes something worthwhile. Being part of a team suggests a sense of value, which a worker is required and desired to have. As an oversimplified illustration, imagine a leadership team with many seasoned managers and one new, youthful manager. The new manager could feel like an outcast with little to contribute. However, if the other managers keenly urge the new manager to share opinions, provide this manager an equal opportunity to lead projects and develop, etc., this makes the new manager feel appreciated and valued (Chiou et al., 2022; Rothwell et al., 2022).

Understanding Staffing

Supervision is inherently people oriented. When individuals are promoted to supervisor, they are no longer judged on their ability to carry out tasks on their own as individual contributors. Instead, they are judged on their ability to work with and through others to accomplish group objectives. Obviously, the people comprising the group or team influence the relative ease of accomplishing group or team objectives. For this reason, staffing decisions made by supervisors or team members have important implications for group or team success.

Steps in the Staffing Process

Think of the staffing process as a series of steps in which supervisors or team members establish a long-term staffing plan for the work group or team, analyze and describe the work to be performed in each job or position in the work group or team, recruit and select people to perform the work, ensure fair treatment of individuals and groups, and orient and train people for their work.

Basic Issues

What are the duties and responsibilities of the work group or team? What kind of competencies, knowledge or skills are needed to carry out those duties? How many people are needed? Should those people work full-time, part-time, or as temporary (temp) employees? Will the duties and responsibilities of the work group or team change dramatically in the future, making it necessary to change the number and types of workers who carry out the work? Supervisors or team members should periodically give these questions some thought. The process of deliberately thinking about—and planning for—people needed in the work group or team is called **staff planning**.

Staff Planning

This process is useful because it forces managers, supervisors, and team members to consider the work group or team's overall duties, the people needed to carry out those duties, and the means of losing any gaps between the kind and amount of work performed and the type/number of workers performing it. This process can be tremendously useful in implementing strategic plans, cooperative plans, and operational plans. It can be a tool for reengineering work processes, ensuring that an optimal match is achieved between work demands and workers available to meet the demands. It can also be an important way to plan for recruiting, selecting, hiring, orienting, and training people for work.

When to Do Staff Planning? Supervisors and team members (under the guidance of team facilitators) should consider the overall work group or team staffing periodically—every year or so—even when no vacancies occur or when no hiring is contemplated. Staffing should also be a focal point of attention immediately after any major change in the organization—such as after an announced change in company business strategy, reporting relationships, or work group or team duties (Kold, 2011). After all, whenever there is a fundamental change in how an organization competes with other organizations or serves its customers, it may be time to re-evaluate what skills are needed by the group or team to meet its responsibilities. How might a change in the strategy of an organization affect the skills required to perform the work of each department? What can supervisors or team members do if and when the organization's strategic plans change? (Rothwell & Kazanas, 2003).

If an organization undergoes a restructuring, supervisors or team members might find themselves reporting to new managers and undertaking new responsibilities. At that time supervisors—or, in teams, the team members with the help of the team facilitator—will need to clarify what new responsibilities they are expected to shoulder. They will also need to review the skill mix of people in the work group or team to ensure that those skills are appropriate for the work to be performed (**Skill mix** refers to the sum of all skills of the individual members of a work group or team) (Levi, 2017).

If a work group or team is given a new list of duties or if new machines change the way the work is done, supervisors or the team will also need to review the kinds of people needed to do the work and assess the kinds of people already available in the group or team. In this way supervisors or team members can begin to plan for recruiting and/or developing the people they need in order to meet a new challenge (Kold, 2011).

Developing a Staffing Plan. To develop a staffing plan, supervisors or team members should do the following (Rothwell & Kazanas, 2003):

1. Estimate the kind and amount of work to be performed.
2. Estimate the kind and number of people needed for performance by the work group.
3. Compare steps 1 and 2.
4. Determine how to match step 2 with 1, over time, through such actions as training, hiring, transferring, and assigning work to prepare people for the future.
5. Establish a long-term staffing plan, complete with staffing goals, a time-table for achieving those goals, and a budget that considers expenses associated with training, hiring, and transferring people.
6. Implement the plan over time.
7. Evaluate progress periodically.

It is not essential to use fancy techniques to do a good job of staff planning. In fact, *any* effort is better than *none*. Supervisors or team members may wish to estimate staffing requirements based on the following data (Collings et al., 2019):

■ ***Production data.*** Given the historical link between production output and staffing levels, how many people will be needed in the work group or team to meet expected production demand over the next year?
■ ***Percentage data.*** How much time is the work group or team spending on each major step in its production or service delivery process? What are the major steps in this process? (In short, what happens from the time material enters and leaves the group or team or from the time a customer makes a service request, and it is met?) What kind and how many people are needed to carry out each step?
■ ***Supervisory or team guesswork.*** What kind of people does the supervisor or team wish were available in the group or team? What number of people does the supervisor or team feel are needed? Does this vary, depending on time of year, work cycle, or some other variable?

Use the simple worksheet illustrated in Table 5.1 to do some brainstorming on staffing issues.

Table 5.1 A Worksheet on Staffing Planning for the Work Group or Team

A Worksheet on Staffing Planning for the Work Group or Team
Directions: Use this worksheet to structure your thinking about appropriate staffing for a work group. When you have completed the worksheet, discuss it with your manager and prepare a memo to project the number and type of people needed over the next two to three years to carry out the duties of the work group or team.
1. What is the primary purpose of your work group or team?
2. What are the major duties and responsibilities of your work group or team? *(List them)*.
3. What are the job titles in your work group or team? What are the major activities performed by each title *(List them below)*.
4. What kinds of jobs and how many people are presently carrying out duties of your work group or team? Prepare a simple staffing table in the space below that illustrates the duties, responsibilities, and major work activities of your work group or team in the left margin, the job titles of people in your group or team in the top margin, and the number of people devoting time to the activity *(Add paper if necessary)*.

Major Duties:	Job Titles:

5. How can you show the relationship between production level and staffing level in your work group or team? What, for example, is the present production rate of your group or team relative to the number of people in the group or team? (Explain below how you can link output of products and number of people. If possible, prepare a chart on a separate sheet that depicts daily production and daily staffing level.)

(Continued)

Table 5.1 (Continued)   A Worksheet on Staffing Planning for the Work Group or Team

A Worksheet on Staffing Planning for the Work Group or Team
6. Explain in the space below what staffing, by number and job title, should exist in your work group or team at present.
7. What major changes, if any, do you expect in the duties or production demands of the work group or team over the next one, two, or three years? Why do you expect them?
8. Describe in the space below how you would like to close any gap between the number/kinds of work and types/number of workers in your group or team. What would you like to do in the way of hiring, transferring, training, or other changes in the work or workers?

Note: Authors' original creation.

Analyzing and Describing the Work

Work Analysis

This connotes any organized, systematic effort to identify the nature of the work performed. **Job analysis** is more restricted, is a type of work analysis, and is focused on organized efforts directed to describe work performed by a group of workers sharing the same title. When supervisors or team members work in a medium to large organization, the Human Resources department will probably analyze jobs and prepare written descriptions of them. In small organizations, supervisors or team members may have to prepare job descriptions on their own. In either case, supervisors or team members should be familiar with analyzing and describing jobs performed in their work group or teams (Phillips & Rothwell, 1998).

Job Description

This is simply a description of the work to be done. It lists work activities, duties, and responsibilities... It may also list what physical requirements are necessary to carry out those activities, what percentage of time is devoted to each activity, or how critical the activities are considered to be. Job descriptions are usually written in broad, general terms. The reason is that not everyone with the same job title performs exactly the same tasks. For example, a secretary working for the production manager probably does not do exactly the same things as a secretary working for the sales manager. However, the tasks they perform in their jobs are comparable. As a result, they share the same title and may have the same job description.

Job Specification

This list enumerates minimum skills needed at entry by someone hired to do a job. A job specification describes the education, experience, and other requirements needed to be qualified for the job. Although job specifications are usually placed at the end of a job description, they do not have to be. They help screen people applying for a job; they do not describe the work performed.

Position Description

This is different from a job description. It lists tasks performed by *one* person performing the job and the approximate amounts of time devoted to each task. The secretary in the production department will therefore have a *position* description different from that of the secretary in the sales department, even though they may share the same *job* description. If there are 123 secretaries in the organization, then there are 123 secretarial positions. Each is unique.

Recruiting and Selecting People

After preparing job descriptions and specifications, supervisors or team members should turn to the next step—locating, screening, and selecting candidates. **Recruitment** means "getting the right person to apply for job openings." **Selection** means "screening, interviewing, and choosing the best candidate for a job" (Rothwell & Kazanas, 2003).

There are two sources for recruitment: (1) inside and (2) outside the organization. The Human Resources department usually handles recruitment in large organizations—particularly for entry-level jobs or those requiring little advanced preparation. In small organizations and for advanced positions, recruitment is typically handled directly by those who will make the ultimate employment decision—that is, the managers to whom the positions will report.

The best place to start looking is on the inside. People already employed in the organization have some advantages over outsiders: they know what business the organization is in and probably already know who does what. If they have been with the organization for any time at all, their supervisors or team members already have some sense of their unique strengths and weaknesses. Recruiting from within can also maintain good morale, demonstrating the employer's loyalty to employees.

It would be a mistake to assume, without asking, that "nobody here would be interested in that job." Indeed, some people might be interested. Appearances can be deceiving. A secretary or janitor might rather be a production worker, a forklift operator, a secretary, a truck driver, or a welder. In fact, it is possible that people in the organization have even had prior experience in doing the job for which applicants are presently being sought. To recruit internally, post a job description on a bulletin board and ask if anyone would like to apply (of course, if the organization is unionized, special restrictions may apply due to collective bargaining agreements). Many organizations have their own job posting programs to encourage internal recruitment and transfers.

A good recruitment campaign should produce a large stack of résumés or completed applications. If the organization does not have employment applications, purchase some and modify them. Many organizations sell blank applications. Applications are preferable to relying on candidate résumés because the application structures information as the recruiter wants it, not as an applicant wishes to present it. Applications can also save time by gathering information that might otherwise take up valuable time in an interview.

Many supervisors or team members end up wasting time once they have a large stack of applications. Probably the most common reason is that they have not clearly specified, in advance of receiving the applications, precisely what kind of skills and what kind of person they are looking for. Some supervisors or team members spend days, even weeks, wading through an endless procession of applications. Some are so cautious that even the slightest flaw—such as an unaccounted-for time gap in an applicant's employment dates—prompts them to disregard an application of an otherwise well-qualified candidate.

A better approach is for supervisors or team members to write out, before they begin looking at résumés or applications, just what standards they plan to apply in screening. Some useful standards may include the following:

- ***Experience.*** What kind and how much is absolutely necessary? If none, say so; if specialized experience is desirable, indicate what it should be.
- ***Education/Training.*** What kind(s)? How much? Remember that it is important to start with the absolute minimum.
- ***Evidence of Motivation.*** How much motivation is indicated by the individual's track record? Did the applicant get high grades while in school? Receive awards from previous employers? Work two jobs at once, or attend school while working full-time?
- ***Salary History.*** Is it worth considering someone who has earned more than the present job pays? Much less than the present job?

(Rothwell & Kazanas, 2003).

Based on this list, develop a scale from one (poorly qualified) to five (highly qualified). Photocopy the list so that there are enough copies for all résumés or applications. Armed with the list, go through the applications in an organized way. Rate each application using the standards and rating scale previously developed. Average the ratings for each applicant. Then rank applicants from highest to lowest. Pick the top three applicants to interview.

Of course, in many large organizations the Human Resources department will handle initial applicant screening. Nevertheless, supervisors or team members should always have an opportunity to make the final decision. If the work group is one in which teamwork is crucial, supervisors should involve one or more team members in making the selection decision. (In team-based organizations, an entire team may interview prospective employees in a panel interview.)

To conduct an employment interview, supervisors or team members should keep the following points in mind:

- Review résumés or completed applications in advance.
- Develop questions unique to each applicant based on prior experience, education, training, salary, or other job-related matters.
- Develop a standard list of questions for all applicants.
- Set each applicant at ease at the opening of each interview. Offer him or her a cup of coffee or a soft drink—and a comfortable chair. Make small talk for a few minutes.

- Lead into the questioning gradually. Begin with a description of the job. If the applicant is from outside the organization, summarize what the organization and/or the team does.
- Let the applicant do most of the talking.
- Be sure to find out about the applicant's wage/salary requirements and future career aspirations, if applicable.
- Close the interview cordially, making clear what will happen next. Inform the applicant how quickly a decision will be reached. Avoid answering applicant questions such as "Did you like me?" or "Do I have an edge on getting the job?"

(Collings et al., 2019).

Once supervisors or team members have finished interviewing job applicants, they are then ready to select a finalist. Most supervisors or team members do this by "gut feel"—that is, on the basis of whether they like or do not like an applicant. The trouble with this approach is that, too often, a single facet of an applicant's background is weighed too heavily.

A better approach is to consider each applicant's **background** holistically. To do that, prepare a list of standards, which set out the job requirements. If possible, use the same list for all applicants to ensure consistency.

Complete an overall evaluation of each applicant by working through this applicant evaluation. This process does force supervisors or team members to consider *all* aspects of each applicant. Bias can be reduced if supervisors ask one or more employees to participate in the selection process. Separate, individual scores of each applicant can be averaged, thereby reducing the possibility for bias by spreading the rating process across multiple raters. By giving representatives of the work group a say in the selection process, supervisors or team members can also:

- *Improve morale.* Group members will feel their ideas are important and have been considered.
- *Increase the likelihood of success for the new hire.* When members of the work group participate in a hiring decision, they will be more committed to helping the newcomer "get up to speed" because they will not want to have to admit later that they made a mistake about the person they helped select.
- *Decrease the likelihood of turnover.* When a new hire is readily accepted in a work group, the applicant is unlikely to leave as quickly as one who has trouble gaining work group acceptance.

■ ***Groom future leadership.*** When promoted, supervisors should already have one or more staff members ready to step up to supervision. By giving members of the work group a role in making selection decisions, supervisors are gradually developing others to take their places.

(Dubois & Rothwell, 2004).

Once all applicants have been rated and ranked, the supervisor or team is ready to choose one and check references. The best way to check references is by phone. (Be sure to have a written waiver signed during the application or interview process to permit reference checks.) Former supervisors are the best sources of information about employees, but they are not always able to release what they know due to organizational policy. Many organizations have strict rules preventing all but the Human Resources department from releasing information about former employees. If references must be checked on someone who is already employed, the supervisor or team should be sure to ask the applicant to sign a written permission first (Sharma & Sharma, 2018). At minimum the applicant's dates of employment and job title should be checked. Often that is the only information that may be obtained.

Assuming references are in order, the supervisor or team should decide on the applicant of choice and call or write him or her to extend an employment offer (in some organizations, the Human Resources department must do that). The supervisor or team should be sure to find out whether the applicant is still available, and state this information:

■ When should the person report to work?
■ To whom should the person report?
■ What will the job title be?
■ What pay rate will the person receive?

The last step in this process involves sending out letters to unsuccessful applicants. Some supervisors find this task unpleasant. The result is that many find themselves hounded by disappointed job seekers who want to know whether a decision has been made. Remember: applicants turned away today might be good prospects for future openings. They are also members of the community served by the organization. They buy the organization's products or receive its services. Therefore, applicants should be eliminated politely so their goodwill is preserved.

Orienting and Training

Once hired, the new employee will need help to become fully productive. Employee orientation is the process of helping employees learn the organization's way of doing things and establish effective relationships with coworkers, supervisors, and others. On-the-job training (OJT) is planned learning experiences conducted by supervisors or coworkers at the site where the employee works—usually while the work is being done (Rothwell & Kazanas, 2003). Off-the-job training is conducted away from the job site and is any planned learning experience intended to improve present job performance, prepare the new hiree for advancement, or point out new developments in the profession, occupation, or industry.

A good orientation can set the tone for high performance and set the stage for more detailed on-the-job and off-the-job training. A supervisor or team can greatly reduce the initial learning period of a new employee in the work group with these activities:

■ Providing a structured discussion of organizational policies (for example, vacation, benefits, and work rules).
■ Describing the structure of the organization and the business it is in.
■ Explaining basic work expectations.
■ Assigning an experienced worker to show newcomers around and help them get to know the work setting and become acquainted with their coworkers.

(Collings et al., 2019).

Many organizations conduct formal orientations. Usually handled by the Human Resources department and carried out on or near the newcomer's first day of employment, such an orientation provides a good way to introduce the new employee to the organization. A first-day orientation usually focuses on employee benefits and work rules.

On-the-job training (OJT) is sometimes praised highly by supervisors or team members, who favor it over off-the-job training. Unfortunately, OJT is not always well-handled. Some supervisors or team members think newcomers can learn just by sitting at a desk or following others around while they work. More effective OJT is planned (structured) around these steps (Rothwell & Kazanas, 2003):

1. ***Preparation.*** Make sure the trainee is ready to learn and has at hand equipment or tools needed to perform.
2. ***Discussion.*** Go through what the learner needs to know. First explain it, then show (or demonstrate) it, and finally ask the trainee to explain it.
3. ***Demonstration.*** Ask the trainee to demonstrate the task. Provide feedback on how well the task was performed. Repeat an explanation or a demonstration if necessary.
4. ***Observation.*** Let the trainee take over. At first, the trainer should provide close supervision and observe how well the trainee performs. Later, the amount of observation may be reduced as the trainee demonstrates the ability to perform up to standards.

The checklist shown in Table 5.2 can help make sure supervisors or team members do a good job in structuring OJT. Once employees have mastered basic job requirements, they may need additional training to prepare for future advancement, deal with a performance deficiency, or learn about recent advances in their field (especially if they are college-trained). Off-the-job training can serve these purposes.

To plan this kind of training, supervisors or the team should do some brainstorming. About what sort of topics should employees learn in order to prepare them for advancement? If the supervisor has employees in more than one job class, can a semi-permanent list of off-the-job courses be developed for each job class? To this list supervisors or team members may wish to add any other items or questions they might find appropriate or needed.

Now use Table 5.3 to provide actions to increase your understanding of Table 5.2.

What's Next?

The next chapter, "Understanding Human Relations," looks into how human relations stem from the ability to deal with individuals through the effective use of such interpersonal skills as listening, questioning, paraphrasing, dealing with feelings, and influencing. Before you move on, don't forget to review the key takeaways and take a moment to reflect on what you learned in this chapter by completing Table 5.4, End of Chapter 5 Discussion Questions and Inquiries.

Table 5.2 A Checklist for On-the-Job Training

A Checklist for On-the-Job Training		
Directions: Use this checklist to prepare an offer on-the-job training		
Employee Name:	Supervisor Name:	
Date:	Team/Department:	
Topics:		
Have you:	*Yes*	*No*
Decided what the employee must be taught to learn the job?		
Assembled the necessary tools, equipment, and supplies to do the training and the work?		
Made the employee feel at ease at the outset of the training?		
Determined what or how much the employee already knew about the job?		
Aroused the employee's interest in learning?		
Told the trainee what to do? And why should it be done this way?		
Show the trainee how to perform the task?		
Checked to make sure that the trainee was paying attention?		
Asked the trainee to explain what to do? And why should it be done this way?		
Asked the trainee to demonstrate the task?		
Observed the trainee as the task was performed?		
Provided feedback on how well the task was performed?		
Asked questions to make sure the trainee understood what to do? And why to do the task as it has been demonstrated?		
Continued these steps until sure that the task was being handled appropriately by the trainee?		
Made sure to observe the trainee closely at first as he or she performed the task on the job?		
Made sure to closely observe the trainee as he or she demonstrated competence in performing the task?		
Other comments:		

Note: Authors' original creation.

Table 5.3 APLI-Connected to Table 5.2

Action Plan for Learning and Improving	
Area of Learning and Improving: *A Checklist for On-the-Job Training*	
Reference: *Table 5.2*	
Three learning and improvement actions for this month that will raise my understanding and awareness in regard to "A Checklist for On-the-Job Training" to enhance my understanding and clarity by at least one on the next rating:	
Action 1:	By When:
Action 2:	By When:
Action 3:	By When:

Note: Authors' original creation.

Key Takeaways

1. A company's human resources (HR) department finds, evaluates, hires, and trains job candidates. It also manages employee terminations, salary and benefits, and training.
2. Supervision is inherently people oriented. When individuals are promoted to supervisor, they are no longer judged on their abilities to carry out tasks on their own as individual contributors. Instead, they are judged on their abilities to work with and through others to accomplish group objectives.
3. Another responsibility of the Human Resources department is implementing and managing the application and presence of all aspects of DEI&B in their organization. DEI&B is a very large concept with many related elements which would not fit in the construct of this chapter; however, in this section we briefly explain the DEI&B and the role of human resources related to it.
4. Work analysis connotes any organized, systematic effort to identify the nature of work performed. Job analysis is more restricted, is a type of work analysis, and is focused on an organized effort directed to describe work performed by a group of workers sharing the same title.

Table 5.4   End of Chapter 5 Questions and Inquiries. Your Perspective on What You Learned in Chapter 5

Your Perspective on What You Learned in Chapter 5	
Area of Inquiry	*What Did You Learn, and How Are You Going to Implement It in Your Position?*
Major roles of Human Resources department	
Diversity, equity, inclusion, and belonging (DEI&B)	
What is the role of human resource in DEI&B?	
Steps in the staffing process	
Staffing planning for the work group or team	
Recruiting and selecting people	
Orienting and training	

Discussion Questions and Inquiries

Please take a minute to answer the following inquiries and questions in Table 5.4. From your point of view, what have you learned about the following areas?

References

Adjo, J., Maybank, A., & Prakash, V. (2021). Building inclusive work environments. *Pediatrics (Evanston), 148*(Suppl 2), 1. https://doi.org/10.1542/peds.2021-051440E

Bundy, R. A. (1997). Changing role of human resources has vast implications. *BizJournals*. Retrieved January 24, 2023, from https://www.bizjournals.com/wichita/stories/1997/07/14/focus1.html

Carasco, M., & Rothwell, W. J. (2020). *The Essential HR Guide for Small Business and Startups*. Alexandria, VA: SHRM-Society for Human Resources Management.

Chiou, E. K., Holden, R. J., Ghosh, S., Flores, Y., & Roscoe, R. D. (2022). Recruitment, admissions, hiring, retention, and promotion: Mechanisms of diversity, equity, inclusion (DEI) and belonging in higher education. *Proceedings of the Human Factors and Ergonomics Society Annual Meeting, 66*(1), 135–138. https://doi.org/10.1177/1071181322661026

Collings, D. G., Scullion, H., & Caligiuri, P. M. (2019). *Global Talent Management*. New York, NY: Routledge.

Commons, J. R. (1893). *The Distribution of Wealth*. New York and London: Macmillan.

Dubois, D. D., & Rothwell, W. J. (2004). *Competency-Based Human Resource Management*. Palo Alto, CA: Davis-Black Publishing.

Foy, C. M. (2021). Successful applications of diversity, equity, and inclusion programming in various professional settings: Strategies to increase DEI in libraries. *Journal of Library Administration, 61*(6), 676–685. https://doi.org/10.1080/01930826.2021.1947057

French, W. L. (2007). *Human Resources Management* (6th ed.). Boston, MA: Houghton Mifflin Company.

Jiang, K., Hu, J., Liu, S., & Lepak, D. P. (2017). Understanding employees' perceptions of human resource practices: Effects of demographic dissimilarity to managers and coworkers. *Human Resource Management, 56*(1), 69–91. https://doi.org/10.1002/hrm.21771

Kold, J. A. (2011). *Small Group Facilitation: Improving Process and Performance in Groups and Teams*. Amherst, MO: HRD Press.

Levi, D. (2017). *Group Dynamics for Teams* (5th ed.). Thousand Oaks, CA: Sage Publications, Inc.

O'Connor, D. (2021). The role of HR in driving diversity and inclusion. ICA (International Compliance Association). Retrieved January 25, 2023, from https://www.int-comp.org/insight/2021/january/hr-diversity-and-inclusion/

Oxford Language. (2023). *Human Resources*. Retrieved January 24, 2023, from https://languages.oup.com/google-dictionary-en/

Phillips, J. J., & Rothwell, W. J. (Eds.). (1998). *Linking HRD Programs with Organizational Strategy*. Alexandria, VA: ASTD.

Rothwell, W. J., & Kazanas, H. C. (2003). *Planning & Managing Human Resources. Strategic Planning for Personnel Management* (2nd ed.). Amherst, MA: HRD Press, Inc.

Rothwell, W. J., Ealy, P. L., & Campbell, J. (2022). *Rethinking Organizational Diversity, Equity, and Inclusion*. New York, NY: Routledge.

Sharma, R. C., & Sharma, N. (2018). *Human Resources Management Theory and Practice*. Los Angeles, CA: SAGE.

Vocabulary. (2023). *Orienting*. Retrieved January 2023, from https://www.vocabulary.com/dictionary/orienting

Chapter 6

Understanding Human Relations

Introduction

Human relations stem from the ability to deal with individuals through the effective use of such interpersonal skills as listening, questioning, paraphrasing, dealing with feelings, and influencing. In a work group or team, human relations also mean that people want to get along, cooperate, and achieve a common goal.

Most individuals value their connections to their families, coworkers, clients, and friends. People concerned about the quality of their relationships are aware that these traits need effort and ongoing nurturing. Over time, good relationships are formed and grown. Relationships develop when individuals show interest in one another, open channels of communication, and build a strong rapport on mutual respect and understanding.

As highlighted in Chapter 1, your role as a supervisor has significantly evolved, largely influenced by the human relations movement of the 1930s. This paradigm shift brought human factors to the forefront as critical drivers of organizational success. Consequently, there was a significant transformation in management philosophies; organizations now prioritize the well-being of employees, nurturing their motivation, and enhancing job satisfaction. The importance of your ability to be inclusive, empathetic, and deeply connected to your team is undeniable.

DOI: 10.4324/9781003413493-6

Empathy, in particular, stands out. It allows you to see and feel what others are experiencing from their perspective as if you are experiencing it yourself. It helps maintain any type of relationship, whether personal or professional, and can influence our success in those relationships. The term "inclusion" refers not only to the extent to which each individual feels supported, appreciated, and valued as a team member but also to the sense of belonging that each team member feels. The relational leadership approach is a management style that emphasizes the relationships between individuals, teams, and groups within an organization. Relational leadership places a high importance on process orientation, purposefulness, inclusivity, and empowerment. When making decisions, inclusive leaders consider the experiences and views of everyone.

As shown in Figure 6.1 of the *Successful Supervisory Leadership Series Book II Structure*, this chapter examines human relations and the connections between supervisors and their employees. We'll examine the various types of interpersonal relationships that form the foundation of our social existence, discuss the significance of building rapport for teamwork and productivity in the workplace, and introduce key human relations skills such

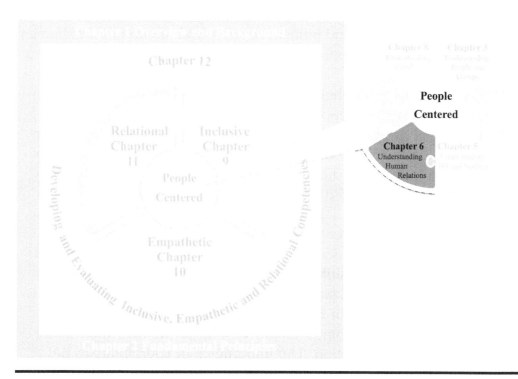

Figure 6.1 *Successful Supervisory Leadership Series Book II Structure.* **Note: Authors' original creation.**

as emotional intelligence and conflict resolution. Recognizing the collective responsibility in fostering a supportive environment, we provide actionable tips for developing and maintaining strong connections. Additionally, we outline the overarching goals for effective human relations that contribute to a positive organizational culture. Finally, we offer strategies to identify and break down barriers to effective relations.

Key Concepts

This chapter will cover the following key concepts:

- The Importance of Human Relations
- Different Types of Interpersonal Relationships
- Rapport and Its Importance at Workplace
- Human Relations Skills
- Responsibilities for Maintaining Effective Human Relations
- Tips for Creating and Maintaining Effective Human Relations
- Goals of Human Relations
- Identifying and Overcoming Barriers to Effective Human Relations

Definitions

The following definitions of key terms will help to better understand the main elements of this chapter:

Human Relations

- "Relations with or between people, particularly the treatment of people in a professional context" (Oxford Language, 2023, n. p.).
- Human relations are the art of managing on-the-job relationships between people (Rothwell et al., 2016).

Relatedness

- "the state or fact of being related or connected" (Lexico.com, 2023, n.p.).
- "to the social nature of human beings and the connectedness with others. Both can be considered as being part of the panhuman psychology, and both are intrinsically intertwined" (Keller, 2016, p. 1).

Interpersonal Relationships

American Psychological Association (APA, 2023) defines Interpersonal Relationships as follows:

- "the connections and interactions, especially ones that are socially and emotionally significant, between two or more people" (n. p.).
- "the pattern or patterns observable in an individual's dealings with other people" (n. p.).

Interpersonal Skills

- "Ability to work with groups and teams, developing and teaching others to add their jobs and tasks, serving customers, leading teams, negotiating positions or contracts, and working effectively with others from different backgrounds and cultures" (SCANS Report-2000, in Bakhshandeh, 2021, p. 62).
- The personal traits and actions we exhibit when interacting with others are known as interpersonal skills. Some personality traits are intrinsic and may be cultivated, while others have been picked up in particular social settings (APA, 2023).

Rapport

- "The relation characterized by harmony, conformity, accord, or affinity" (Merriam-Webster, 2021).
- "I like to define rapport as a deep emotional connection and understanding between two people" (Gilmore, 2019, p. 2).

Figure 6.2 represents the key elements of effective human relations.

The Importance of Human Relations

Effective human relations are essential to any relationship. But why should supervisors or team members be concerned about it? The importance for supervisors to understand interpersonal relationships and have a connection with their employees boils down to the following reasons (Rothwell & Bakhshandeh, 2022):

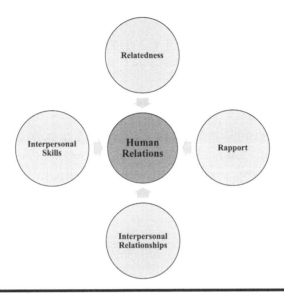

Figure 6.2 Elements of effective human relations. *Note*: **Authors' original creation.**

First, supervisors and team members work with and through other people. How workers feel about their supervisors and coworkers affects their willingness to exert extra effort and willingly accept direction. It also affects their willingness to remain with, or quit from, the organization, work group, or team.

Second, supervisors and teams gain influence when their employees support what they do and how they approach meeting work group or team goals. A supervisor's workers or members of a team talk to other people, and they make known their support (or lack of support) for a supervisor or for the team. This rarely escapes the notice of higher-level managers and is sometimes a factor in decisions about promotions, transfers, or special work assignments.

Third, and finally, the ability to work effectively with others is essential for supervisors who aspire to promotion. Managers and executives must know how to work as team players. They cannot do so if they are deficient in their ability to manage on-the-job relationships with others.

Let's look at different types of interpersonal relationships because not all types of relations would apply to a professional relationship at the workplace.

Different Types of Interpersonal Relationships

Relationships begin when two people realize they like one another's company and want to remain together. Interpersonal relationships are tight associations between people with similar interests and aspirations. An interpersonal relationship is formed when two people are compatible. To have a solid and healthy relationship, people must get along well (Bakhshandeh & Zeine, 2012). Let's review the several kinds of interpersonal relationships:

Friendship

Friendship is an open-ended kind of connection that people choose to join of their own free will. Friendship is a connection in which there are no formalities, and participants enjoy one another's company.

Romantic Love Relationship

Romantic and love are terms used to describe an interpersonal connection marked by ardor, closeness, trust, and respect. Romantic partners have a strong emotional attachment and a unique bond based on passion, attraction, and intimacy.

Platonic Relationship

A platonic relationship is one in which the two people involved have no sexual or emotional attachments. People in such a relationship are just friends and they will not combine friendship and love.

Relationship with Family

A family is defined as a group of people linked via marriage or blood.

Work-Related and Professional Relationship

It is believed that coworkers employed by the same company have a professional relationship. Colleagues are people with whom you have a shared occupation. Whether or not coworkers get along depends on them.
    (Bakhshandeh & Zeine, 2012).

Rapport and Its Importance at the Workplace

Regardless of the type of interpersonal relationship you are involved in, there is always the need for establishing a rapport with another person or persons. This would make rapport an essential element of effective and productive human relations at the workplace.

According to Angelo (2012), rapport refers to two people connecting, which would result in ongoing communication and collaboration. Sometimes trust which is essential to develop rapport may be built right away, and other times it takes some time. To establish a functional rapport, however, requires two parties. The level of trust and rapport between managers and the people they train determines how effectively managers function as coaches (Whitmore, 2017; Rothwell et al., 2016; Cummings & Worley, 2015; Bakhshandeh, 2008).

Rapport is more than just polite expressions of friendliness or joking acquaintanceship. Being emotionally aware, or having empathy, compassion, and a connection with people by being aware of their feelings, is a prerequisite for building rapport (Gilmore, 2019; Whitmore, 2017; Bakhshandeh, 2009). "It is a relationship that brings people together, facilitates dialogue, and most importantly fosters greater understanding" (Gilmore, 2019, p. 2). Given the range of explanations presented, it is reasonable to say that rapport refers to people's interactions and emotional ties with those in their life. Building such connections and partnerships based on shared experiences or views requires first developing rapport. When developed, it can last for a very long time (Gilmore, 2019; Angele, 2012; Bakhshandeh, 2009).

Rapport and Organizational Values

Organizational values are a collection of ideals that guide behavior and may be personal or socially desirable (Schwartz, 1992). Organizational values show what is significant to the organization. Values are connected to ethical standards, to what is good or wrong.

Employees are able to create a clear route to results with the aid of organizational values. Values serve as the foundation for developing an organizational culture that values good performance and productivity in the workplace. The ideals of a business greatly influence the attitudes and behaviors of employees. In reality, "organizations must communicate their work principles and expectations with personnel, and organizational values must be able to suit the demands of diverse employees" (Cennamo & Gardner, 2008, p. 891).

Rapport and Organizational Culture

Rothwell et al. (2016) defined organizational culture as

Mindset is to individuals as culture is to organizations. A strategy to change culture is often required, one that assesses which aspects of the current culture already support the desired future, which block it, and what may need to be created to better serve it.

(p. 73)

Organization culture consists of deeply ingrained behaviors, a history of interactive employee-to-employee dynamics, and sensitivity to the traditions and norms of an organization and its workforce. Organizational culture is a vigorous force rooted in a variety of facets of personal and professional life, including employee behavior, organizational structure, and business strategies. In light of this overarching dynamic, organizational culture and its business strategy should be in line with all phases of a company to ensure that its workforce is working toward the firm's aims and intended outcomes (Aristotelous, 2019).

Understand Relatedness before Establishing Rapport

Many people struggle to manage their relationships (personally or professionally) because they rush into such relationships before learning how to get related and comprehend the true meaning of connectedness. Both home and work settings are affected by this phenomenon (Bakhshandeh, 2006, 2009).

Aristotelous (2019) asserts that there is strong evidence in the study of literature to support the idea that encouraging relatedness among individuals via the development of deeper human relationships promotes optimism in workplace settings and organizations. It was a difficult challenge to maintain our humanity and feeling of interconnectedness in these times of extraordinary technological advancement. Keller (2016) paired autonomy and relatedness as two fundamental human wants:

… the definition of self and others can be regarded as embodying the two dimensions of autonomy and relatedness. Autonomy and relatedness are two basic human needs and cultural constructs at the same time. They may be differently defined yet remain equally important. The respective understanding of autonomy and relatedness is socialized during the everyday experiences of daily life routines from birth and beyond.

(p. 1)

Human Relations Skills

The ability to relate to others is necessary for productive collaboration and the achievement of shared objectives. This comprises the capacity for understanding and sympathy, as well as the capacity for clear communication. The foundational ability of communication serves as the foundation for all other interpersonal abilities. Strong interpersonal skills are crucial in any job, but they will be much more crucial in the workplace of the future, where teams will be more cross-functional, diverse, and collaborative.

These are only a few instances of the kinds of interpersonal abilities that will be crucial in the workplace of the future. It is critical to keep in mind that, at our core, we are all social creatures who require the ability to connect with and communicate with one another, even as technology continues to transform the way we engage with one another.

Emotional Intelligence

The capacity to recognize and control both your own emotions and those of others is known as emotional intelligence. It requires having the capacity to comprehend and react to others in a way that fosters connections. The ability to manage stress and sustain morale in the ever-changing workplace of the future will require emotional intelligence (Hockenbury & Hockenbury, 2007).

Effective Communication

Organizations, managers, and team members all depend on communication. Information is crucial for outperforming rivals and managing internal business operations. (Bakhshandeh, 2008).

Active Listening

Active listening is the capacity to pay attention to what another person is saying without allowing your own prejudices, opinions, or presumptions to interfere. It is time to comprehending another person's viewpoint and then replying in a way that respects their emotions and viewpoint (Leonard, 2020).

Problem-Solving

Identification, analysis, and implementation of the best solutions are all aspects of problem-solving abilities. A worker skilled at solving problems is both self-motivated and a cooperative team member. They are proactive in identifying the source of an issue and collaborate with others to evaluate a variety of alternatives before selecting how to proceed (Schwartz, 2021).

Conflict Resolution

The capacity to recognize conflict and manage it in a way that produces a favorable result is known as conflict resolution. It entails comprehending the underlying reasons of conflict as well as the many points of view of individuals involved. Excellent communication and problem-solving abilities are necessary for successful conflict resolution (Lencioni, 2002).

Positive Attitude

Optimism is a state of mind and an associated attitude that expresses a leader's ideas, beliefs, or expectations that a task, an event, or an endeavor will have a favorable outcome. They convey optimism and assurance in the future or a positive result. Pessimists give attention to negative elements of things and search for what is wrong, while optimists focus on the positive and bright side of things and hunt for what is good with the situation (Gordon, 2017).

Empathy

Because empathy is the capacity to comprehend and experience the sentiments of another person, it plays a significant role in conflict resolution. Understanding what somebody is going through in the office, whether it is a challenging professional scenario or a personal issue, can be a sign of empathy. It can also entail being considerate of other people's needs, both in terms of their professional requirements and personal preferences. An environment that is helpful and empathetic at work may be advantageous for both employees and employers.

Patience

Along with compassion, being patient with other people is a valuable asset in enabling the client to navigate periods of self-awareness and self-realization on their own terms. Knowing that not everyone discovers their personalities, actions, and attitudes at the same rate, one may fully accept responsibility and accountability for who they become as quickly as their coach or other people (Bakhshandeh, 2015).

Cultural Awareness

Cultural awareness is the capacity to comprehend and collaborate well with individuals from various cultural backgrounds. This ability will be crucial for fostering effective interactions across multifarious teams and distant employees from many cultures in the future's diversified workplace (Rothwell & Bakhshandeh, 2022).

Personal Responsibility

It is important to encourage others to accept responsibility for their decisions. The cause of misery is frequently either choosing not to make decisions or choosing not to stick with our decisions. Making a decision is simple. Maintaining and strengthening the decisions we made is difficult. Unfortunately, a great number of individuals exist in the world who don't accept responsibility for anything! They just want to place the blame for their lack of personal or professional success, contentment, or happiness on something or someone (Bakhshandeh, 2009).

Now use Table 6.1 to list a series of actions to increase your understanding of Table 6.2.

Responsibilities for Maintaining Effective Human Relations

Occupying positions of authority, supervisors should work to establish and maintain good human relations between–

- Themselves, managers, and peers.
- Employees within the work group or team.
- Employees they supervise and those who report to other supervisors.
- The work group or team which they lead and groups outside the organization—such as customers, suppliers, and distributors.

Creating and maintaining effective human relations is not the sole responsibility of supervisors. Others play important parts as well. However, supervisors do establish a climate through their leadership styles. Of

Table 6.1 Monthly Supervisor's Human Relations Skills Self-Rating Process

Monthly Supervisor's Human Relation Skills Self-Rating Process						
Supervisor:		Month/Year:				
Manager:		Team/Department:				
Rating Scale: 1 = Poor, 2 = Marginal, 3 = Acceptable, 4 = Good, 5 = Excellent						
	Rating Scale	*1*	*2*	*3*	*4*	*5*
#	*Skills*	*Ratings from 1(lowest) to 5 (highest)*				
1	Emotional intelligence					
2	Effective communication					
3	Active listening					
4	Problem-solving					
5	Conflict resolution					
6	Positive attitude					
7	Empathy					
8	Patience					
9	Cultural awareness					
10	Personal responsibility					
Monthly Total per Scale						
Monthly Total (Total of above totals per scale))						
Monthly Average (above monthly total divided by 10)						

Note: Authors' original creation.

course, **climate** refers to the psychological feel of the work group or team (Cennamo & Gardner, 2008).

In team-based organizations, each team member bears the same responsibilities for maintaining effective human relations as supervisors bear in traditional organizations. They must work effectively together if the team is to maintain team *esprit de corps* (Hove & Risen, 2009).

Table 6.2 APLI-Connected to Table 6.1

Action Plan for Learning and Improving	
Area of Learning and Improving: Monthly Supervisor's Human Relations Skills Self-Rating Process	
Reference: *Table 6.1*	
Three learning and improvement actions for this month that will raise my understanding and awareness in regard to "Monthly Supervisor's Human Relations Skills Self-Rating Process" to enhance their understanding and clarity by at least one on the next rating:	
Action 1:	By When:
Action 2:	By When:
Action 3:	By When:

Note: Authors' original creation.

Tips for Creating and Maintaining Effective Human Relations

What can supervisors or team members do to create and maintain effective human relations? Research revealed the following elements have a very positive effect on establishing powerful human relations between supervisors and managers and their employees, peers, and higher managers (Rothwell & Bakhshandeh, 2022; Rothwell et al., 2016; Hove & Risen, 2009; Cennamo & Gardner, 2008; Bakhshandeh, 2002):

With Managers

Supervisors or team members should keep these things in mind to create and preserve relations with their managers:

■ Familiarize themselves with the job description and problems facing those to whom they report. By making middle managers and coworkers look good, supervisors and team members look good, too.
■ Treat with respect those with whom they work. Once a decision is made, responsible supervisors and team members do not complain about it.

- Think about the feelings of other people once in a while. Praise others when the praise is warranted.
- Do not openly criticize a coworker or a middle manager to others. If a problem exists, voice it to the person who is perceived to be creating it. Do so privately. Be straightforward but tactful.
- Find out what kinds of decisions they should make and what kinds others should make.
- Perform assignments on time.
- Apply the idea of finished staff work, which means taking responsibility to investigate the facts surrounding a problem or recommendation before delegating it upward to a manager or presenting it to a coworker.
- Try to cut to a minimum the unnecessary leg work of others.
- Provide regular, routine information to others about how things are going with your work or team.
- Participate actively in work groups or team meetings.
- Bring problems and possible solutions to the attention of those who are best positioned to solve the problems or implement the solutions.
- Avoid making excuses for mistakes.
- Work through channels. In a traditional organization, supervisors should talk to their managers before seeing an executive about a problem. In team-based organizations, team members should discuss problems with the team or with a team facilitator before going to higher levels about it.

With Peers

To preserve good relations with other supervisors or other team members they should keep these in mind:

- Always support their peers. Never criticize them publicly.
- Always think in terms of the good of the organization, not in terms of the "turf" of one work group or team or another.
- Be willing to cooperate. If other supervisors need help, give what help is possible; if other team members need help, follow the same advice. Assist willingly rather than grudgingly.
- Praise people when it seems deserved.
- Avoid listening to rumors or spreading rumors about others.
- Do not speak to another supervisor's manager about a problem before speaking directly to the supervisor about it.

With Employees

To create and preserve an effective climate in a work group or team and with individuals, supervisors or team members should keep these in mind:

- Get to know each employee well and treat each one as an individual.
- Provide prompt feedback on tasks that are especially well done or poorly done.
- Avoid emotive or harsh words. (That only draws attention to your behavior, not to the offense that prompted it.)
- Avoid shifting blame. Effective supervisors and team members are willing to accept responsibility and authority.
- Exhibit enthusiasm.
- Let employees know about changes likely to affect them before it is necessary to make the changes.
- Listen closely to employee suggestions. If the suggestions will not work, explain why in a tactful way; if the suggestion will work, praise the employees and give credit where it is due.
- Be loyal to employees. Back them up—especially when they are only following the orders given to them.
- Assume that employees are hardworking, creative, bright, and productive. This will tend to create a self-fulfilling prophecy that will make people that way.
- Expect high performance, high work output, and good interpersonal relations between the employees who work for you.
- Smile.
- Say "Thank you" whenever appropriate.
- Attend ceremonies—such as anniversary parties or retirement celebrations.
- Invite people to meetings.
- Ask employees for their opinions.
- Be pleasant.
- Greet people by name.
- Hold rap sessions or team meetings.
- Nominate workers for awards.
- Say "We missed you" when workers return from having been away.
- Be careful, however, about being too supportive or nurturing of people.

Table 6.3 Are You a Soft Touch?

Are You a Soft Touch?		
Directions: Some supervisors (or team members) find it difficult to deal with human relations problems. Answer the questions below to determine whether you might be prone to these problems.		
Do you:	**Yes**	**No**
1. Make too many excuses for workers who are absent excessively and thereby create problems for the work group or team?		
2. Make too many excuses for others when they are not productive and thereby create problems for the work group or team?		
3. Feel angry at others but do not share their feelings with team members?		
4. Experience frustration with others about how they behave but share those feelings with people other than the one who causes them?		
5. Hear complaints from other workers because they allowed a worker to "get away with" something?		
Scoring: If you checked "yes" to 3 or more of the items above, you are probably too nurturing. You wish to avoid conflict more than confront it. You should learn to be more open about your feelings.		

Note: Authors' original creation.

Some supervisors (or team members) find it difficult to deal with human relations problems. Answer the questions in Table 6.3, *Are You a Soft Touch?* to determine whether you might be prone to these problems.

Goals of Human Relations

While the goals of human relations may seem like a philosophical issue, psychologists contend that there are five ingredients in satisfying relationships: *sincerity, similarity, agreeableness, continuity*, and *shared goals* (Kold, 2011; Bakhshandeh, 2008). While these ingredients are associated with friendships, they can also be viewed as essential to effective human relations between a supervisor and employees, between members of a work team, or between members of separate work groups or teams. Achieving these goals should be considered part of the supervisor's (and team member's) job just as much as achieving satisfactory quantity and quality of production (see Figure 6.3).

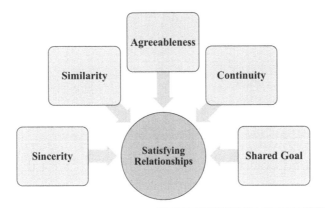

Figure 6.3   Satisfying Relationships. Source: Adapted from Kold (2011) and Bakhshandeh (2006).

The following are brief descriptions for these goals according to APA (2023):

Sincerity

Openness and honesty; the absence of dishonesty or hypocrisy. Sincerity is a blend of gravity and sincerity. People will trust you if you act sincerely in all that you do.

Similarity

An analogy, likeness, resemblance, and similitude are some typical synonyms for similarity. Although all of these phrases refer to agreement or correspondence in specifics, the word "likeness" suggests a deeper relationship than the word "similarity," which frequently suggests that objects are just slightly similar.

Agreeableness

Being agreeable is a personality quality that shows itself in one's actions and is viewed as empathetic, cooperative, kind, and thoughtful. One of the five main aspects of personality structure in modern personality psychology, agreeableness reflects individual variances in social harmony and collaboration.

Continuity

The existence of a whole route for current flow is continuity. When a circuit's switch is closed, the circuit is finished. Check the switches, fuses, electrical connections, conductors, and other parts using a digital multimeter's Continuity Test to check the circuit's mode. For instance, a good fuse should have continuity.

Shared Goal

Actors' shared objectives and a sense of destiny with others are examples of shared goals. Shared objectives serve as a unifying factor that enables participants to organize their efforts and collaborate for mutual gain. They are more than simply formally stated objectives.

Identifying and Overcoming Barriers to Effective Human Relations

People have trouble working together—thus preserving a climate conducive to effective human relations—when they engage in destructive conflict, perceive such matters as goals, time, and status differently, and behave in relationships with other people in ways that give rise to anger or hostility. Hence, there are three chief barriers to effective human relations:

1) Destructive conflict
2) Differences in perceptions
3) Poor interpersonal behaviors

But what are these barriers, and how can they be identified and overcome?

Types of Conflict

All work groups or teams experience some conflict, defined as a confrontation between people stemming from differences. There are two kinds. **Constructive conflict** leads to improvements and preserves goodwill among group members. **Destructive conflict** neither improves performance nor preserves goodwill. Constructive conflict can be a powerful source of creativity and innovation, leading to increased agreements over group goals, work methods, and company policies and procedures. Without constructive conflict, progress is rarely made.

However, constructive conflict can turn into destructive conflict if problems are left to fester, solutions are forced on unwilling people, or if a conflict escalates beyond issues to include personalities. To overcome destructive conflict and thus surmount it as a barrier to effective human relations, supervisors or team members can rely on numerous, exemplary approaches. One approach is to focus on **problem-solving**. Members of a team or a group can be brought together to focus on identifying what a problem is and how it can be solved.

Problem-Solving Approaches: The following are several approaches to problem-solving between teams and groups:

- *Confrontation Meeting*. This approach aims to clear the air by articulating perceptions and working through them to solutions. Team facilitators should play a lead role in calling together individuals or groups for such meetings, promoting open descriptions of problems, and helping people work through the problems to reach solutions or strategies for improvement.
- *Establish Common Goals*. In many cases, destructive conflict stems from differences of opinion about the means (work methods and procedures) rather than ends (the results to be achieved). Supervisors, team facilitators, or team members should focus attention on the ends to get agreement on the means.
- *Expand the Resources Available*. Conflict often stems from competition over scarce resources such as time, money, staff, or management attention. By obtaining more resources, supervisors or team members can sometimes eliminate this cause of conflict. While often a most desired approach, it can be tough to use in a time of diminishing resources.
- *Avoid the Problem*. While hardly effective as a long-term approach to resolving destructive conflicts, avoidance can sometimes work as a short-term strategy. If problems are avoided long enough, some will get worse and some will work themselves out.
- *Smooth over Differences*. Smoothing means trying to make people feel better without really addressing the cause of their discomfort. This approach is a short-term strategy. It is not very effective because it does not get at the root of the conflict.
- *Compromise*. When compromising, one person or group involved in conflict gives up something and gets something in return. This is the political way of resolving conflict. Neither party to a conflict wins nor

loses completely. Neither party is completely satisfied with the outcome of a compromise.

■ ***Use Authority***. Often tempting to autocratic supervisors or similarly minded team members, this approach means dictating a solution to conflicting individuals or groups. If the issue is not one that provokes strong emotion, the groups or individuals in conflict may cease their bickering and go along with the decision. On the other hand, if the issue evokes strong emotion, then the use of authority will not work. If coerced to accept a decision, the conflicting parties may hide their differences of opinion but seek revenge in more subtle, less desirable ways.

■ ***Change Behavior***. It can be costly and time-consuming. It requires a two-sided solution: one focusing on the cause of conflict and one focusing on the feelings of the people involved in it. To use the approach, supervisors or team members should begin by soliciting information about the nature of conflict from the people involved in it. Information about the feelings of those involved should also be solicited. Supervisors, team facilitators, or team members should then feedback the information that was collected, focus attention on solving problems and on behaviors needed for the conflicting groups or individuals to work together cooperatively, and direct the conflicting groups or individuals to go on the record with a plan for change that is mutually satisfactory, address the conflict and encourage improved relations. In some cases, this process requires assistance by a third-party mediator—someone other than an authority figure like a supervisor or manager.

■ ***Change the Structure***. This approach means changing reporting relationships. It may also mean transferring, exchanging, or otherwise altering the people in the work group or team. By changing group membership, supervisors and teams can sometimes reduce conflict by shifting the boundaries that have created an "us against them" mindset or can separate two people who cannot get along harmoniously.

■ ***Identify a Common Enemy***. Conflicting members of a work group or team will tend to close ranks behind a leader, even when the leader is unpopular, when challenged by threatening or competing forces from outside. Identifying a common enemy is only a short-term technique for resolving conflict. When the external threat is removed, the internal conflict usually resurfaces quickly.

Whatever the source of destructive conflict, however, it can prove damaging to a climate conducive to good human relations. For this reason, supervisors and team members should remain vigilant and act quickly when they spot the symptoms of destructive conflict. In some settings, especially those in which the work is highly creative or in which cohesive teamwork is critical because workers function interdependently, destructive conflict can inhibit productivity because it will lead to a climate in which people are guarded, distrustful, and suspicious. These characteristics are, of course, exactly opposite from those required for creativity or for team *esprit de corps*.

Differences in Perceptions

Another barrier to effective human relations centers around differences in perceptions.

Perception is the process of receiving information from the outside world and interpreting it. Individuals perceive the world differently because they vary in what experiences they have had in it. Past perceptions color present ones.

People constantly receive and interpret information about the world and about the organizations in which they work. They tend to judge, evaluate, and interpret information based on past events or past dealings with others. When they distrust the motives of others or wrongly interpret behaviors they observe, then perceptions can interfere with group relations.

Consider a simple example. Mike Peabody observed his supervisor, Laura Wentling, talking to George Hanson. Mike is intensely jealous of George. He is likely to be considered with George as a possible successor for Laura's position when she is promoted or rotated. Mike is deeply suspicious of Laura because he has observed her speaking in whispers to George on several occasions. When he approaches them to ask Laura a question, she breaks off her conversation with George and looks nervous. Mike suspects that they are conspiring so that, when the time comes, George will be promoted to Laura's job. As this example illustrates, what people perceive can affect their beliefs, attitudes, and behaviors. Mike is suspicious of Laura not because of the present incident but because of past dealings with her or with others. What he perceives at present is rooted in past experiences.

To deal with perceptions, supervisors and team facilitators should surface them, deal with them honestly and forthrightly, and establish grounds for future perceptions based on present experiences with employees.

Methods of surfacing perceptions include staff or team meetings, one-on-one discussions, exit interviews, attitude surveys, training sessions, and interviews during employee performance evaluations. Supervisors or team facilitators should establish the grounds for frank discussions by actively listening.

When employees wrongly perceive events or the behaviors of others, supervisors or team members should take pains to listen to the employees' views and then feedback the meanings to them. By doing this, supervisors and team facilitators establish the grounds for trusting relationships in the future. Trust is very important because it leads to improved personal relations and communication. Lacking it, people will be guarded and uncomfortable and will probably not be very productive because they will be unsure of themselves in the process of interacting with others.

Poor Interpersonal Behaviors

A third and final barrier to effective human relations involves poor interpersonal behaviors. This means behaving toward others in ways that make them feel hostile, angry, or unappreciated. Most people have probably experienced first-hand poor interpersonal behaviors of others at one time or another. Such behaviors may be nonverbal or verbal and may occur in face-to-face interactions or over the telephone.

Examples of poor interpersonal behaviors occurring nonverbally

- Looking away when someone speaks
- Looking at one's watch during a conversation
- Failing to return a smile
- Staring at people while they talk
- Gawking at the hand of one who gestures

Examples of poor interpersonal behaviors occurring verbally

- Talking at people without listening to what they have said
- Responding to others with statements that can be interpreted in several ways
- Finding fault, accusing, or placing blame
- Using a tone of voice that sounds arrogant, whining, disinterested, sarcastic, or otherwise inhibiting

Poor interpersonal behaviors over the telephone

- Cutting people off
- Forgetting to mention one's name, department, or organization

- Putting people on hold for long time periods
- Transferring calls that have already been transferred

Other irritating mannerisms are common and lead to all kinds of problems

- Talking behind people's backs
- Complaining constantly without suggesting improvements
- Praising supervisors or influential team members in ill-concealed efforts to obtain favors or special treatment
- Taking actions without telling people involved

Supervisors or team members can follow a few simple rules to deal effectively with these common problems:

- Do not encourage people to talk behind the backs of others. Simply stop listening—or better yet, offer to invite to the conversation the person who is being discussed.
- Every time people complain, ask them what they suggest should be done to solve the problem. If they present a good solution, then praise them. If they have no solution, then assign them the task of finding one. If they present a poor solution, then explain why it will not work and then ask for a better solution.
- Accept praise or blame from employees without emotion. If praise is offered and appears to be serious, accept it graciously. If it is insincere or self-serving, ignore it.
- Confront people who act without consulting those affected. Explain what problems have been or are likely to be created as a result. Then propose they help solve any problems resulting from what they have done.

What's Next?

The next chapter, "Understanding People's Motivation and How to Delegate," explores motivation as one of the most important reasons that a human being would act for or against any topic, desire, or interest, and how to effectively delegate responsibilities. Before you move on, don't forget to review the key takeaways, and take a moment to reflect on what you learned in this chapter by completing Table 6.4, End of Chapter 6 Discussion Questions and Inquiries.

Table 6.4   End of Chapter 6 Questions and Inquiries. Your Perspective on What You Learned in Chapter 6

Your Perspective on What You Learned in Chapter 6	
Area of Inquiry	*What Did You Learn, and How Are You Going to Implement It in Your Position?*
The importance of human relations	
Different types of interpersonal relationships	
Different types of interpersonal skills	
Human relations skills	
Responsibilities for maintaining effective human relations	
Tips for creating and maintaining effective human relations	
Goals of human relations	
Identifying and overcoming barriers to effective human relations	

Key Takeaways

1. Human relations stem from the ability to deal with individuals through the effective use of such interpersonal skills such as communicating, listening, questioning, dealing with feelings, and influencing. In a work group or team, human relations also means that people want to get along, cooperate with each other, and achieve a common goal.
2. The foundation of rapport and trust is relatedness. Supervisors that are effective won't treat their coachees as inferiors or superiors. They will treat the coachees with respect and compassion, considering where they are in their lives and professions.
3. Interpersonal relationships are tight associations between people who have similar interests and aspirations. An interpersonal relationship is formed when two people are compatible. To have a solid and healthy relationship, people must get along well (Bakhshandeh & Zeine, 2012).
4. Regardless of what type of interpersonal relationship you are involved with, the need exists for establishing rapport with other person or persons. That would make rapport an essential element of having effective and productive human relations at the workplace.
5. Strong interpersonal skills are crucial in any job, but they will be much more crucial in the workplace of the future, where teams will be more cross-functional, diverse, and collaborative.

Discussion Questions and Inquiries

Please take a minute to answer the following inquiries and questions in Table 6.4. From your point of view, what have you learned about the following areas?

References

Angelo, G. (2012). *Rapport; The Art of Connecting with People and Building Relationships.* Middletown, DE: SN & NS Publications.
APA (American Phycological Association). (2023). APA dictionary of psychology. *Interpersonal Relationship.* Retrieved January 25, 2023, from https://dictionary.apa.org/interpersonal-relations
Aristotelous, P. (2019). *The Marvel of Engagement.* Middletown, DE: (self-publishing).

Bakhshandeh, B. (2002). *Business Coaching and Managers Training*. Workshop on coaching businesses and training managers. Unpublished. San Diego, CA: Primeco Education, Inc.

Bakhshandeh, B. (2006). *Potholes on the Highway of Love: Mistakes you Can Avoid in Any Relationship*. 2-Sets CD. San Diego, CA: Primeco Education, Inc.

Bakhshandeh, B. (2008). *Bravehearts; Leadership Development Training*. Training and developmental course on coaching executive and managers. Unpublished. San Diego, CA: Primeco Education, Inc.

Bakhshandeh, B. (2009). *Conspiracy for Greatness; Mastery on Love Within*. San Diego, CA: Primeco Education, Inc.

Bakhshandeh, B. (2015). *Anatomy of Upset: Restoring Harmony*. Carbondale, PA: Primeco Education, Inc.

Bakhshandeh, B. (2021). *Perception of 21st Century 4cs (Critical Thinking, Communication, Creativity & Collaboration) Skill Gap in Private-Sector Employers in Lackawanna County, NEPA* (An unpublished dissertation in workforce education and development. The Pennsylvania State University).

Bakhshandeh, B., & Zeine, F. (2012). *The Power of Two*. 8-Sets DVD. Los Angeles, CA: Primeco Education, Inc. & Dr. Foojan Zeine.

Cennamo, L., & Gardner, D. (2008). Generational differences in work values, outcomes and person-organization values fit. *Journal of Managerial Psychology, 23*(8), 891–906. https://doi.org/10.1108/02683940810904385

Cummings, T. G., & Worley, C. G. (2015). *Organization Development & Change* (10th ed.). Stamford, CT: Cengage Learning.

Gilmore, M. (2019). *The Power of Rapport*. Middletown, DE: Partridge.

Gordon, J. (2017). *The Power of Positive Leadership*. Hoboken, NJ: John Wiley & Sons, Inc.

Hockenbury, D. H., & Hockenbury, S. E. (2007). *Discovering Psychology*. New York, NY: Worth Publishers.

Hove, M. J., & Risen, J. L. (2009). It's all in the timing: Interpersonal synchrony increases affiliation. *Social Cognition, 27*(6), 949–960. https://doi.org/10.1521/soco.2009.27.6.949

Keller, H. (2016). Psychological autonomy and hierarchical relatedness as organizers of developmental pathways. *Philosophical Transactions of the Royal Society B: Biological Sciences, 371*(1686), 20150070.

Kold, J. A. (2011). *Small Group Facilitation: Improving Process and Performance in Groups and Teams*. Amherst, MA: HRD Press.

Lencioni, P. (2002). *The Five Dysfunction of a Team*. San Francisco, CA: Jossey-Bass; A Wiley Imprint.

Leonardo, N. (2020). *Active Listening Techniques*. Emeryville, CA: Rockridge Press.

Levi, D. (2017). *Group Dynamics for Teams* (5th ed.). Thousand Oaks, CA: Sage Publications.

Lexico.com 2023. *Relatedness*. Powered by Oxford. https://www.lexico.com/en/definition/relatedness

Merriam-Webster Dictionary. (2023). Rapport. https://www.merriam-webster.com/dictionary/rapport

Oxford Language. (2023). *Human Relations*. Retrieved January 26, 2023, from https://languages.oup.com/google-dictionary-en/

Rothwell, W. J., & Bakhshandeh, B. (2022). *High-Performance Coaching for Managers. Step-by-Step Approach to Increase Employees' Performance and Productivity*. New York, NY: Taylor & Francis Group; Routledge.

Rothwell, W. J., Stavros, J. M., & Sullivan, R. L. (2016). *Practicing Organization Development: Leading Transformation and Change* (4th ed.). Hoboken, NJ: John Wiley & Sons, Inc.

SCANS Report. (2000). Employment & training administration. United States Department of Labor. https://wdr.doleta.gov/SCANS/whatwork/

Schwartz, J. (2021). *Work Disrupted*. Hoboken, NJ: John Wiley & Sons.

Schwartz, S. H. (1992). Universals in the content and structure of values: Theoretical advances and empirical tests in 20 countries. In *Advances in Experimental Social Psychology*, 25 (pp. 1–65). Academic Press. https://doi.org/10.1016/S0065-2601(08)60281-6

Whitmore, J. (2017). *Coaching for Performance; The Principle and Practice of Coaching and Leadership* (5th ed.). Boston, MA: Nicholas Brealey Publishing.

Chapter 7

Understanding People's Motivation and How to Delegate

Introduction

Motivation is one of the most important reasons that a human being would act for or against any topic, desire, or interest. Motivation is what makes a person engaged with certain behaviors and actions. There are biological and psychological variables on one's motivations, as well as different sources that might cause one to become motivated. At the same time our human perceptions of how we view and relate to ourselves, others around us, and the world itself has an absolute effect on our motivation or lack thereof (Deckers, 2010).

Since supervisors get things done with and through others, they have good reasons to be interested in what prompts people to act and how people can be encouraged to act in predictable, desirable ways. However, supervisors in traditional organizations can rarely increase or decrease individual motivation. As a force coming from within, individuals can only control their motivation. But supervisors *can* affect the work climate and help establish a work climate conducive to unleashing individual energy, productivity, enthusiasm, creativity, and initiative.

A similar principle applies to team facilitators and team members in team-based organizations. While no team member can genuinely "motivate" another, team climate is the responsibility of all team members. By

160   DOI: 10.4324/9781003413493-7

maintaining an open, trusting, and supportive team climate, team members support team motivation.

Your team members will be motivated to take constructive action as a result of your inclusive leadership style, which will promote an innovative workplace culture, higher job satisfaction, better job performance, and reduced attrition rates. Employing and training more talented managers and supervisors who can advance their organizations through both prosperous and trying times is crucial for businesses and motivating their workforces. For this, it is necessary to look beyond conventional management development techniques and build the abilities crucial for success such as being empathetic for one (Wulf & Lewthwaite, 2016).

To lead with empathy, one must be able to comprehend the needs of others and be conscious of their emotions and ideas. Regrettably, as a performance metric, it has long been a disregarded soft skill. But studies have shown that today's effective leaders must be more "person-focused" and able to motivate others and get along with individuals from different teams, departments, nations, cultures, and backgrounds. Effective supervision may guarantee a competitive edge at work. Higher authorities' influence and working hours are seen to be crucial for enhancing employees' performance. Monitoring honorarium payments may boost morale and strengthen team ties (Stander & Rothmann, 2010). However, the success of an organization especially depends on a number of variables, but one of the key variables that affects the company's performance is the leadership style that the leader, such as a supervisor and a manager, exemplifies. The leadership style that establishes the company's culture is crucial for resolving workplace problems and inspiring employees must include competencies such as being empathetic, inclusive, and relational.

Motivation is a desire to achieve a goal, satisfy a need, or rectify a perceived imbalance between *what is* and *what should be*. It stimulates purposeful action by individuals. It is a force or drive coming from inside people rather than imposed from outside on them. Derived from the Latin *movere*— meaning "to move"—motivation guides human behavior. Observations of what people do (*behavior*) can lead to conclusions about what motivates them (*what force or drive guides behavior*) (Wulf & Lewthwaite, 2016).

As shown in Figure 7.1 of the *Successful Supervisory Leadership Series Book II Structure*, this chapter is at the heart of understanding what drives employees in the workplace and how they can be effectively empowered through delegation. We simplify the key theories behind motivation, list the top ten factors that inspire people in the workplace, and dissect the art

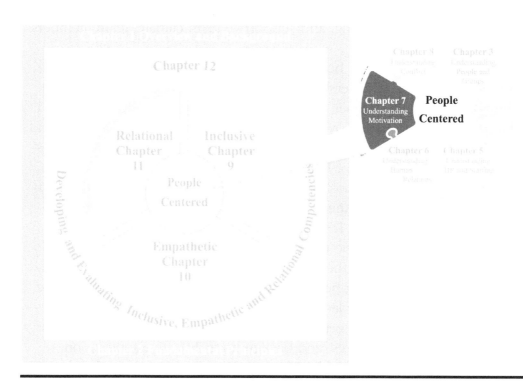

Figure 7.1 *Successful Supervisory Leadership Series Book II Structure.* *Note:* **Authors'** original creation.

of delegation when it is beneficial and not. We will also address common hurdles that can block successful delegation and provide a clear, step-by-step approach to entrusting tasks to others. This chapter gives you the insights and knowledge needed to harness team potential and optimize productivity by aligning individual drives with organizational goals—to achieve the best possible results.

Key Concepts

This chapter will cover the following key concepts:

- Understanding Motivation and What Motivates People at Workplace
- Understanding Motivation Theories
  - Vroom's Expectancy Theory
  - Locke's Goal-Setting Theory
  - Adam's Equity Theory
  - Psychological Empowerment Theory
- Top Ten Motivation Factors Affecting Employees

- Understanding Delegation and Delegating
- When Delegation Is Appropriate or Inappropriate
- Barriers to Delegation and How to Overcome Them
- Steps in Delegating

Definitions

The following definitions of key terms will help to better understand the main elements of this chapter:

Motivation

American Psychological Association (APA) (2023a) defines motivation as:

- "a person's willingness to exert physical or mental effort in pursuit of a goal or outcome" (n. p.).
- "the act or process of encouraging others to exert themselves in pursuit of a group or organizational goal. The ability to motivate followers is an important function of leadership" (n. p.).

Also, APA (2023a) describes motivation as:

> the impetus that gives purpose or direction to behavior and operates in humans at a conscious or unconscious level. Motives are frequently divided into (a) physiological, primary, or organic motives, such as hunger, thirst, and need for sleep; and (b) personal, social, or secondary motives, such as affiliation, competition, and individual interests and goals. An important distinction must also be drawn between internal motivating forces and external factors, such as rewards or punishments, that can encourage or discourage certain behaviors
>
> **(n. p.).**

Oxford Language Dictionary defines Motivation as:

- "the reason or reasons one has for acting or behaving in a particular way."
- "the general desire or willingness of someone to do something."

(Oxford Language, 2023, n.p.).

Delegation

APA on delegation of authority in business:

- "an approach whereby a manager or supervisor assigns tasks to subordinates, along with commensurate responsibility for completion of the tasks, but without relinquishing the ultimate responsibility for any success or failure" (APA, 2023b, n.p.).

Rothwell and Kazanas (2003) described delegation in business as:
- Transferring accountability for certain duties from one person to another is referred to as delegation. From a managerial standpoint, delegation happens when a manager gives their staff members particular tasks to do.

Understanding Motivation and What Motivates People at the Workplace

Motivation is one of the few OB (organizational behavior) subjects that is important to both managers and employees. How many times have you questioned why you couldn't get moving today? Alternatively, how often have you noticed a friend or coworker working slowly and wondered why? Both of these inquiries concern "motivation" (Colquitt et al., 2015). More specifically, motivation is described as a collection of energizing forces that both come from an employee's internal and external environment and affect the direction, level of intensity, and persistence of their work-related efforts. Because effective work performance frequently involves levels of both skill and drive, motivation is an important factor (Colquitt et al., 2015).

The first section of the above definition of motivation demonstrates that it is not just one thing but rather a collection of varied elements. Some of those factors—like a sense of purpose or confidence—are internal to the individual, whereas others—like the objectives or incentives provided to the employee—are external. The next portion of that definition demonstrates how an employee's motivation affects a variety of aspects of their job effort (Colquitt et al., 2015; French & Bell, 1999). The focus of an employee's work is determined by their motivation at any particular time. Choices between task and citizenship-type acts, retreat, and unproductive types of actions are available at every minute of the workday. On a Thursday at 3:00 PM, are you working on the job your employer has given you? Or do you spend some time online browsing or sending emails? (French & Bell, 1999). As Colquitt et al. (2015) pointed out, "Once the direction of effort has been decided, motivation goes on to determine how hard an employee works—the intensity of effort—and *for how long*—the persistence of effort" (p. 168).

Why Do Some Workers Have Greater Motivation than Others?

Many theories and ideas make an effort to explain why certain workers are more driven than others. The parts that follow go into further depth about those theories and notions. While some are better at describing the concentration and perseverance of effort, certain of them are specifically suited to conveying the direction of effort.

Expectancy Theory

According to Victor Vroom's expectation theory, conduct is the result of conscious decisions made between options with the goals of maximizing pleasure and minimizing pain. Vroom came to the realization that a worker's performance is influenced by personal traits including personality, skills, knowledge, experience, and talents. He said that their effort influences a person's motivation, performance, and motivation. To account for this, he employs the variables Expectancy, Instrumentality, and Valence (Fitzgerald et al., 2015). (see Figure 7.2).

Expectancy, or "if I work more than this will be better," is the idea that putting in more effort will result in higher performance. This is impacted by factors like:

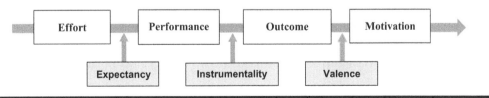

Figure 7.2   Motion and elements of Victor H. Vroom's expectancy theory of motivation. Adapted from http://gaculty.css.edu/dswenson/web/OB/VIEtheory.html.

■ Having the appropriate resources such as more time or material on hand.
■ Possessing the essential support, such as manager's or supervisor's support to complete the task.
■ Possessing the appropriate skills and competencies to perform the task.

Instrumentality is the idea that you will achieve a worthwhile goal if you work hard enough. how much a first-level result will influence a second-level result, i.e., there is something in it for me if I do a good job. This is impacted by factors like:

■ A clear grasp of how performance and results are related, such as the rules of the reward game.
■ Have faith in those making decisions about who will receive what results.
■ Transparency of the procedures used to determine who receives what results.

Valence is the weight that a person gives to the anticipated result. The person must prefer achieving the outcome over not achieving it for the valence to be positive. People who are primarily driven by money, for instance, might not be interested to offers of more time off.

Importantly, Vroom's expectation theory relies on perceptions; as a result, even if an employer believes they have supplied all the necessary incentives and even if this strategy works for the majority of employees there, it doesn't guarantee that someone else won't feel the same way.

At first appearance, expectancy theory would appear to be most applicable to traditional work environments where an employee's motivation hinges on if they choose the prize offered for doing well and if they feel putting in more effort will result in that reward. Hence, the associations people establish with anticipated results and the influence they believe they can make to those outcomes are the focus of Vroom's expectation theory of motivation rather than self-interest in rewards (Fitzgerald et al., 2015; Hersey & Blanchard, 1993).

Edwin Locke Goal-Setting Theory

Edwin Locke proposed the goal-setting theory of motivation in the 1960s. According to this hypothesis, task performance and goal setting are fundamentally related. It claims that clear, difficult objectives and useful feedback help people do tasks more effectively. In plain English, goals outline and instruct an employee as to what must be performed and how much endeavor must be expended. Locke's Goal-Setting Theory establishes a connection between the accomplishment of a goal and its five distinct guiding principles. According to Locke's study and the consequent study that was based on it, organizations and employees would do better if goals followed the following five guidelines (see Figure 7.3) (Colquitt et al., 2015):

Establishing Clear Goals. It is crucial that a goal is transparent so that you and everyone else understand what it is, how to monitor it, and when it will be completed. If your goal is unclear, it will be tough to agree on its accomplishment and it won't inspire others. You can adhere to the following guidelines to make sure your goals are clear:

■ Instead of using unclear wording for measurement, attempt to employ metrics like numbers, time, dates, or percentages.
■ Double-check your specificity by using the SMART (Specific, Measurable, Achievable, Relevant, and Timely) approach for goal setting as a reference.
■ If you're in a team, don't be hesitant to clarify things if necessary or ask questions if you don't understand.
■ Share your goal with your peer or manager for support and clarity.

Figure 7.3   Principles of Edwin Locke's goal-setting theory of motivation. Adapted from Colquitt et al. (2015).

Establishing Challenging Goals. Make sure your goals are both tough and attainable. It will increase motivation and give you that satisfying sensation when you achieve your goals! To assist you in reaching a tough goal, take into account the following:

- How does the goal stack up against your current or prior progress?
- Is it plausible? Is it a bold enough goal?
- What will the prize be if it is successful?
- Are you able to incite friendly competitiveness among teammates or teams?

Ensuring Commitment to Goals. This is crucial because without dedication, it's very probable that you won't reach your full potential and accomplish your goals. There are certain important elements to keep in mind as the entire team must be involved and committed to the goal:

- Share the wider strategy with the team so they can understand how they fit into the larger plans for the success of the organization.
- Share the incentive for the goal being accomplished.
- Communicate why this goal is essential.
- Ensure that everyone feels it is achievable to hit the goal.

Collecting Feedback on Goals. For his you must pay attention to feedback and organize your goals appropriately; this concept touches on the commitment and challenging aspects of goal design. This will make them feel involved and provide you with useful information into the team's current well-being and outlook on future success. Think about the following:

- Include time in your schedule for your team to go through the goals.
- Review your prior progress and solicit their opinion.
- Collect feedback in a disciplined manner using tried-and-true techniques or software.
- If necessary, break down larger goals into smaller ones.

Managing Task Complexity. Overwhelming goals can only lower your final performance, and employee mental and psychological health and wellness are really vital. To achieve the greatest result for everyone, be careful to take into account your team and how they handle various goals. Think about the following:

- Don't overburden any one individual with all the goals.
- Break bigger goals down into smaller, more attainable objectives.
- Keep track via progress reports and catch-ups.
- Assign coaches or mentors to your team and ask them how they feel about the goals and progress.

Adam's Equity Theory

Adam's Equity Theory, commonly referred to as the equity theory of motivation, was created in 1963 by workplace behavioral psychologist John Stacey Adams. The foundation of equity theory is the notion that people are driven by justice. Simply said, according to equity theory, if a person notices an unfairness between themselves and a peer, they will change what they do to make the situation right in their view. As an illustration of equity theory, if a worker discovers that a colleague receiving the same amount of money as them, they can decide to work less to make things seem more equitable in their view (Wulf & Lewthwaite, 2016) (see Figure 7.4).

According to the equity idea, fair treatment motivates people. Fairness perceptions are typically the product of social comparison. In other words, we contrast our efforts (inputs) and the outcomes of those efforts (outputs) with those of others (referents). These are each defined below (Fitzgerald et al., 2015). From this, Adam's Equity Theory extrapolates that a person will be more driven if they see equity (fairness) as being higher. If someone feels unfairly treated, on the other hand, they will get demotivated.

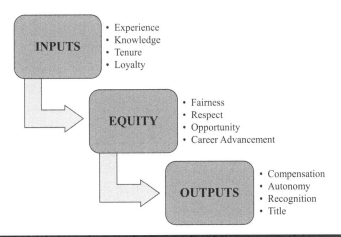

Figure 7.4 Elements of John Stacey Adams's equity theory of motivation. Source: Authors' original creation.

Hersey and Blanchard (1993) describe the main elements of Adams's equity theory below.

- ▪ ***Inputs.*** This refers to any contribution a person makes to a formal activity. This might include specific expertise, experience, length of service with the company, hours worked, opportunities passed up, job prioritizing, etc.
- ▪ ***Outputs.*** These are the benefits reaped from the input. This can refer to pay, a position title, acceptance, autonomy, etc.
- ▪ ***Referent.*** The referent may be a single individual or a group of individuals. It's crucial that the referent is relevant to each employee's condition, such as those with comparable jobs, titles, and responsibilities.

It's critical to realize that subjective views of inputs and outputs exist. They could be predicated on fact or the outcome of misinterpretation or prejudice. It is not fair, in our opinion, if our input-to-output ratio differs from or is not equal to that of others. Actions to lessen injustice are motivated by perceptions of inequity.

The equity theory proposes a wide range of possible responses to the alleged unfairness (French & Bell, 1999):

- ▪ ***Warp Perceptions.*** Consider the scenario in a new way to explain the unfairness of the input/output ratio.
- ▪ ***Increase Inputs.*** This might entail pushing yourself harder or learning new skills.
- ▪ ***Reduce Inputs.*** This might include working less or producing work of lower quality.
- ▪ ***Increasing Outputs.*** This might involve bargaining for more pay, obligations, authority, status, and other benefits.
- ▪ ***Alter the Referent.*** Alter the standard against which you judge yourself.
- ▪ ***Leave the Situation***. This usually involves resigning from your position.
- ▪ ***Seek Legal Action.*** File a lawsuit for a specific instance of discrimination based on membership in a protected class.

An intriguing feature of equity theory is that, in most cases, people do not react in the same ways when they feel they have received more compensation for their work than they reasonably should have given the input. In conclusion, being overcompensated simply does not have a detrimental effect on individuals.

Psychological Empowerment Theory

Psychological empowerment is the appearance of individuals inner motivation in relationship to the following four cognitive elements (see Figure 7.5). A proactive attitude and sense of control over one's job are reflected in the four cognitive components. According to psychological empowerment theory, empowered workers are more enthusiastic about their jobs. This displays a culture in which staff members desire and truly possess confidence in defining their job function and context. Therefore, feeling empowered and intrinsically motivated might lead to improved work output (Spreitzer et al., 1997; Spreitzer, 1995).

Mcaning. When used in a professional setting, the definition of meaningfulness is "the worth of a work aim or purpose, considered in connection to an individual's own id." Job duties become meaningful when one believes they are worthwhile and have an impact. People are creative and self-expressive; therefore, they look for jobs that allow them to act in ways that reflect their self-concepts (Stander & Sebastiaan, 2010). Work responsibilities and activities that fit with how people view themselves should be linked to more fulfilling work experiences. Employees who feel more empowered find

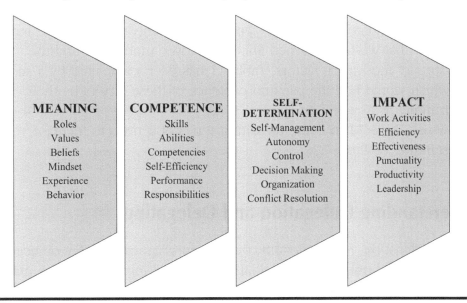

Figure 7.5   Elements of psychological empowerment. Source: Authors' original creation.

more significance in their job. A strategy to increase an employee's motivation and commitment to their job, which leads to engagement, is said to be the restoration of meaning in the workplace (Macey & Schneider, 2008).

Competence. Research has demonstrated that feeling competent and confident in regard to important goals is connected with increased intrinsic motivation and well-being, according to Macey and Schneider (2008). Engaged workers believe they are fully capable of handling the responsibilities of their positions (self-efficacy). Engagement and self-efficacy go hand in hand very well.

Self-Determination. Employee involvement will increase with self-endorsed objectives but not with heteronomous goals, even when implemented successfully. Self-determined goals are independent and well-integrated inside the individual. Gagne and Deci (2005) contend that it is impossible to remain independent while pursuing one's actual self (Macey & Schneider, 2008).

Impact. Impact denotes organizational participation and measures how individuals perceive their level of contribution to their organization (Spreitzer et al., 1997). Employee engagement is influenced by impact, which suggests a sense of progress toward a goal and people's conviction that their activities are having an impact on their businesses (Greasley et al., 2005).

Top Ten Motivation Factors Affecting Employees

Let's talk about some of the most significant elements that influence motivation now that we have learned about employee motivation and the many sorts of motivating factors. Table 7.1 has been completed by a supervisor which would rate the use and presence of these factors by their organization.

Now use Table 7.1 to come up with a series of actions to increase your understanding of Table 7.2.

Understanding Delegation and Delegating

Without delegation, nothing could occur in an organization. Theoretically speaking, all authority for managerial decision-making rests with owners (in privately held enterprises), shareholders (in publicly held enterprises), or voters (in government agencies). In turn, owners and shareholders elect Boards of Directors. Boards, in turn, hire Chief Executives—and voters elect public

Table 7.1   Supervisor's Rating on Top Ten Employees' Motivation Factors in Their Organization

Supervisor's Rating on Top Ten Employees' Motivation Factors in Their Organization								
Supervisor's Name		Date		Supervisor's Manager		Department		
*Rating Scale: **1** = Poor, **2** = Marginal, **3** = Acceptable, **4** = Good, **5** = Excellent*								
	Factors	*Descriptions*			*1*	*2*	*3*	*4*	*5*
1	*Display of respect*	People always react to a respectful manner and when they have a feeling of being respected regardless of their work title or place in the organization's hierarchy. As a supervisor displaying respect to everyone in your team or group is essential to an individual motivation.							
2	*Recognition and reward*	To show your workers that you value and respect their accomplishments, you might give them compliments. Simply praising employees for their additional effort is insufficient; they should also be rewarded. Your staff members are more likely to continue or repeat their conduct when you give them favorable comments on their performance.							
3	*Opportunities for growth*	When there are prospects for growth, employees are more driven to work. Promotion and development are intrinsic motivators. Employees are more likely to be motivated and committed if they are given freedom to improve and a career ladder to climb.							
4	*Work environment*	For employees to effectively perform their tasks and obligations, the work environment must be encouraging, welcoming, and empowering. They will lose motivation rapidly if they operate in a hostile setting and don't feel valued or welcomed.							

(Continued)

Table 7.1 (Continued)   Supervisor's Rating on Top Ten Employees' Motivation Factors in Their Organization

Supervisor's Rating on Top Ten Employees' Motivation Factors in Their Organization							
Supervisor's Name		Date	Supervisor's Manager		Department		
Rating Scale: *1* = Poor, *2* = Marginal, *3* = Acceptable, *4* = Good, *5* = Excellent							
Factors		Descriptions	*1*	*2*	*3*	*4*	*5*
5	*Financial benefits*	Most employees are motivated by money in one form or another. Offering employees a variety of cash perks increases their motivation and work incentive. Additionally, it gives your staff members a feeling of recognition and success.					
6	*Nonmonetary benefits*	Some employees just choose nonmonetary advantages, gestures, and benefits, despite the fact that most employees prefer monetary rewards. They resemble employee awards in certain ways. Let them take pleasure in the present and the advantages of their non-cash earnings.					
7	*Work and life balance*	An excellent motivation is ensuring that your staff members have a healthy work–life balance and a reasonably flexible work schedule. They are more motivated to ensure the task is completed well and are less inclined to make excuses. Keep in mind that happy, effective employees are those who have a healthy work–life balance.					
8	*Presence of DEI&B*	Employees will get more motivated when they are experiencing the presence of respect to diversity, equity, and inclusion which would cause experiencing of belonging with their small work community.					

(Continued)

Table 7.1 (Continued)   Supervisor's Rating on Top Ten Employees' Motivation Factors in Their Organization

Supervisor's Rating on Top Ten Employees' Motivation Factors in Their Organization							
Supervisor's Name	Date	Supervisor's Manager	Department				
Rating Scale: 1 = Poor, 2 = Marginal, 3 = Acceptable, 4 = Good, 5 = Excellent							
Factors		*Descriptions*	*1*	*2*	*3*	*4*	*5*
9	*Interpersonal relationships*	The majority of an employee's day is spent at the workplace with their coworkers and peers. At least five days a week, they devote the majority of their time to work. Their attitude and mood are greatly influenced by how their coworkers interact with them.					
10	*Leadership inspiration*	Having a leader, the employees can look up to for inspiration and guidance is one of the best motivating factors for employees. As a leader, it is your duty to guide your employees as needed. Your leadership style also dictates a lot of motivating factors.					
Individual Columns' Totals							
Total of above Individual Columns							
Final Average (above total divided by 10)							

Note: Authors' original creation.

officials—to carry out daily decision-making. Chief Executives, in turn, appoint managers and supervisors to help them meet their responsibilities.

In traditional organizations, failure to delegate may be the single most common reason that supervisors fail in their jobs. Supervisors who do not delegate find themselves overburdened with tasks that they cannot possibly complete alone. Often, they also lack detailed technical skill to carry out the work. Yet many supervisors do not delegate because they accept the old adage that "if you want things done right, do them yourself." Another common reason: supervisors who are promoted from within are accustomed to functioning as individual contributors and have never been properly trained

Table 7.2 APLI-Connected to Table 7.1

Action Plan for Learning and Improving	
Area of Learning and Improving: Supervisor's Rating on Top Ten Employees' Motivation Factors in Their Organization	
Reference: *Table 7.1*	
Three learning and improvement actions for this month that will raise my understanding and awareness in regard to "Supervisor's Rating on Top Ten Employees' Motivation Factors in Their Organization" to enhance their understanding and clarity by at least one on the next rating:	
Action 1:	By When:
Action 2:	By When:
Action 3:	By When:

Note: Authors' original creation.

by their organizations how to transition into a new role in which they work with and through others.

Professional Definition of Delegation in Business

The following text includes some definitions and descriptions of some terminologies relevant to the concept of delegation:

Delegation is the deliberate redirection of authority. It is *deliberate* because no delegation occurs without explicit direction. (Employees who take it upon themselves to act on their supervisor's behalf or on a team's behalf without explicit direction are said to *usurp* authority.) Delegation is the *redirection of authority* because the supervisor or team bestows the employee with a temporary ability to act on the supervisor's or team's behalf. The supervisor or team is not relieved of responsibility; rather, the employee is given only temporary authority to act on others' behalf (Rothwell, 2015; Gagne & Deci, 2005).

Authority is the right to give orders and exact obedience. There are three kinds of authority:

■ *Legal authority* is vested in public officials, who are granted rights to act by virtue of election or appointment to office.

- ***Managerial authority*** stems from an individual's position in an organization.
- ***Expert authority*** stems from specialized knowledge, skill, or talent. Only managerial authority can be delegated. Managerial authority may reside with a supervisor (in traditional organizations) or with a team (in team-based organizations).

(Rothwell, 2015; Gagne & Deci, 2005).

Responsibility is an obligation to perform tasks or carry out duties assigned to an individual or position. If supervisors or teams carry out duties assigned to them, they are acting responsibly. Responsible behavior is highly prized because it relieves pressure for all decision-making from individual supervisors or from a whole team (Rothwell, 2015; Gagne & Deci, 2005).

Classical management theorists asserted that authority must match responsibility. This principle is called **parity**. It means that, if individuals are held responsible for an activity, they must also possess sufficient authority to ensure that the activity is performed. It makes little sense to delegate responsibility (*obligation to perform*) without delegating authority (*the right to give orders*). Nor is it wise to delegate authority without also endowing commensurate responsibility.

There is a practical limit to delegation, however. In carrying out their jobs, supervisors cannot do everything by themselves. They must delegate some managerial authority to others. They can also hold employees responsible. But supervisors never completely relinquish responsibility. If employees act improperly, supervisors are held accountable by others for the misguided action or its unfortunate consequences. For instance, a government employee who embezzles public funds is accountable to an elected official, but the public holds the official responsible for having created conditions that permitted the crime to occur. Likewise, executives are legally liable for endangering the lives of employees by exposing them to hazardous substances, even when they have delegated responsibility for action to others and are unaware that employees are being exposed to those substances.

The same basic principle also applies in self-directed teams. The team is ultimately responsible for the work performed and the results achieved. If the team delegates a work duty to one member and that duty is subsequently handled poorly, the individual is responsible to the team. However, the team ultimately bears responsibility for the actions of its members.

A related problem is **reverse delegation**, which is an employee's willful transfer of responsibility back to his or her supervisor. It occurs when employees lack confidence in their own abilities and would rather shift the responsibility for action to a supervisor, who is viewed by the employee as better equipped to handle a tough problem. Unfortunately, supervisors who permit reverse delegation will find that they must do everything themselves because their employees have never learned how (Akinola et al., 2018).

When Delegation Is Appropriate or Inappropriate

How can a supervisor tell whether he or she is not delegating enough? One way is to perform a simple diagnostic (see Table 7.3); another way is to examine how well he or she is presently delegating (see Table 7.4).

Appropriate delegation. The following list depicts some reasons for delegating:

- Possess necessary knowledge or skills to act for their supervisors or teams—or can acquire necessary knowledge or skills quickly.
- Are positioned closer than their supervisors or teammates to events, situations, or problems requiring prompt decisions and actions.
- Can carry out duties or make decisions at a lower cost than a supervisor or another team member because the employee's hourly wage or salary is lower.
- Frequently request guidance on the same issue, indicating that it is an area in which they may require cross-training or development.

Inappropriate delegation. The following list depicts some reasons for not delegating:

- ***Assigning personnel.*** The final decision on staff hiring, training, and evaluating rests with the supervisor in traditional organizations and should not be delegated lower. The same general principle holds true in teams: team members should reach a consensus about assignments before one person assigns another to a duty.
- ***Resolving conflicts among employees.*** Supervisors cannot delegate authority for resolving conflicts to someone co-equal to them in status. (This practice will create more problems than it solves.) In team settings, the team facilitator's role is to help employees work out their own conflicts.

Table 7.3 Evidence That a Supervisor Is Not Delegating Enough

Evidence That a Supervisor Is Not Delegating Enough		
Directions: Review each item in the Evidence column below. Then, place a checkmark to indicate your response as either a Yes or a No.		
Evidence	**Yes**	**No**
1. You are work longer hours than others.		
2. You are taking work home.		
3. You are impatience with others.		
4. You are rushing at work.		
5. Finding yourself doing many routine tasks.		
6. You are feeling stressed.		
7. Frequently meeting with employees so they can discuss what they should do.		
8. Frequently missing deadlines.		
9. Finding yourself struggle to plan your future work.		
10. Receiving complaints about the speed that work progresses you're your team or work group.		
Results: If the answers to 4 or more of the above evidence are "yes," then you may not be delegating enough.		

Note: Authors' original creation.

- ***Establishing direction for the work group or team.*** Supervisors are responsible for establishing the direction of their work group and for obtaining needed resources to realize those plans. Team members must usually reach a consensus on this issue.
- ***Dealings with peers or supervisors.*** Supervisors are always responsible for their work groups or teams. They should not delegate activities to employees involving coordination with the supervisor's peers or manager. Team members, on the other hand, may delegate responsibility for cross-functional teamwork to one of their members. However, they are ultimately accountable for decisions made by that member as a team representative.
- ***Meeting responsibilities delegated explicitly from above.*** If the manager gives the supervisor a special assignment, the supervisor is responsible

Table 7.4   Appropriate Levels of Delegation for a Task or Function

Appropriate Levels of Delegation for a Task or Function		
Directions: Use this worksheet when determining the appropriate level of delegation for a project, assignment, or job. Describe the task or function to be delegated. Then indicate *at what level of delegation* the task or function is to operate. Review this worksheet with an employee *before* the task or function is undertaken.		
Task or Function Description		
Should the Employee?	**Description**	**Appropriate?**
Investigate and report back	Employee obtains facts; supervisor uses the facts to frame the problem, make a decision, and take action.	
Investigate and recommend action	Employee obtains facts and recommends what to do; supervisor reviews facts and recommendations, makes decision, and takes action.	
Investigate and advise on action planned	Employee obtains facts and recommends action; supervisor approves or disapproves recommendation.	
Investigate and take action; advise on action taken	Employee obtains facts, makes decision, takes action, and advises the supervisor later.	
Investigate and take action	Employee obtains facts, makes decision, takes action, but does not advise the supervisor.	

Note: Authors' original creation.

for it. While employees may help in information-gathering or advice-giving, the supervisor should not delegate such an assignment.

Barriers to Delegation and How to Overcome Them

Barriers to delegation stem from organizational policies, management expectations, supervisors themselves, and employees.

Organizational policies may prevent delegation on some matters. For example, they may explicitly state that certain documents, forms, or reports must be submitted by the supervisor. For instance, budget forms, production reports, attendance records, travel vouchers, and hiring/dismissal notices may have to bear the supervisor's signature. Employees may supply information, but supervisors have to submit the paperwork (Lauring & Kubovcikova, 2022).

Managers may have their own expectations about what should and should not be delegated by supervisors in their department. Some managers prefer to make hiring decisions for their departments, for example, and then send new employees to supervisors. Some managers participate in hiring decisions as an equal partner with the supervisor. Some delegate hiring to supervisors but reserve for themselves only the decision about who is to be named the supervisor (Lauring & Kubovcikova, 2022).

As Akinola, Martin, and Phillips (2018) pointed out, supervisors may create their own barriers to delegation because they

- distrust employees,
- lack confidence in employees' abilities,
- lack patience to develop employees so that duties can be delegated to them,
- lack time to provide guidance on decisions before delegating authority,
- lack ability to delegate because they do not know how to structure decisions or communicate expectations to employees, and
- lack guidance from their own managers about what they may or may not delegate.

According to Akinola, Martin, and Phillips (2018), employees may also pose barriers to delegation. While these barriers can be an issue in traditional organizations, they are serious matters in team-based organizations in which employees must be willing to function cohesively. Common barriers to delegation may stem from employees if they

- express unwillingness to accept more responsibility,
- demand higher pay in line with every additional duty they are asked to assume,
- see no benefit to themselves stemming from added responsibility and are unwilling to develop themselves,
- fear criticism stemming from what they do in a role delegated to them, and
- encounter poor guidance, unwillingness to help, or punishment for what they do from their supervisor or teammates.

Overcoming barriers to delegation requires analysis and action. First, supervisors or team members must determine why problems with delegation exist. Second, they must act on the causes of problems, if they can (Lauring & Kubovcikova, 2022).

Organization policies. To deal with organizational barriers to delegation, they should clarify organizational policies. For example, what actions are limited only to supervisors without the possibility for delegating? What reasons lie behind these policies?

Managers' expectations. To deal with barriers to delegation stemming from the expectations of their managers, supervisors should clarify these expectations. What guidance can the manager provide about tasks and duties supervisors should delegate, may delegate, and should not delegate?

Supervisors' issues. To deal with barriers to delegation stemming from supervisors themselves, supervisors should make it a point to seek improvement. If they have difficulty with delegating—or try it and encounter difficulties—then they should seek coaching from their managers about effective ways to do it.

Employees' issues. To deal with barriers to delegation stemming from employees, supervisors or team members should focus attention on the barriers. They should ask employees for their opinions about how these issues could be effectively addressed. They should then follow through to see that employees' advice is followed.

Steps in Delegating

There are four steps in the delegation process whether the organization is traditionally structured or is team-based. Supervisors or team members should (Akinola et al., 2018)

1. allocate duties,
2. clarify responsibilities,
3. provide employees with necessary background information on delegated duties, and
4. establish a means of monitoring employee performance on delegated duties.

Allocating duties is the first step. Supervisors decide what duties they will delegate—and to whom. They then discuss the matter with their employee(s). If appropriate, they also inform the manager or other people affected.

According to Akinola, Martin, and Phillips (2018), when allocating duties, supervisors should take special care to consider:

1. ***The effect of delegating on others.*** What consequences will stem from delegating the duty? How are others likely to react? Why?
2. ***The feelings of others.*** Will someone feel slighted if the duty is delegated to one employee but not to another? If so, why?
3. ***The priority of delegating.*** Is there anything which prevents allocating this duty to another? What is the organization's policy? What sections of collective bargaining agreements may be relevant?

In team settings, team members typically discuss important delegation decisions in team meetings. Examples of such delegation decisions may include which team member will be selected as a representative to a cross-functional team or which team member will oversee service delivered to an important customer.

The process of delegation is critically important. It can influence how willingly employees carry them out and how successfully they achieve results. There are at least five ways of delegating (Jiang & Men, 2017):

1. ***The guess approach.*** Employees are not specifically told that duties have been delegated to them and are left guessing.
2. ***The order approach.*** Supervisors "order" employees to assume duties on their behalf and leave no room for dispute, comment, explanation, or hesitation.
3. ***The order-and-listen approach.*** Supervisors issue orders but then allow employees to discuss the matter if they wish.
4. ***The request-and-persuade approach.*** Supervisors request help and then try to overcome any employee objections through persuasion.
5. ***The request-and-listen approach.*** Supervisors request employees to receive delegated duties, listen to employee comments or objections, and make decisions accordingly.

The guess approach is rarely if ever appropriate because employees are unaware of what they have been delegated and how they are responsible for achieving results. The order approach is appropriate in times of emergency. In those cases there is little time for explanation: the supervisor should designate an employee to assume a duty, explain what results are desired, and then move on to more pressing matters. If used in times other than emergencies, employees will often resent the highly authoritarian tone of orders and will respond unwillingly. The order-and-listen, request-and-persuade, and request-and-listen approaches are appropriate on most occasions. In team-based organizations, the request-and-persuade approach may be used in team meetings as one team member "nominates" another—and then other team members either endorse the nomination or suggest alternatives (Stander & Rothmann, 2010).

Providing employees with necessary background information is the third step in the delegation process. Employees should know about the present status of the duty delegated to them, any pertinent historical information about how the present status was reached, and background on desired objectives and company policies. At this point, after the employee has assumed responsibility for the duty, supervisors should brief them as completely as possible. Without complete information, employees may waste time, make the wrong decisions or assumptions, or otherwise handle delegated duties improperly—through no fault of their own (Tansey et al., 2017).

In team-based organizations, team members may have to assume the responsibility for investigating the background surrounding duties delegated to them by the team. One reason is that other team members may not know the background. Monitoring employee performance on delegated duties is the final step in the delegation process. Supervisors or team members should establish a means for monitoring how well employees are carrying out delegated duties and for providing corrective feedback when duties are not being handled successfully. It is generally a good idea for the supervisor or team to establish a timetable to review progress with the employee. In team organizations, team facilitators may assume the role of reminding the team of the need to review the performance of individual team members on duties delegated to them.

What's Next?

The next chapter, Chapter 8, "Understanding Employment Conflicts and the Disciplinary Process," looks at the supervisor's (or team's) responsibility to ensure adherence to policies, procedures, work rules and standards, and other requirements affecting employees in organizations. Because without discipline, employees may act in illegal, unsafe, unethical, or otherwise improper ways. But before you move on, don't forget to review the key takeaways and take a moment to reflect on what you learned in this chapter by completing Table 7.5, End of Chapter 7 Discussion Questions and Inquiries.

Table 7.5   End of Chapter 7 Questions and Inquiries. Your Perspective on What You Learned in Chapter 7

Your Perspective on What You Learned in Chapter 7	
Area of Inquiry	*What Did You Learn, and How Are You Going to Implement It in Your Position?*
What is motivation?	
Expectancy theory of motivation	
Goal-setting theory of motivation	
Equity theory of motivation	
Psychological empowerment theory of motivation	
Top ten motivation factors affecting employees	
What is delegation?	
When delegation is appropriate or inappropriate	
Barriers to delegation	

Key Takeaways

1. Motivation is one of the most important reasons that a human being would act for or against any topic, desire, or interest. Motivation is what makes a person engaged with certain behaviors and actions.
2. Motivation is one of the few organizational behavior (OB) subjects that is important to both managers and employees.
3. Motivation is a desire to achieve a goal, satisfy a need, or rectify a perceived imbalance between *what is* and *what should be*. It stimulates purposeful action by individuals. It is a force or drive coming from inside people rather than imposed from outside on them.
4. Delegation is the deliberate redirection of authority. It is *deliberate* because no delegation occurs without explicit direction.
5. Responsibility is an obligation to perform tasks or carry out duties assigned to an individual or position.

Discussion Questions and Inquiries

Please take a minute and come up with your own answers to these inquiries and questions. From your viewpoint, briefly express what you have learned about these areas and write it in Table 7.5. After completing Table 7.5 and answering these questions, discuss your learning with your higher manager. Your discussion with your manager about your new knowledge and understanding would be a great pathway to your development as a positive and effective supervisor.

References

Akinola, M., Martin, A. E., & Phillips, K. W. (2018). To delegate or not to delegate: Gender differences in affective associations and behavioral responses to delegation. *Academy of Management Journal, 61*(4), 1467–1491. https://doi.org/10.5465/amj.2016.0662

APA (American Psychological Association). (2023a). Motivation. Retrieved January 29, 2023, from https://dictionary.apa.org/motivation

APA (American Psychological Association). (2023b). Delegation of authority in business. Retrieved January 29, 2023, from https://dictionary.apa.org/motivation

Colquitt, J., LePine, J., & Wesson, M. (2015). *Organizational Behavior. Improving Performance and Communication in the Workplace* (4th ed.). New York, NY: McGraw Hills Education.

Deckers, L. (2010). *Motivation; Biological, Psychological and Environmental* (3rd ed.). New York, NY: Allyn & Bacon. Imprint of Pearson.

Fitzgerald, S., Chan, F., Deiches, J., Umucu, E., Hsu, S., Lee, H., Bezyak, J., & Iwanaga, K. (2015). Assessing self-determined work motivation in people with severe mental illness: A factor-analytic approach. *The Australian Journal of Rehabilitation Counselling, 21*(2), 123–136. https://doi.org/10.1017/jrc.2015.12

French, W. L., & Bell, C. H. (1999). *Organization Development: Behavioral Science Interventions for Organization Improvement* (6th ed.). Upper Saddle River, NJ: Prentice Hall.

Gagne, M., & Deci, E. L. (2005). Self-determination theory and work motivation. *Journal of Organizational Behavior, 31*, 331–362. https://doi.org/10.1002/job.322

Greasley, K., Bryman, A., Price, A., Soetanto, R., & King, N. (2005). Employee perceptions of empowerment. *Employee Relations, 27*, 354–368. https://doi.org/10.1108/01425450510605697

Hersey, P., & Blanchard, K. H. (1993). *Management of Organizational Behavior: Utilizing Human Resources* (6th ed.). Englewood Cliffs, NJ: Prentice Hall.

Jiang, H., & Men, R. L. (2017). Creating an engaged workforce: The impact of authentic leadership, transparent organizational communication, and work-life enrichment. *Communication Research, 44*(2), 225–243. https://doi.org/10.1177/0093650215613137

Lauring, J., & Kubovcikova, A. (2022). Delegating or failing to care: Does relationship with the supervisor change how job autonomy affect work outcomes? *European Management Review, 19*(4), 549–563. https://doi.org/10.1111/emre.12499

Macey, W. H., & Schneider, B. (2008). The meaning of employee engagement. *Industrial and Organizational Psychology, 1*(1), 3–30. https://doi.org/10.1111/j.1754-9434.2007.0002.x

Oxford Language. (2023). *Motivation*. Retrieved January 29, 2023, from https://languages.oup.com/google-dictionary-en/

Rothwell, W. J. (2015). *Beyond Training & Development (3rd ed.). Enhancing Human Performance Through a Measurable Focus on Business Impact.* Amherst, MA: HRD Press, Inc.

Rothwell, W. J., & Kazanas, H. C. (2003). *Planning & Managing Human Resources. Strategic Planning for Personnel Management* (2nd ed.). Amherst, MA: HRD Press, Inc.

Spreitzer, G. M. (1995). Psychological empowerment in the workplace: Dimensions, measurement, and validation. *Academy of Management Journal, 38*(5), 1442–1465. https://doi.org/10.2307/256865

Spreitzer, G. M., Kizilos, M. A., & Nason, S. W. (1997). A dimensional analysis of the relationship between psychological empowerment and effectiveness, satisfaction, and strain. *Journal of Management, 23*(5), 679–704. https://doi.org/10.1016/S0149-2063(97)90021-0

Stander, M. W., & Rothmann, S. (2010). Psychological empowerment, job insecurity and employee engagement. *SA Journal of Industrial Psychology, 36*(1). Retrieved February 1, 2023, from https://sajip.co.za/index.php/sajip/article/view/849/886

Tansey, T. N., Iwanaga, K., Bezyak, J., & Ditchman, N. (2017). Testing an integrated self-determined work motivation model for people with disabilities: A path analysis. *Rehabilitation Psychology*, *62*(4), 534–544. https://doi.org/10.1037/rep0000141

Wulf, G., & Lewthwaite, R. (2016). Optimizing performance through intrinsic motivation and attention for learning: The OPTIMAL theory of motor learning. *Psychonomic Bulletin & Review*, *23*, 1382–1414. https://doi.org/10.3758/s13423-015-0999-9

Chapter 8

Understanding Employment Conflicts and the Disciplinary Process

Introduction

A healthy and effective workplace might include both a required and desirable element of disciplinary action. Knowing when to take disciplinary action and how to effectively implement it may help you and your staff get the most out of it. As early as 1930 when Henri Fayol described the importance of discipline, its importance in organizations was recognized. Supervisors or team members and other members of the organization bear the responsibility to ensure that employee behavior leads to safe, efficient, and effective working conditions. Without discipline, employees may act in illegal, unsafe, unethical, or otherwise improper ways; with discipline, employees behave in ways that are consistent with organizational policies and procedures, work rules or standards, governmental laws and regulations, and collective bargaining agreements.

Discipline is the supervisor's (or team's) responsibility to ensure adherence to policies, procedures, work rules, standards, and other requirements affecting employees in organizations. According to Sharma and Sharma (2018), there are generally two kinds of discipline:

1) **Positive Discipline**, equated with educating employees about the organization's policies, procedures, rules, and job standards so that they can monitor their own behavior to ensure conformity with organizational requirements.

DOI: 10.4324/9781003413493-8

2) **Negative Discipline**, equated with corrective actions designed to bring improper, unsafe or illegal employee behavior in line with organizational, departmental, work group, or team requirements. Positive discipline emphasizes prevention before problematic behavior is exhibited; negative discipline emphasizes corrective action after problematic behavior occurs.

Supervisors and managers with a high-empathy level are adept at seeing things from another person's point of view and responding in a compassionate manner. Simply said, empathy in the workplace refers to the capacity of your employees to build genuine, empathic connections with one another that improve interactions and output, even at the time of a disciplinary action.

Talking with the individuals who have acted inappropriately or performed poorly is an important part of applying discipline with empathy. It involves hearing their side of the story and presenting your own. You will collaborate with them to assist in their recovery through a disciplinary dialogue that incorporates empathy and relatedness. Here are some steps you can take to handle a disciplinary action process with empathy and understanding:

- Don't enter the talk intending to eventually have the individuals' employment terminated; instead, focus on helping them become better employees.
- Be careful to consider their perspective. To identify the cause of the issue, ask questions. Was there miscommunication? Were they unaware of the rules? Are they not appropriately trained to manage the situation?
- Spend some time outlining your future expectations. Discuss the workers' future with the organization as well as your expectations of them.
- Get their consent to the modification. A shared agreement to proceed considering the talk you just had should be the conversation's conclusion.

(Fleischer, 2018)

As shown in Figure 8.1 of the *Successful Supervisory Leadership Series Book II Structure*, in this chapter, we focus on the importance of grasping the nuances of workplace conflicts and the disciplinary measures that follow. We guide you through the disciplinary process, break down the duties of the supervisor in maintaining discipline, and guide you through each step.

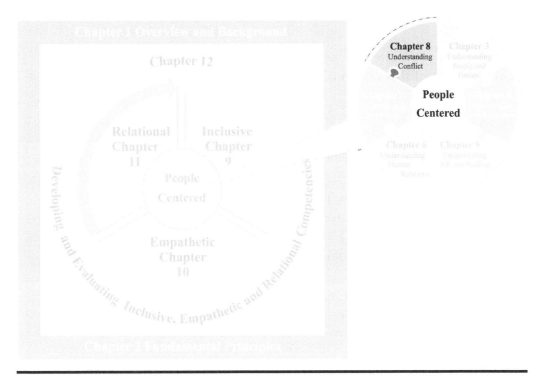

Figure 8.1 *Successful Supervisory Leadership Series Book II Structure. Note:* **Authors' original creation.**

In addition, we will provide a supervisor's checklist to ensure that discipline and dismissal procedures are properly handled.

Key Concepts

This chapter will cover the following key concepts:

- Understanding Conflict and Disciplinary Process
- Supervisory Roles and Responsibilities Regarding Maintaining Discipline:
  - To the organization
  - To managers
  - To other supervisors
  - To employees
  - To themselves
- Necessary Steps in the Disciplinary Process
- What to Pay Attention to before and during the Disciplinary Action Process
- Problems to Avoid when Disciplining Employees
- Supervisor's Checklist of Discipline and Dismissal

Definitions

The following definitions of key terms will help to better understand the main elements of this chapter.

Discipline

Oxford Language (2023) defines discipline as follows:

■ "The practice of training people to obey rules or a code of behavior, using punishment to correct disobedience."

"Merriam-Webster" (2023) defines discipline as follows:

■ "Control gained by enforcing obedience or order"
■ "Orderly or prescribed conduct or pattern of behavior"
■ "Self-control"

Disciplinary Actions

Below you will find descriptions of disciplinary actions by two HR and HRD professionals:

■ A reprimand or disciplinary action taken in reaction to an employee's misbehavior, a rule violation, or subpar performance is known as a disciplinary action. Depending on the seriousness of the situation, disciplinary actions may include verbal or written warnings, unsatisfactory performance reviews or evaluations, rank or pay reductions, or even termination (French, 2007).
■ When an employee violates corporate rules and regulations, the employer may take disciplinary actions to stop them from doing so in the future. It is put in place to make sure that workers are safe and that workplace disturbances (such as improper conduct and goal-setting failures) are kept to a minimum (Fleischer, 2018).

Understanding Conflict and the Disciplinary Process

The purpose of disciplinary action is to tell employees of the problem, provide them the chance to fix it, stop them from negatively affecting other workers, and safeguard the company's and the employees' interests. Primarily, discipline in the workplace discourages workers from acting in a way that could be detrimental to a company's growth.

The expectations you have for employee performance and behavior should be spelled out in your business handbook. The disciplinary measures you will deploy if staff members act in a manner inconsistent with these standards should also be mentioned. This guarantees that workers are aware of what is suitable and inappropriate in the workplace. Employees are prompted by disciplinary action to meet organizational standards, follow rules and regulations, and behave and perform better in the future in a team-based setting.

Supervisory Roles and Responsibilities in Disciplining Employees

By virtue of positions, supervisors in traditional organizations bear specific responsibilities for disciplining employees. In team-based organizations, team members bear similar responsibilities for maintaining discipline in the team. In self-directed teams, team members (collectively) may have to exercise exactly the same responsibility for discipline that falls to supervisors in traditional organizations. Responsibility means, of course, an obligation to behave in certain ways. What are the traditional supervisory responsibilities in disciplining employees? These responsibilities can be considered from the standpoint of obligations to the organization, managers, other supervisors, employees, and supervisors themselves. These responsibilities were indicated in many research sources, such as O'Connell et al. (2017), Dubois and Rothwell (2004), Rothwell and Kazanas (2003), and Wren et al. (2002).

Supervisory Responsibilities to the Organization for Maintaining Discipline

Responsibilities are based by virtue of their position in the organization:

(1) Supervisors should identify what policies, procedures, work rules, governmental laws, rules, and regulations they should help enforce.
(2) They should act as agents of the organization to ensure that employee behavior is in compliance with organizational and governmental requirements.

Supervisory Responsibilities to Managers for Maintaining Discipline

Supervisors bear five key responsibilities to their managers for maintaining discipline:

(1) They should monitor the behavior of employees reporting to them.
(2) They should administer discipline in a way that does not cast anyone in an unfair light.
(3) Supervisors should never tell an employee that discipline was ordered by the department manager in order to avoid blame or try to stay on the employee's good side when discipline is called for.
(4) Supervisors should call attention to organizational policies, procedures, work rules, or other requirements that are not being consistently administered in the department.
(5) Supervisors should suggest improvements in policies or procedures when necessitated by changing conditions or conflicting priorities.

Supervisory Responsibilities to Other Supervisors for Maintaining Discipline

Supervisors bear three key responsibilities to other supervisors:

(1) They should administer policies, procedures, rules, and other requirements in the same way as other supervisors. (This may necessitate communication among supervisors so as to allow them to compare notes about how similar disciplinary situations should be handled.)
(2) Supervisors should avoid criticizing other supervisors behind their backs for their handling of disciplinary matters.
(3) Supervisors should avoid creating their own rules that differ substantially from rules imposed by other supervisors.

Supervisory Responsibilities to Employees for Maintaining Discipline

Supervisors bear ten key disciplinary responsibilities to their employees:

(1) They should identify what rules, policies, procedures, and laws are applicable to them.
(2) They should clarify job standards and their own expectations.

(3) They should communicate to employees the rules, policies, procedures, job standards, and supervisory expectations to which employees should adhere.

(4) They should clarify what kind of discipline will be meted out for various infractions of rules, departures from policies, and violations of standard procedures.

(5) Supervisors should provide timely feedback to employees when they act improperly.

(6) Supervisors should clarify to employees how they should behave and model that behavior themselves.

(7) Supervisors should fairly investigate charges that could lead to punishment.

(8) They should match punishment, when warranted, to the offense.

(9) They should typically exercise progressively harsher punishments for each subsequent repetition of the same violations of organizational policies, procedures, work rules, or job standards.

(10) Supervisors should make every effort to treat all employees the same under similar circumstances.

Supervisory Responsibilities to Themselves for Maintaining Discipline

Supervisors are also responsible to themselves:

(1) They should have clear consciences about the disciplinary actions they take.

(2) Supervisors should not discipline employees when they (the supervisors) have been guilty of the same offense and have thus failed in setting a good example.

(3) They should not suddenly punish employees without warning—or the chance to improve—unless employees have previously been warned in advance of the consequences of their actions.

Necessary Steps in the Disciplinary Action Process

Like many other facets of supervision, discipline may be thought of as a process, that is, ongoing activities that are carried out on a day-by-day basis rather than one-shot efforts resulting from specific employee behaviors or situations. According to Fleischer (2018) to encourage workplace efficiency and harmony, it is critical to continuously penalize employees who don't follow rules. Consider these actions when disciplining an employee (Fleischer, 2018; O'Connell et al., 2017):

Understand the National and State Laws about Disciplinary Actions

Subject to the state you work and live in and the offense for which you are disciplining an employee, the laws regarding employee punishment may change. Most statutes do not define what offenses can result in employee punishment. However, some requirements which are set forth by federal and state legislation comprehensively address employee reprimand and termination. So before you start the disciplinary procedure, it is crucial to study the legislation your state requires you to follow. You can get help on this from your HR department and your HR director (Carasco & Rothwell, 2020).

Review the Company's Employee Handbook

Your disciplinary procedures and rules should be explained in depth in your employee handbook. These policies should clearly define the expectations for your staff so they are aware of what is acceptable behavior. If employees have any concerns regarding the regulations they broke, be sure to highlight them and link them to the employee handbook when you meet with them. Usually, the employee handbook covers policies and regulations of many elements of employment, such as dress codes, attendance, absenteeism, productivity, performance, behavior, use of mobile devices, or non-mingling. Make sure you have a copy of the company's employment handbook and study it.

Inform the HR Department

As soon as you are aware of effective actions and broken policies by an employee, inform the HR department with your initial information and evidence. Follow HR department's suggestions and role of engagement with the employees in these kinds of situations.

Have an Initial Meeting with the Accused Employee

A verbal warning is frequently the initial step in a process of disciplinary action. Prepare yourself to be receptive and supportive before meeting with the employee. Instead of looking at discipline as a punishment, try to consider it as a corrective action that supports your employees' development and growth. Inform the employees of the disciplinary action and go over the reasons why you are having it with them. Prepare yourself to respond to their inquiries and to lay out what you're willing to do to assist them in changing their behavior. Make sure you hold the meeting in private so that no one may overhear the conversation. Along with documenting your talks in writing, you should think about alerting HR to this initial warning or include them in the dialogue.

Document and Record Employee Discipline Process

As you proceed through the disciplinary process, you might want to consider documenting any employee punishment. Just in case the disciplinary action results in termination or legal action, include signatures, notes, and assertions in the employee file. Keeping track of problems as they arise can help you have precise dates, location, and records of policy infractions. For instance, you may make a note of each occurrence in which your employee arrived late and address your expectations on policies each time it happens. This enables the worker to gauge the severity of the situation.

Follow-Up with the Employees

After you've disciplined employees, follow-up with them a week or two later to gauge their development and see how they're doing. The workers could be more receptive to queries and concerns once some time has gone over the punishment you meted out.

Submit an Official Written Warning

The following stage in the procedure is usually a more official and written notification after you follow-up and noticed any progress after a fair amount of time. Create and use a disciplinary action form to record the problem, explain it, and spell out the remedial steps that will be taken if nothing changes. It is frequently beneficial to make reference to past meetings with the workers and to alert them of a potential suspension or termination of their privileges.

To demonstrate an understanding of the document's terms, employees must read it and sign it. This official notification serves as the start of the employees' probationary term, which will be monitored by you or another member of management.

Conduct a Recorded Disciplinary Meeting

At this time an official meeting with the employee, an HR professional, and yourself is typically the following step. Discuss the event during this discussion and let the employee know that, in accordance with your disciplinary policy, there may be termination if there is no change.

Sanctions on Employees' Incentives

Employees often get sanctions defined in your employee disciplinary policy if their conduct or performance continues to be poor. These sanctions could be suspension using a company's credit card, or use of a company car, or even a cutback on compensation.

Termination or a Performance Improvement Plan

Termination could be a possibility if no improvement is achieved or if unacceptable conduct persists. Before issuing a formal warning, if you believe the underperforming employee can get better, you might present a performance improvement plan. A formal document that outlines performance objectives is known as a performance improvement plan (PIP). It has a timetable and specific objectives. Recorded discussions and meetings with the supervisor and HR representative are required under a PIP in order to monitor the employee's progress toward performance goals (Voxted, 2017).

Take a moment and use Table 8.1 to rate yourself on understanding the above steps for conducting a disciplinary action process.

Now use Table 8.2 to devise a series of actions to increase your understanding of Table 8.1.

Table 8.1 Supervisor's Rating on Understanding the Disciplinary Action Process

Supervisor's Rating on Understanding the Disciplinary Action Process								
Supervisor's Name	Date		Supervisor's Manager		Department			
*Rating Scale: **1** = Poor, **2** = Marginal, **3** = Acceptable, **4** = Good, **5** = Excellent*								
					1	*2*	*3*	*4*	*5*
1	Understand the National & State Laws about Disciplinary Actions								
2	Review the Company's Employee Handbook								
3	Inform the HR Department								
4	Have an Initial Meeting with the Accused Employee								
5	Document and Record Employee Discipline Process								
6	Follow-Up with the Employee								
7	Submit an Official Written Warning								
8	Conduct a Recorded Disciplinary Meeting								
9	Sanction Employee's Incentives								
10	Terminate or a Review Performance Improvement Plan								
Individual Columns' Totals									
Total of above Individual Columns									
Final Average (above total divided by 10)									

Source: Adapted from Fleischer (2018) and O'Connell et al. (2017).

What to Pay Attention to before and during the Disciplinary Action Process

The following suggestions from Hatchuel and Segrestin (2019), Wren et al. (2002), and Phillips and Rothwell (1998) are what a supervisor should pay attention to while conducting a disciplinary action process:

Identifying Pertinent Organizational Policies and Procedures

The first step in effective discipline is identifying what policies and procedures exist and how they should be interpreted. Proper discipline can be maintained

Table 8.2   APLI-Connected to Table 8.1

Action Plan for Learning and Improving
Area of Learning and Improving: *Supervisor's Rating on Understanding the Disciplinary Action Process*
Reference: *Table 8.1*
Three learning and improvement actions for this month that will raise my understanding and awareness in regard to *"Supervisor's Rating on Understanding the Disciplinary Action Process"* to enhance my understanding and clarity by at least one on the next rating:

Action 1:	By When:
Action 2:	By When:
Action 3:	By When:

Note: Authors' original creation.

only when it is clear what policies and procedures govern behavior and how they are to be interpreted. It helps to make a list of the policies and procedures that employees are expected to follow and keep them in prominent places such as employee handbooks, collective bargaining agreements, procedural manuals, management manuals, memos from top and middle managers, notices posted on company bulletin boards, signs posted around the work area ("No horseplay," "Fighting is grounds for immediate dismissal," "No smoking"), and proper verbal instructions from supervisors or team members. If applicable, certain government laws, regulations, rules, and city ordinances should also be identified. These may differ by jurisdiction.

Identifying Job Standards

In addition to policies, procedures, and governmental laws and regulations, employees are also accountable for meeting fair and reasonable job performance standards. They must maintain adequate quantity and quality of work output in a reasonable time period and carry out their work in a way that does not jeopardize the safety or work of others. An effective employee performance appraisal system, based on setting standards and holding employees accountable for them, is an important part of maintaining effective discipline.

Communicating Policies, Procedures, and Job Standards

It does little good to *identify* what policies, procedures, and job standards employees should be accountable for if these policies, procedures, and job standards are not communicated to those affected by them. Educating employees about organizational policies, procedures, and job standards is an important role of the supervisor. In team-based organizations, each team member has the responsibility to do likewise. Quite often, when employees are being disciplined for breaking rules or not meeting job standards, they defend themselves by claiming that they were not informed. If what they say is true, then supervisors or team members cannot reasonably discipline them.

In one organization, for example, a college graduate defended failing to call in when sick on the grounds that "nobody told me who to call, when to call, or what to say." The employee's supervisor, stunned by this defense and unable to respond, began requiring all newly hired workers to read a one-page description of their responsibilities for calling in when sick and to sign statements for inclusion in their human resource files that they had been apprised of what to do under these circumstances. This procedure may seem drastic and does not set a positive tone conducive to the beginning of the work relationship or work group or team morale. Yet it does eliminate the possibility of employees defending their improper behavior on the grounds that they were unaware of their responsibilities.

Perhaps a better approach is to prepare a checklist of policies, procedures, work rules, governmental regulations, and other matters for discussion with each newly hired employee. In this way, new employees are familiarized with them at the outset. Supervisors or team members may even require employees to sign the checklist upon completion to show that they have been made aware of the policies and the consequences of acting in ways at odds with them. As employees gain experience, they may forget specific work rules. It is the supervisor's job to remind them periodically. Common methods of doing that may include sending out a routine memo each year, covering matters routinely in one staff (or team) meeting each year, putting signs in visible places in the work area, and providing training on policies, procedures, work rules, and other matters.

Clarifying Consequences of Noncompliance before It Occurs

It is not enough for supervisors or team members to tell employees what they are accountable for. Supervisors or team members should also routinely clarify what will happen if employees break rules, depart from policies or procedures, fail to perform at acceptable levels, or otherwise act in noncompliance.

Clarifying the Supervisor or Team Leader's Role in the Disciplinary Action Process

Not every department manager shares the same views about the appropriate role of supervisors or team members in disciplining employees. Some managers prefer to take disciplinary action themselves; some only wish to be consulted before a supervisor takes action; some prefer to leave disciplinary matters entirely to supervisors or team members, holding them accountable for exercising even-handed treatment; and some managers wish to be consulted before specific actions (such as suspension or dismissal) but otherwise prefer to leave lesser disciplinary matters in the hands of the supervisors or team members. Managers may also vary in how much they wish to be consulted on disciplinary matters, depending on the experience and ability of a supervisor (Valcik, 2012).

It is important to clarify the preferences of the manager. This should be done before any specific problems arise. For example, if a fight breaks out in the work group or team, what does the manager want the supervisor to do? If an employee is caught stealing, drinking alcohol on the job, selling or using drugs, or sabotaging equipment, what is the supervisor empowered to do? Will the organization support the actions of their supervisors or team members, or are they on their own? Just what does the manager expect? Supervisors or team members are well-advised to discuss that at length with their managers before problems occur so that they can stand on firm ground, knowing precisely what they are—and are not—authorized to do by the manager, the organization, the human resources department, and the legal department.

Figure 8.2 displays supervisors' role in the disciplinary actions process.

Investigating Charges of Noncompliance

Imagine that you are a supervisor who is sitting at your desk one day and one of your most trusted employees walks in and accuses several other employees of violating important organizational policies. What should you do?

Some supervisors would take the word of their trusted employee at face value and assume that the other employees are guilty.

Figure 8.2 Supervisors' role in the disciplinary action process. Source: Adapted from Voxted (2017), Tanguy (2013), and Valcik (2012).

That is not an advisable course of action. A better approach is to investigate charges of noncompliance in a fair, thorough, confidential, and objective manner. That is, admittedly, tough to do. Perhaps it is the word of one employee against another with no witnesses. In that case, innocence should be assumed. In such cases, however, supervisors or team members should restate organizational policy and make clear that, if violations can be substantiated, disciplinary action will result. Supervisors or team members should also clarify the exact nature of that disciplinary action so that it is completely clear and that there will be no surprises.

Barring an open admission of guilt by an employee, supervisors or team members should seek substantiating evidence. Physical evidence is the best, like examples of poor work performed. Next best is testimonial evidence by several reliable sources, not just one. Supervisors or team members should ask several employees to explain, independently, what happened or how an employee behaved. Then they should confront the individual with this information. If the employee confesses, supervisors or team members should act confidently. If the employee professes innocence, supervisors or team members should look into the matter further if evidence is not sufficient to warrant immediate action notwithstanding a profession of innocence.

Using Progressive Discipline

Progressive discipline is the principle that punishments for offenses should become increasingly severe as offenses recur. For example, an employee is warned orally (by verbal reprimand) on the first occurrence. If the individual repeats the offense, a written warning is given. If the offense occurs again, the employee is suspended. On the fourth offense the individual is dismissed. Generally speaking, supervisors or team members should exercise the principle of progressive discipline unless the organization's disciplinary policies and procedures call for alternative approaches, or an offense is so severe that, having made the consequences of it clear in advance, supervisors can initiate immediate termination when they catch an employee in the act (Tanguy, 2013).

Avoiding Charges of Favoritism

Charging a supervisor with favoritism is a popular defense for employees who have been disciplined. They are likely to conclude that "the supervisor doesn't like me" or "is gunning for me" and appeal for sympathy from co-workers on the grounds that "the supervisor is treating me more harshly than others." Members of protected labor groups may also try to stand behind their protected status, citing evidence of discrimination.

What can supervisors do to avoid these charges or give them little chance of being viewed seriously? The first question supervisors or team members should ask themselves is this: *Am I treating this person differently from others?* If the answer is yes, then they should re-evaluate what they are doing. There is no room for personal favoritism in discipline. Using such an approach will come back to haunt supervisors later.

If the answer is no, then supervisors or team members should consider past situations when the same problem had arisen. How was it handled? Are there enough similarities between that situation and the present one to warrant similar treatment? If not, what circumstances make it different enough to warrant different action? Supervisors should be prepared to explain to other members of management how this situation differs from others. Why *do* they warrant different action?

Get the Facts Straight

Nothing is so potentially damaging to supervisory credibility—or an investigation of improper behavior—than for a supervisor to confront an employee only to discover that the facts unquestionably differ from the supervisor's initial understanding of them.

Supervisors should avoid that serious problem by getting the facts straight at the outset. They should seek answers to such questions as these:

- What happened? What sequence of events led up to the situation?
- What policy, procedure, rule, law, or another requirement was breached? Exactly how?
- Who was involved in the situation? Who was nearby and may have observed it?
- When did it happen?
- Where did it happen?
- Why was the breach important? What consequences, if any, stemmed from it?
- How did these consequences affect the organization? Other employees? Customers? Suppliers?
- What subsequent effects may result from the breach of policy, procedure, rule, regulation, or other mandate?

Identifying Causes of Improper Behavior

Supervisors or team members should make a diligent effort to ascertain the underlying causes of problematic behaviors or violations of policy. Without understanding the cause(s), supervisors or team members may have difficulty coaching employees to avoid such problems or violations in the future.

Common causes of disciplinary problems—like common causes of other employee performance problems—are frequently traced to lack of knowledge, unclear interpretations, variations in practices across the organization, changing conditions, conflicting priorities, or personal problems. To conduct troubleshooting, supervisors should ask questions such as these:

- Have employees been informed what policies they are expected to follow? If not, the problem may be traceable to a lack of knowledge.
- Are policies, procedures, and directives clear? If not, the problem may be traceable to an unclear interpretation.
- Are conditions now the same as those at the time a policy or procedure was adopted? If not, the problem may be traceable to changing conditions.
- Do employees understand how to set priorities? If not, the problem may be traceable to misplaced or conflicting priorities.

■ Are employees feeling underpaid, overworked, or otherwise stressed out? If so, the problem may be traceable to personal problems.

Supervisors or team members should take care to identify the causes of any behavior problems and act accordingly. Disciplinary problems stemming from a lack of knowledge should be rectified by training. Problems stemming from unclear interpretations can be solved by clarification, preferably in writing so that the information can be widely distributed in a form unaltered by oral interpretations. Those stemming from variations in practices across the organization can be handled by increasing coordination among departments, work groups, or teams and communication between managers and supervisors. Those stemming from changing conditions can be solved by periodic, systematic reviews of all policies and procedures. Those stemming from conflicting priorities can be solved by improved methods of giving orders. Finally, problems stemming from the personal problems of employees can be solved by informal counseling or referral to qualified professionals (Voxted, 2017).

While finding a cause does not ameliorate the problem, it does help avert recurrences. A good approach is to ask employees why they did what they did. Supervisors should listen carefully to the response, probing to go beyond superficial responses or no responses at all.

Documenting Repeated Offenses

If oral warnings are not adequate to modify employee behavior, then supervisors or team members should resort to written documentation.

The most common form of documentation is a memo to the human resources file along with a copy to the employee. A memo of this kind should clearly set forth the problem behavior and describe the facts of the situation. (It should answer all journalistic questions: who? what? when? where? why? how?)

Supervisor's Checklist on Discipline and Dismissal

Use the checklist appearing in Table 8.3 to guide your actions when disciplining or terminating an employee.

Table 8.3   Supervisor's Checklist on Discipline and Dismissal

	Supervisor's Checklist on Discipline and Dismissal		
	Directions: Complete the following checklist in the event that you consider disciplining or dismissing an employee. For each question in the left column, check a yes or no in the right column. If you check no, then you have additional action to take before dismissal is warranted.		
	Questions	*Answers*	
#	**Have you. . .**	Yes	No
1	Clearly established and communicated standards for employee performance?		
2	Discussed organization/department/work group or team policy procedures with employees?		
3	Communicated the consequences of violating policies, procedures and performance standards with employees before negative discipline (punishment) is necessary?		
4	Discussed with the manager what role you are expected to play in employee discipline on a continuing basis?		
5	Made an effort to verify from several sources that a rule, policy, or procedure was violated or that the employee is not performing in line with reasonable job standards established in advance?		
6	Made sure to treat the same rule violation in the same way for all employees, allowing for extenuating circumstances that may justify special treatment in some cases?		
7	Made sure to note any written documentation extenuating circumstances to employees about their misconduct?		
8	Taken care to ensure that the punishment matches the offense?		
9	Taken care to ensure the punishment matches the individual's level of experience and length of service?		
10	Considered the circumstances surrounding misconduct and allowed for any causes that were not under the individual's control?		
11	Provided timely feedback on what the employee did wrong?		
12	Made explicit, in clear and unambiguous terms, what the employee should do to avoid future misconduct or what the employee should do to perform in line with job standards?		

(Continued)

Table 8.3 (Continued) Supervisor's Checklist on Discipline and Dismissal

Supervisor's Checklist on Discipline and Dismissal			
Directions: Complete the following checklist in the event that you consider disciplining or dismissing an employee. For each question in the left column, check a yes or no in the right column. If you check no, then you have additional action to take before dismissal is warranted.			
Questions		*Answers*	
#	Have you. . .	Yes	No
13	Prepared three written warnings or otherwise complied with the organization's disciplinary policy prior to dismissal (unless the circumstances warrant special treatment)?		
14	Made sure that any written warnings that are issued clearly spell out: • What led up to the written warning? • What the employee did (or failed to do) that constitutes misconduct? • What policy, procedure, or job standard was violated? • What consequences will result if the employee's misconduct is repeated? • What the employee should do in the future? • What disciplinary action will be taken if the employee's misconduct is repeated?		
15	Made sure documentation to support dismissal has been placed in the employee's human resources file prior to dismissal?		
16	Discussed problem performance with an employee before dismissal or taking disciplinary action?		
17	Discussed the case with the department manager before taking dismissal action?		
18	Discussed the case, as appropriate, with the Human Resources manager before taking dismissal action?		

Note: Authors' original creation.

Problems to Avoid When Disciplining Employees

Supervisors and team members should avoid five specific problems whenever they discipline employees:

1) They should never act emotionally. They should not discipline people while in the heat of anger. They should not allow offenders to provoke

them into doing something that will gain them support (or even a reprieve) when supervisory or team actions are appealed to a higher level. If the wrongdoing is serious but the facts surrounding it are unclear, supervisors should suspend the suspects until the facts can be gathered. If the wrongdoers are subsequently exonerated, they should be prepared to reinstate them with full back pay. Above all, supervisors and team members should never become sarcastic, crude, or rude. They should keep their emotions in check. Their emotions may undercut their actions.

2) They should avoid acting without regard to the individual's level of experience. Supervisors should know their people. They should match the punishment according to the level of experience. Employees who just entered a job or the work group or team may be unaware of special rules or restrictions. Newcomers should be given the benefit of the doubt. They should know the rules before being disciplined.

3) Supervisors should avoid acting without considering the circumstances. Was an offense willful—or accidental? Was this a first offense or a repeated one? Were there mitigating circumstances, and (if so) what were they? As a general rule of thumb, they should treat willful or repeated offenses more harshly than accidental or first offenses.

4) Supervisors should avoid acting without regard to other employees or other consequences. They should always remember that, while it is wise for them *not* to discuss disciplinary actions taken with individuals due to individual privacy rights, other employees will eventually become aware of their actions. Supervisors should strive to become known as even-handed but firm.

5) Supervisors should never handle discipline in public. They should always follow this rule: Praise in public, but discipline in private.

What's Next?

The next chapter, "Inclusive Supervisor: Supervising Diversity, Equity, Inclusion, and Belonging," looks at the supervisor's responsibility and conduct on ensuring the presence and application of DEI&B by employees at the workplace. But before moving on, don't forget to review the key takeaways, and take a moment to reflect on what you learned in this chapter by completing Table 8.4, Chapter 8 Discussion Questions and Inquiries.

Table 8.4   End of Chapter 8 Questions and Inquiries. Your Perspective on What You Learned in Chapter 8

Your Perspective on What You Learned in Chapter 8	
Area of Inquiry	*What Did You Learn, and How Are You Going to Implement It in Your Position?*
What is positive discipline?	
What is negative discipline?	
Supervisory roles and responsibilities in disciplining employees	
Necessary steps in the disciplinary action process	
What to pay attention to before and during the disciplinary action process	
Problems to avoid when disciplining employees	
Supervisor's checklist on discipline and dismissal	

Key Takeaways

1. A healthy and effective workplace might include both a required and desirable element of disciplinary action. Knowing when to take disciplinary action and how to effectively implement it may help you and your staff get the most out of it.
2. The purpose of disciplinary action is to tell employees of the problem, provide them the chance to fix it, stop them from negatively affecting other workers, and safeguard the company's and the employees' interests.
3. By virtue of positions, supervisors in traditional organizations bear specific responsibilities for disciplining employees.
4. Like many other facets of supervision, discipline may be thought of as a process—that is, ongoing activities that are carried out on a day-by-day basis rather than one-shot efforts resulting from specific employee behaviors or situations.
5. Supervisors or team members should take care to identify the causes of any behavior problems and act accordingly.

Discussion Questions and Inquiries

Please take a minute to answer the following inquiries and questions in Table 8.4. From your point of view, what have you learned about the following areas?

References

Carasco, M., & Rothwell, W. J. (2020). *The Essential HR Guide for Small Business and Startups*. Alexandria, VA: SHRM-Society for Human Resources Management.

Dubois, D. D., & Rothwell, W. J. (2004). *Competency-Based Human Resource Management*. Palo Alto, CA: Davis-Black Publishing.

Fleischer, C. H. (2018). *The SHRM Essential Guide to Employment Law: A Handbook for HR Professionals, Managers, Businesses, and Organizations* (First ed.). Alexandria, VA: Society for Human Resource Management (SHRM).

French, W. L. (2007). *Human Resources Management* (6th ed.). Boston, MA: Houghton Mifflin Company.

Hatchuel, A., & Segrestin, B. (2019). A century old and still visionary: Fayol's innovative theory of management. *European Management Review, 16*(2), 399–412. https://doi.org/10.1111/emre.12292

Merriam-Webster. (2023). Dictionary. Discipline. Retrieved February 6, 2023, from https://www.merriam-webster.com/dictionary/discipline

O'Connell, M., Delgado, K., Lawrence, A., Kung, M., & Tristan, E. (2017). Predicting workers' compensation claims and disciplinary actions using Securefit®: Further support for integrative models of workplace safety. *Journal of Safety Research, 61*, 77–81. https://doi.org/10.1016/j.jsr.2017.02.010

Oxford Language Dictionary. (2023). Discipline. Retrieved February 6, 2023, from https://languages.oup.com/google-dictionary-en/

Phillips, J. J., & Rothwell, W. J. (1998). *Linking HRD Programs with Organizational Strategy* (2nd ed.). Alexandria, VA: ASTD.

Rothwell, W. J., & Kazanas, H. C. (2003). *Planning & Managing Human Resources. Strategic Planning for Personnel Management* (2nd ed.). Amherst, MA: HRD Press, Inc.

Sharma, R. C., & Sharma, N. (2018). *Human Resources Management Theory and Practice*. Los Angeles, CA: SAGE.

Tanguy, J. (2013). Collective and individual conflicts in the workplace: Evidence from France. *Industrial Relations, 52*(1), 102–133. https://doi.org/10.1111/irel.12013

Valcik, N. A., & Benavides, T. J. (2012). *Practical Human Resources for Public Managers: A Case Study Approach*. CRC Press. https://doi.org/10.4324/9781315089560

Voxted, S. (2017). 100 years of Henri Fayol. *Management Revue, 28*(2), 256–274. https://doi.org/10.5771/0935-9915-2017-2-256

Wren, D. A., Bedeian, A. G., & Breeze, J. D. (2002). The foundations of Henri Fayol's Administrative Theory. *Management Decision, 40*(9), 906–918. https://doi.org/10.1108/00251740210441108

Chapter 9

The Inclusive Supervisor: Supervising Diversity, Equity, Inclusion, and Belonging

Introduction

As a supervisor, you must be aware of your impact in creating a culture of inclusivity within your workplace. The definitions of diversity, equity, inclusion, and belonging (DEI&B) are always changing, but at its core, the idea is to recognize and value the unique perspectives, experiences, and identities of every individual in an organization. Diverse teams are more innovative and excel in problem-solving due to the diverse perspectives they bring, leading to enriched brainstorming and creative solutions. Numerous studies confirm that inclusive teams consistently outperform others in innovation and profitability. Such teams are better positioned to understand and serve a diverse global customer base. Organizations recognized for their DEI&B initiatives attract a broader spectrum of top talent, and when these employees feel valued and included, they display greater commitment, leading to increased engagement and reduced turnover. Many jurisdictions enforce DEI&B-related laws and regulations, so adherence is essential to avoid legal complications. This chapter also touches upon equal employment opportunity (EEO) laws across federal, state, and local levels, highlighting their role in employee relations and personnel management (Foy, 2021; O'Connor, 2021; Adjo et al., 2021).

DOI: 10.4324/9781003413493-9

As a supervisor, you should be aware of some criticisms surrounding DEI&B initiatives. Some argue that these initiatives can lead to tokenism, where organizations might appear inclusive on the surface without making genuine changes. Others may view DEI&B as preferential treatment, not recognizing its intention to create a level playing field. This resistance can foster a belief that decisions are based on identity rather than merit. Such misunderstandings can promote subversive stereotypes and perpetuate prejudices. Understandably, resistance to change can emerge, especially if individuals feel their positions or chances for promotions are under threat.

However, if you have a clear understanding of DEI&B, you can be confident that the decisions you make will always be in the best interests of your team as a whole. Furthermore, you are in a pivotal position to set the tone for your team, significantly influencing the organizational culture. By promoting open communication, you can gather feedback about DEI&B initiatives and continually refine your approach based on that feedback.

Building on the key concepts introduced in Chapter 2, including intersectionality, cultural dimensions, generational cohort, critical race theory, and gender norms, this chapter further explores the role of DEI&B in the ever-evolving business landscape. You'll gain insights into how new organizational environments and global dynamics present both challenges and opportunities for supervisors like you.

As shown in Figure 9.1 of the *Successful Supervisory Leadership Series Book II Structure*, we focus on being an inclusive supervisor. A supervisor who creates a workplace where diversity is not only present, but is valued, where equity is the norm, and where everyone feels involved and has a sense of belonging. We'll examine current issues challenging organizations, share strategies for managing and celebrating diversity, and underscore why diversity, equity, inclusion, and belonging (DEI&B) is critical in today's workplaces. Additionally, we'll look at how Human Resources can lay the groundwork for DEI&B and the specific actions supervisors should take to manage and bring these principles to their teams.

Key Concepts

This chapter will cover the following key concepts:

- ■ What Issues Are Affecting Organizations?
- ■ Managing and Celebrating Diversity
- ■ The Importance of DEI&B in the Workplaces

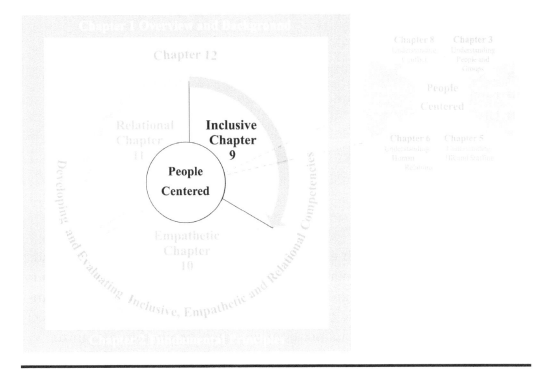

Figure 9.1 *Successful Supervisory Leadership Series Book II Structure. Note: Authors' original creation.*

- Role of Human Resources in Establishing DEI&B in Organizations
- Role of Supervisors in Managing and Implementing DEI&B

Definitions

The following definitions of key terms will help to better understand the main elements of this chapter:

Diversity

Various definitions exist for diversity. Organizations frequently alter the phrase to match their own environment. In general, diversity refers to the differences and similarities that exist among individuals, taking into account every aspect of each individual's personality and sense of who they are. The following list according to Chiou et al. (2022), and Rothwell et al. (2022) displays common aspects of diversity from Chapter 5:

- Age
- Ethnicity or national origin

- Race and color
- Family status
- Gender identity
- Sexual orientation
- Language
- Disability
- Physical characteristics
- Religion and spirituality
- Veteran status

Equity

Workplace equity gives each employee the same access, opportunities, and advancement. This action entails identifying and trying to overcome barriers that prevent disadvantaged groups from getting equal treatment, from team-level adjustments to systemic changes in organizations and sectors. To effect change via an equity lens, organizations are often required to recognize that the social structures in which we now function are not equitable and that these injustices are reflected in our organizations (Chiou et al., 2022; Rothwell et al., 2022).

Inclusion

The level of each person's support, appreciation, and value as a member of a group or team is referred to as inclusion. Each individual has a duty to seek out and acknowledge inclusion from others. In such a culture, everyone has a tendency to feel more involved and more eager to contribute to the firm's commercial objectives. In this type of context, people from diverse origins must communicate, work together, and grasp one another's requirements and opinions; in other words, they must demonstrate cultural competence (Chiou et al., 2022; Rothwell et al., 2022).

Belonging

Regarding how employees feel about being welcomed at work, the idea of belonging is at its core. Team members should feel that their opinions are valued and that they have something valuable to offer. Being a member of a team implies a sense of worth, which is something that employees should and want to have. Imagine a leadership team with several experienced managers and one new, young manager. This is an oversimplified example. As a result, the new boss could feel like a nobody with little to offer. Yet, the new manager will feel valued and respected if the existing managers strongly encourage them to offer their thoughts, provide them equal opportunities to lead projects, etc. (Chiou et al., 2022; Rothwell et al., 2022).

What Issues Are Affecting Organizations?

Emerging issues lead to change, sometimes small and sometimes profound. Today's organizations have been affected by many emerging issues that are taking them in many new directions and are leading to many new systems in order to address them. Six emerging issues are of particular importance: (1) growing global markets; (2) demanding customers; (3) competing on the basis of time; (4) increasing flexibility in working arrangements; (5) changing technology; and (6) re-engineering work processes (Rothwell et al., 2016). In the following sections, you will find brief descriptions of each emerging issue. Each of them should be understood as a major influence on how organizations function. They should also be understood as a backdrop affecting supervisory leadership today. In addition to all these mentioned issues, we need to pay greater attention to the role of DEI&B in dealing and working to resolve these issues.

Growing Global Markets

A global market refers to trade across nations. It occurs through the flow of money, goods, services, jobs, and technology across international borders. A global market is not restricted to the goods that pass through customs. Indeed, a market can include financial transactions occurring electronically across borders or even the exchange of engineering diagrams over the Internet.

Globalization refers to the intensification of world trade and cultural exchange. Globalization has been intensifying since the mid-1980s. Unfortunately, not everyone has recognized that (Rothwell et al., 2016).

Globalization has produced multifaceted consequences. One is that competition globally is fierce. This, in turn, has forced organizations in the United States and other nations to re-examine how efficiently and effectively they operate. In some cases, this has led to downsizing and the reduction of workforces without corresponding reductions in productivity so as to reduce expenses and increase profits (Pieterse, 2004).

Another result of globalization has been the development and use of first-rate technology and infrastructure outside the developed world. High productivity is not the exclusive province of nations like the United States. It can be found elsewhere. At the same time, a nation that invents a new technology may not necessarily be positioned to benefit the most from it. Indeed, "there is money in developing products, making small improvements in efficiency and quality, and developing new applications for existing technologies, products, and services" (Carnevale, 1991, p. 19). Moreover, small nations can often carry out these activities with comparative advantage, meaning they can do it better than other nations can.

Globalization will not cease. Indeed, it will accelerate over the years to come. As a result, organizations and individuals alike must prepare to compete internationally rather than just domestically (Cummings & Worley, 2015).

Demanding Customers

To survive, any organization must be able to carry out complex transactions with its external environment and benefit from those transactions. In other words, organizations must end up adding more value than they used to produce. In business, the organization must make a profit or realize a return on investment. In nonprofit enterprises and government agencies that do not make profits, the organization must satisfy its users, service recipients, and constituents.

The importance of adding value is a simple principle. But it is easily forgotten amid the pressure of daily crises. Managers and employees can easily lose sight of it as they struggle to get the work out. When Henry Ford perfected the principles of mass production, he decreased product specialization. All cars were black. Customers suffered that inconvenience because it gave them cars at an attractive price. Today, cars vary dramatically in color. Manufacturing processes across automakers remain similar, but they have been able to add diversity to the products they offer.

Customers have grown to expect that diversity. Two decades ago, three networks supplied all the television shows. With cable entry, some customers now expect between 40 and 500 channels. The tendency in markets is to achieve growing complexity to appeal to increasingly sophisticated and demanding customers.

While an organization's decision-makers and employees must deal with many stakeholders (those who are affected by the organization's decisions), the most important single stakeholder group is the organization's ultimate customer, who stands at the end of the organization's production or service delivery process. In the automobile industry, for example, the purchaser of a car is the ultimate customer. However, to be successful, the organization must also satisfy the demands of other stakeholders. These stakeholders include those who sell the cars (called distributors), those who make parts and offer essential services necessary to assemble the cars (called suppliers), those who supply funds for company operations (called investors), those from the government who regulate the company's compliance with laws (called regulators), and even citizens and prospective customers in the communities in which the companies manufacture or sell the automobiles.

The final consumer, in the opinion of quality expert Deming (2018), is the most crucial step in the manufacturing process. The goals of quality should be the present and long-term demands of the consumer. To survive, today's organizations must be capable of meeting or even exceeding customer expectations. Increasingly, however, customers are becoming more discriminating in their tastes and more demanding in their expectations. They are no longer willing to accept a "one-size-fits-all" mentality. Instead, they want products and services that are uniquely geared to them—often as individuals and not even as representatives of various groups. Several reasons account for escalating customer demands and diversified tastes:

Competing Based on Time

Time emerged as a major strategic issue in the recent decades; it is an issue both for individuals and organizations.

For individuals. Time is an issue for individuals because they simply have less of it. A General Motors plant went on strike because the workers were tired of excessive and mandatory overtime for many weeks. It is a sign of the times in the downsized organizations of the 1990s: Americans are devoting more time to work and less to everything else: "both men and women are spending a little less time with their children and less time eating at home. Men have lost a little more than two hours free time per week and women more than three" (Carnevale, 1991, pp. 20–21). As a result, the time-pressured consumers of the 1990s want everything fast; they want to walk up to a counter and receive fast foods immediately, drop in one-hour dry cleaners, drive in for a quick oil change, and go to an Emergency Room for immediate medical attention. At the same time, "busy people have neither time nor patience for shoddy products or second-rate services" (Carnevale, 1991, p. 21), and many would rather take their business elsewhere than waste even a moment's time complaining about the poor quality of products or services they receive.

For organizations. Time has also become a competitive issue for organizations. Any organization that can offer a high-quality product or service in less time than its competitors will enjoy a significant advantage. Those that cannot keep up with time demands will not survive. As Chairman and Chief Executive Officer Jack Welch of General Electric has said, "for example, in the computer business, if you miss a cycle, you lose your company" (O'Boyle, 2011, p. 25).

Organizations are really competing on the basis of time in four different ways. These four ways can be expressed as questions:

- First, *who can innovate fastest?*
  - To win this race, the organization must be able to develop a new technology, product, service, or work process before others.
- Second, *who can apply the innovation fastest?*
  - To win this race, the organization must be able to implement the innovation before others.
- Third, *who can refine the innovation and implementation?*
  - To win this race, the organization must be capable of progressing up the learning curve faster than its competitors, offering more variations at the same or lower price and in less time.
- Fourth and finally, *what organization can use its success with one innovation to achieve others without becoming complacent?*
  - To win this race, the organization must be able to find new applications and even new technologies stemming from existing (and sometimes cutting-edge) products, services, and work methods.

Emerging Flexibility in Working Arrangements

In the 1950s, most people in the United States expected to find a job and remain with the same employer throughout their working lives until retirement. And employers expected workers to be loyal and to refrain from "jumping ship" even when pay or working conditions were less than safe or ideal. Such expectations no longer exist. People are changing not just their *jobs* but also their *careers* (Rothwell et al., 2016).

Maximizing employee loyalty is crucial for any company that wants to enhance retention and lower turnover, according to Flynn's recent study on job happiness and loyalty (2023). Unfortunately, it appears that employee loyalty to employers has been declining recently. These changes will undoubtedly impact businesses, companies, and the employment market. Flynn (2023) has compiled all the pertinent trends and data on employee loyalty in the United States to learn more. According to the in-depth research:

- Workers who don't feel appreciated are twice as likely to be looking for work.
- About 40% of workers leave their employment for lack of advancement opportunities.
- Non-financial recognition accounts for 55% of employee engagement.
- 64% of workers concur that having trust in senior management is crucial for job happiness.
- Loyalty rates among employees are 27% higher when they feel that their employer is driven by goals other than financial success.

(Flynn, 2023).

We all have a lot of discussions about the profound change that COVID-19 has forced the workplace to undergo. Although the epidemic dramatically expedited the change, it had already begun to gain speed; a wealth of data shows that many employees favored flexible and remote work arrangements.

Gallup report stated that 39% of personnel performed remotely in 2012, which feels like a century ago, considering the rate of digital transformation in the workplace. By 2016, that number had climbed to 43%, and the proportion of time spent working remotely also grew. Society for Human Resource Management (SHRM) documented increased firms giving choices to work remotely starting in 1996. By 2016, three times as many businesses were doing this (Biro, 2020).

Forward-thinking employers were already planning strategies to let employees work when and where they chose by essentially opening the front doors. Already, job seekers recognize the appeal of remote and flexible work options. But it goes without saying that the global health crisis entirely changed remote and flexible work hours from just prospects to economic imperatives, thereby killing co-working (Biro, 2020).

Flexible working arrangements are being explored in many work settings as a way for organizations to hold down salary and benefit costs and match labor needs precisely to labor demands on a just-in-time basis. Such arrangements go well beyond such earlier experiments with new job designs as job enlargement (adding more of the same work to an employee's job),

job enrichment (adding higher-level duties to an employee's job), flextime (allowing workers freedom in scheduling their working hours), or flexplace (allowing workers to pick work locations). More common in today's work setting is the temporary worker or consultant, who is hired briefly to undertake a specific work assignment and then is discarded upon the assignment's completion.

Virtual office. One approach to flexible working arrangements is a move toward the virtual office or virtual corporation in which necessary resources are acquired and used at the time they are needed. Such resources, including workers, are then discarded for other resources that are immediately applicable to present needs (Wellins et al., 1991).

Team-based organizational structures. A second approach to flexible working arrangements is a move toward team-based organizational structures, which may have varied meanings. For example, more than 40% of *Fortune 500* industrial firms have experimented with teams (Wellins et al., 1991). This approach eliminates bureaucratically defined and rigid jobs in which individuals will not perform duties not specifically identified in their job descriptions.

Like managing and working with a virtual workforce, team-based structures place new, unique demands on an organization's long-term workers and management employees. For example, more time than has been traditional must be devoted to cross-training workers and crafting performance-related incentives and rewards tied to the team rather than individual contributors and performance. To be effective, teams also require more attention to interpersonal relations, group dynamics, and team processes since cooperation within and across teams (rather than competition across individual contributors) becomes the key to success.

Changing Technology

If you own a personal computer or a mobile phone, you should already know how quickly technology changes. The device seems outdated the minute you remove it from the box. Constant updating to keep pace with new technology is time-consuming and expensive—but essential for competitive success. The organization that fails to keep pace will probably not be in business for long.

Historically, organizations and nations have achieved advantages by their natural resources and labor-capital ratios. But technology is quickly emerging as a key competitive issue. Technology does not mean just machines. It also means the know-how to make machines and organizations operate. To survive, organizations must know how to apply technology better than others. That means they must be able to unleash the brainpower of workers and take advantage of the ideas of those who are closest to work operations.

Re-engineering Work Processes

In today's organizations, constant attention must be paid to the time it takes to do anything. In response to external pressures, many decision-makers have started business process re-engineering efforts in their organizations. A business process re-engineering effort seeks quantum leaps in productivity improvement by fundamentally re-examining (and slashing) the time it takes to design, make, and deliver products or offer services. By doing that, organizations can compete more successfully (Bhatt, 2000).

There is no one right way to conduct re-engineering. However, a frequent starting point of a re-engineering effort recognizes that "the way we have always done it before" is not good enough. New ways must be found to achieve increased productivity and result in less time, reduced cost, and improved quality. The frequent focal points of re-engineering efforts are work processes (repeatable activities), structure (reporting relationships), technology (evolving tools and techniques), and people (human resource policies and practices of the organization) (Bhatt, 2000).

Focusing on Quality. Amid fierce global competition and increasingly demanding customers, organizations can only compete effectively by continuously improving what they do and how they do it. For this reason, quality improvement has become a byword for organizations of the 21st century. While business process re-engineering may be the means to this end, quality improvement is the ultimate goal. Quality is not just "checked" at the end of a process or after a service to ensure that defects are missing; rather, it is built in from the beginning, starting with the recognition that no mistake is desirable and that ultimately customers are the absolute arbiters of quality.

Managing and Celebrating Diversity

Besides the growing issue of incorporating the above-mentioned issues in organizations, they must also be responsive to many viewpoints to appeal to increasingly demanding customers and function effectively across the spectrums of beliefs found in global business culture. Decision-makers must go beyond the mere recognition of differences across cultures, races, sexes, and other groups. They need to be prepared to handle diversity, which entails being open to a thorough managerial approach for creating an atmosphere that benefits all employees (Westover, 2022). Managing diversity is not built on the assumption that individuals must "fit in" to be accepted; rather, it recognizes that individuals are proud of their racial, sexual, religious, and other differences and wish to continue acting in line with their differences both inside and outside the workplace. For this reason, organizations must be willing to go beyond mere efforts to manage diversity and be willing to **celebrate diversity**, which means effectively and positively unleashing the immense creativity and synergy stemming from many different people working together.

Managing and celebrating diversity begins with the recognition that the US workforce is changing dramatically. Additional impetus is created by globalization in which the appreciation of cultural differences is the starting point for business success. This includes the changing median age of the labor force.

The average age of the US workforce was 39.6 in 2001; it was 41.9 in 2011, it was 41.7 in 2021, and it will reach the age of 42.6 by the year 2031; this phenomenon is called **the Graying of America** (see Table 9.1).

The US workforce no longer looks like it did in the 1950s. Gone are one-income families in which white male breadwinners dominated work settings outside the home and white female homemakers single-handedly nurtured children and worked full time at home.

According to the US Department of Labor (2022b), the Current Population Survey (CPS), a monthly sample survey of around 60,000 homes, gathers information on nativity. The term "foreign born" refers to people who were not born citizens in the United States but now live in the country. They were born abroad (or in one of its overseas territories, such as Puerto Rico or Guam), and neither parent was a citizen of the United States. The term "foreign born" refers to people who were born abroad, including legal immigrants, refugees, temporary residents like students and temporary employees, and illegal immigrants. The study does not, however, specifically identify those who fit into these groups (see Table 9.2).

These and other changes have prompted organizations to take action to train workers and management employees on how to work more effectively together. Such efforts are called **diversity programs**.

Table: 9.1 Median Age of Labor Force by Sex, Race, and Ethnicity

Median Age of the Labor Force by Sex, Race, and Ethnicity				
Group	*2001*	*2011*	*2021*	*2031*
Men	39.6	41.6	41.7	42.6
Women	39.7	42.2	41.7	42.7
White	40.1	42.5	42.4	43.3
Black	37.8	39.4	39.6	41.0
Hispanic Origin	34.0	36.7	38.4	39.8
Total	**39.6**	**41.9**	**41.7**	**42.6**

Note: US Department of Labor (2022a). Last updated September 8, 2022.

The Importance of DEI&B in the Workplaces

Collaboration, innovation, creativity, decision-making, and both individual and team performance and productivity are all improved by diversity. Researchers frequently concentrate their attention on variables including ethnicity, gender, religion, sexual orientation, and socioeconomic background. Although variety is equally vital, it's also crucial to keep in mind. Organizations must cultivate a culture that accepts and values individuals from a range of social, economic, and political origins as well as those with different experiences, educational backgrounds, and communication and learning styles. The open, trustworthy, and mutually respectful atmosphere that leaders should foster enables the respectful and fruitful exchange of ideas (Westover, 2022).

In order to recruit and keep the finest talent and guarantee that every member is treated with decency and respect, we must go past workplace diversity and equity challenges, including supporting the diversity of opinion. We must go beyond diversity to create a vibrant, inclusive culture for our business. We must intensify these efforts to establish an organizational culture of belonging as we go past diversity and equity concerns and establish an inclusive workplace. Everyone will benefit greatly from creating an inclusive atmosphere that fosters a real sense of belonging for each

Table 9.2   Foreign-Born Workers: Labor Force Characteristics—2021

	Some Highlights from the 2021 Foreign-Born Workers Report and Labor Force Characteristics Data
1	The proportion of foreign-born workers in the civilian labor force in the United States increased from 17.0% in 2020 to 17.4% in 2021, which was pre-pandemic levels.
2	The workforce of people who were not native-born rose by 671,000 from 2020 to 2021, while the labor force of those who were born here remained largely stable.
3	Overall employment grew by 4.8 million from 2020 to 2021. Employment among those who were born abroad climbed by 1.6 million or 6.5%.
4	In 2021, Asians made up one-quarter of the foreign-born workforce, with Hispanics continuing to make up roughly half.
5	In 2021, males who were born abroad continued to enter the labor market at a rate that was much greater (76.8%) than that of men who were born domestically (65.8%).
6	In 2021, foreign-born employees were more likely than native-born workers to work in service occupations, professions involving the use of natural resources, building and maintenance, and occupations involving the movement of goods.
7	In 2021, the median normal weekly wages for full-time wage and pay workers who were not native-born Americans were $898 instead of $1,017 for those who were.

Note: US Department of Labor (2022b).

employee. This would be one of the things that will be managed by an inclusive supervisor (Westover, 2022).

With a diverse corporate culture, a sense of belonging and inclusion are crucial for any business to succeed in the long run. The development, promotion, and maintenance of a safe and inclusive workplace necessitate procedures and programs, but I believe that we also need to assist all organizational leaders in modeling people-oriented values such as dignity and respect for everyone in their interactions with their workforce. While it is undoubtedly crucial, trying to employ a diverse staff and ensuring pay fairness is insufficient. Even while it is crucial, it is not enough to include a diverse workforce in strategy creation and decision-making (Westover, 2021).

Figure 9.2 Elements of DEI&B as an organizational culture. *Note*: **Authors' original creation.**

We must expand on our DEI initiatives to develop a lasting corporate culture of belonging for everyone. Ultimately, we hope to reach a point where all employees can feel a sincere and genuine sense of organizational belonging and are empowered to do their best work and realize their full human capital potential (Westover, 2021) (see Figure 9.2).

Role of Human Resources in Establishing DEI&B in Organizations

The responsibility of Human Resources management is to support inclusive workplace cultures that provide opportunities for all staff members while also coming up with innovative ways to combat discrimination in the workplace. The purpose of workplace DEI&B is difficult, and it goes beyond simply having a diverse staff. The HR department should make sure that efficient techniques penetrate all aspects of people management since it has a unique aerial view of how DEI&B will affect the firm (Rothwell et al., 2022).

Employees' buy-in and understanding during implementation are more likely to occur when they are aware of the efforts being made to incorporate different perspectives in establishing company plans. When people with different backgrounds and ways of thinking are exemplified in strategic, advisory, and oversight roles, silo mentality barriers are reduced, knowledge management is strengthened, and problem-solving is improved. This also lowers the risk of business failure due to a lack of innovation (O'Connor, 2021).

HR & Senior Management Partnership in Encouraging DEI&B at the Workplace

We hear too often about businesses that truly want to integrate DEI&B activities into their corporate objectives but are unsure of where to begin. Reviewing where they are now, creating goals, and then agreeing on the necessary adjustments are often the first steps in the process. There are numerous ways that may be put into practice right away, even though it's helpful to have a basic awareness of what a varied, fair, and inclusive atmosphere looks like and why it's vital (Chiou et al., 2022; Barnes, 2020).

So many people become paralyzed by inaction because they are unsure of what to do or where to begin. How can they make goals if they don't know where they are? Since they have never collected any data, how can they begin gauging where they are? Just getting started is the key. While a comprehensive plan is great, getting started is the secret to success. You will arrive sooner than you could have anticipated if you start with little steps (Chiou et al., 2022; Barnes, 2020).

You may take a lot of actions right away to start. These ten suggestions can help you immediately promote diversity, fairness, and inclusion in your workplace. To succeed, simply start right away. Begin modestly and progress. Choose one action you can do right away to promote a more inclusive, egalitarian, and diverse culture. Next, go to the subsequent steps. Never stop learning and aiming for quality, justice, and belonging (Minott, 2021; Foy, 2021).

Table 9.3 represents ten practices HR departments, and senior management can encourage DEI&B in their organizations and at their workplace.

Role of Supervisors in Managing and Implementing DEI&B

The unfortunate reality that HR practitioners must face is that all the effort put into developing and improving policies and programs can be undone by one conceited manager. The diversity program at your business is similar (Chiou et al., 2022).

Your leadership as a supervisor is crucial to fostering an inclusive workplace and assisting staff in their efforts to participate in your programs for workplace DEI&B. You cannot expect your supervisors to completely grasp and incorporate your diversity effort or policy into their everyday activities by just writing it down and handing it to them. You should teach your supervisors how to participate in the project, just like any other program or policy you wish to start (Holder-Winfield, 2007).

Table 9.3   Ten Practices to Encourage DEI&B in the Workplace by HR and Senior Management

Ten Practices to Encourage DEI&B in the Workplace by HR & Senior Management		
#	*Practice*	*Description*
1	Hiring process	Blind hiring is a technique used to avoid prejudices based on names, ages, genders, races, and ethnicities during the earliest phases of the employment process.
2	Interviewing team	Less discrimination will likely occur when your interview teams are more diverse, leading to more diverse hiring.
3	Sourcing approach	A solid diversity sourcing approach involves leveraging various sources and targeted keywords and phrases while looking for individuals.
4	Decision-making process	Make sure everyone is involved and has the chance to progress professionally to promote inclusion and equity. Consult with workers for advice and comments before making essential choices.
5	Vision, mission, and values	Integrate your vision, mission, and values with a diversity, equity, and inclusion statement. Then, reiterate the assertion and support it.
6	Work flexibility	Provide as flexible scheduling as possible. Being adaptable is crucial now more than ever since many kids are learning virtually at home, and more individuals are working from home.
7	Fair compensation	Be as open and honest as you can about your pay. For example, if you base compensation on experience, devise a fair and consistent system for crediting experience to prevent pay gaps due to race, ethnicity, gender, disability, sexual orientation, age, or other variables.
8	Accountability	Establish metrics for your DEI&B goals and hold individuals accountable for meeting them whenever feasible. Sending out questionnaires to collect feedback from your staff is one approach to gauge the success of your efforts.
9	Foster conversations	Much better is encouraging discussions on DEI&B particularly. Create a DEI&B chat room in your communication platform of choice, such as Slack, where individuals may contribute articles and news items. Promote discussion during meetings.
10	Leaders buy-in	Leadership supports are essential to a DEI&B initiative's success since leaders set the tone for the organization. A company's morale suffers if the leaders advocate but do not implement improvements.

Source: Adapted from Minott (2021) and Barnes (2020).

Table 9.4 Suggestions for HR in Developing Supervisors in Their Role on Overseeing DEI&B at the Workplace

Suggestions for HR in Developing Supervisors in Their Role on Overseeing DEI&B at the Workplace		
#	*Suggestions*	*Descriptions*
1	Display respect for everyone	Supervisors shall display respectful behavior and communication for everyone, free of any inappropriate comments and suggestions.
2	Be an informational resource and advocate	Ensure that all of your supervisors have received thorough training on the company's diversity effort and the notion of diversity. They must be ready to respond to inquiries from staff members on the company's diversity program.
3	While filling positions, take diversity into consideration	Supervisors should take into account diversity sooner in the recruiting process than only when making an offer. Supervisors need to consider where and how they will seek applicants.
4	Take action and get involved when necessary	Supervisors may hesitate to step in when two team members engage in seemingly harmless activity, such as jokes or hazing. Get involved and stop it anyway.
5	Do not take sides regarding nepotism or partiality	Supervisors should lead the charge in demonstrating to workers that they have an equal chance of success and progression. Supervisors shall stay away from taking sides in favor of one employee over another.
6	Show employees the ways to grow	Employees should sit down with their supervisors and be fully informed of the organization's promotion requirements. Inform employees about the many jobs and possibilities the organization offers to dependable employees.
7	Provide acknowledgment and positive feedback	Supervisors should take the time to speak with staff members one-on-one about how well they are doing or how they may better position themselves for more opportunities.
8	Give assignments and ask for high quality	Employees will know you're serious about offering them the chances to grow the way they want if you assign work based on their skills, and capacity and indicate a willingness to manage additional work.

(Continued)

Table 9.4 (Continued)   Suggestions for HR in Developing Supervisors in Their Role on Overseeing DEI&B at the Workplace

	Suggestions for HR in Developing Supervisors in Their Role on Overseeing DEI&B at the Workplace	
#	*Suggestions*	*Descriptions*
9	Hold employees accountable for their actions	Supervisors should hold employees accountable for their inappropriate behaviors and actions related to breaking DEI&B regulations and policies.
10	Be an example of practicing DEI&B	Supervisors should refrain from acting improperly. For example, working with individuals who are typically underrepresented in the workplace includes offensive jokes, behavior, and remarks.

Source: Adapted from Chiou et al., (2022), Holder-Winfield (2015), and Holder-Winfield (2007).

The supervisors are actually the crucial missing connection between the workforce and the diversity officers. Even if diversity officers do all within their powers to outline and develop a strategic vision, if the supervisors do not take meaningful and brave action to promote diversity, all of the diversity officers' efforts will ultimately amount to nothing more than efforts on paper (Holder-Winfield, 2015).

Table 9.4 provides some suggestions for HR directors and diversity officers in hiring, training, and developing supervisors in their role in managing and overseeing DEI&B at the workplace.

Use Table 9.5 to rate yourself on understanding the above roles of overseeing DEI&B at the workplace.

Now use Table 9.6 to devise a series of actions to increase your understanding of Table 9.5.

What's Next?

The next chapter, "Empathetic Supervisor: Supervising with Interpersonal and Intrapersonal Skills," looks at the supervisor's abilities to utilize their understanding of interpersonal and intrapersonal skills to build mastery in being an empathetic supervisor. But before moving on, don't forget to review the key takeaways and take a moment to reflect on what you learned in this chapter by completing Table 9.7, Chapter 9 Discussion Questions and Inquiries.

Table 9.5   Supervisor's Rating on Understanding Their Roles in Overseeing DEI&B at the Workplace

Supervisor's Rating on Understanding Their Roles in Overseeing DEI&B at the Workplace							
Supervisor's Name		Date	Supervisor's Manager		Department		
*Rating Scale: **1** = Poor, **2** = Marginal, **3** = Acceptable, **4** = Good, **5** = Excellent*							
Supervisor's Role about DEI&B				*1*	*2*	*3*	*4*	*5*
1	Display equal respect for everyone							
2	Be an informational resource and advocate							
3	While filling positions, take diversity into consideration							
4	Take action and get involved when necessary							
5	Do not take sides regarding nepotism or partiality							
6	Show employees the ways to grow in the organization							
7	Provide acknowledgment and positive feedback							
8	Give assignments and ask for high-quality work							
9	Hold employees accountable for their actions							
10	Be an example of practicing DEI&B							
Individual Columns' Totals								
Total of above Individual Columns								
Final Average (above total divided by 10)								

Source: Adapted from Chiou et al. (2022), Holder-Winfield (2015), and Holder-Winfield (2007).

Key Takeaways

1. Another supervisor's duty is to manage the application and presence of all diversity, equity, inclusion, and belonging (DEI&B) aspects with their teams.
2. DEI&B guarantees employees fair and decent treatment and opportunities in all areas of employment.

Table 9.6 APLI-Connected to Table 9.5

Action Plan for Learning and Improving	
Area of Learning and Improving: *Supervisor's Rating on Understanding Their Roles in Overseeing DEI&B at the Workplace.*	
Reference: *Table 9.5*	
Three learning and improvement actions for this month that will raise my understanding and awareness regarding *"Supervisor's Rating on Understanding Their Roles on Overseeing DEI&B at Workplace"* to enhance my knowledge and clarity by at least one on the next rating:	
Action 1:	By When:
Action 2:	By When:
Action 3:	By When:

Note: Authors' original creation.

3. Emerging issues lead to change, sometimes small and sometimes profound. Today's organizations have been affected by many emerging issues that are taking them in many new directions and that leads to many new systems to address.

4. The new directions facing organizations from outside and the new systems created in response to those directions inside organizations call for new roles, responsibilities, and duties from American workers and from those who supervise them.

5. Managing and celebrating diversity begins with the recognition that the US workforce is changing dramatically. Additional impetus is created by globalization in which the appreciation of cultural differences is the starting point for business success.

Discussion Questions and Inquiries

Please take a minute to answer the following inquiries and questions in Table 9.7. From your point of view, what have you learned about the following areas?

Table 9.7   End of Chapter 9 Inquiries. Your Perspective on What You Learned in Chapter 9

Your Perspective on What You Learned in Chapter 9	
Area of Inquiry	*What Did You Learn, and How Are You Going to Implement It in Your Position?*
What is diversity?	
What is equity?	
What is inclusion?	
What is belonging?	
Role of HR in establishing DEI&B	
Role of supervisors in managing the DEI&B	

References

Adjo, J., Maybank, A., & Prakash, V. (2021). Building inclusive work environments. *Pediatrics (Evanston)*, *148*(Suppl 2), 1. https://doi.org/10.1542/peds.2021 -051440E

Barnes, S. (2020). 10 ways to foster diversity, equity & inclusion at work. Retrieved March 1, 2023, from https://stephanie-barnes.medium.com/10-ways-to-foster -diversity-equity-inclusion-at-work

Bhatt, G. D. (2000). Exploring the relationship between information technology, infrastructure and business process re-engineering. *Business Process Management Journal*. https://doi.org/10.1108/14637150010324085

Biro, M. M. (2020). On-site vs. remote: Balancing flexible work arrangement. Indeed. LEAD. Retrieved March 8, 2023, from https://www.indeed.com/lead/ remote-flexible-work-arrangements?

Carnevale, A. P. (1991). *America and the New Economy*. Alexandria, VA: American Society for Training and Development.

Chiou, E. K., Holden, R. J., Ghosh, S., Flores, Y., & Roscoe, R. D. (2022). Recruitment, admissions, hiring, retention, and promotion: Mechanisms of Diversity, Equity, Inclusion (DEI) and belonging in higher education. *Proceedings of the Human Factors and Ergonomics Society Annual Meeting*, *66*(1), 135–138. https://doi.org/10.1177/1071181322661026

Cummings, T. G., & Worley, C. G. (2015). *Organization Development & Change*. Stanford, CT: Cengage Learning.

Deming, W. E. (2018). *Out of the Crisis, Reissue*. Cambridge, MA: MIT Press.

Flynn, J. (2023). ZIPPIA website. 20+ vital employee loyalty statistics [2023]: Engagement trends + Data. Retrieved March 8, 2023, from https://www.zippia .com/advice/employee-loyalty-statistics

Foy, C. M. (2021). Successful applications of diversity, equity, and inclusion programming in various professional settings: Strategies to increase DEI in libraries. *Journal of Library Administration*, *61*(6), 676–685. https://doi.org/10.1080 /01930826.2021.1947057

Holder-Winfield, N. (2007). *Recruiting and Retaining a Diverse Workforce*. New York, NY: First Books.

Holder-Winfield, N. (2015). *Exclusion: Strategies for Improving Diversity in Recruitment, Retention and Promotion*. New York, NY: American Bar Association.

Minott, L. (2021). 9 proven strategies to improve diversity, equity & inclusion at your workplace. Retrieved March 1, 2023, from https://www.greatplacetowork .com/resources/blog/9-proven-strategies-to-improve-diversity-equity-inclusion -at-your-workplace

O'Boyle, T. F. (2011). *At Any Cost: Jack Welch, General Electric, and the Pursuit of Profit*. New York, NY: Vintage.

O'Connor, D. (2021). The role of HR in driving diversity and inclusion. ICA (International Compliance Association). Retrieved January 25, 2023, from https://www.int-comp.org/insight/2021/january/hr-diversity-and-inclusion/

Pieterse, J. N. (2004). *Globalization or Empire?* New York, NY: Routledge.

Rothwell, W. J., Ealy, P. L., & Campbell, J. (2022). *Rethinking Organizational Diversity, Equity, and Inclusion.* New York, NY: Routledge.

Rothwell, W. J., Stavros, J. M., & Sullivan, R. L. (2016). *Practicing Organization Development: Leading Transformation and Change* (4th ed.). Hoboken, NJ: John Wiley & Sons, Inc.

US Department of Labor. (2022a). Median age of the labor force, by sex, race and ethnicity. US Bureau of Labor and Statistics. Employment Projections. Retrieved March 8, 2023, from https://www.bls.gov/emp/tables/median-age-labor-force.htm

US Department of Labor. (2022b). Foreign-born workers: Labor force characteristics-2021. News Release. Bureau of Labor and Statistics. Retrieved March 8, 2023, from https://www.bls.gov/news.release/pdf/forbrn.pdf

Wellins, R. S. (1991). *Empowered Teams: Creating Self-Directed Work Groups that Improve Quality, Productivity, and Participation.* San Francisco, CA: Jossey-Bass Inc.

Westover, J. (2021). *'Bluer than Indigo' Leadership: The Journey of Becoming a Truly Remarkable Leader (The Remarkable Leadership Series).* New York, NY: HCR Press.

Westover, J. (2022). *The Future Leader: Creating & Transforming Next Gen Organizations (The Remarkable Leadership Series).* New York, NY: HCR Press.

Chapter 10

The Empathetic Supervisor: Supervising with Interpersonal and Intrapersonal Skills

Introduction

Leading organizations with empathy present a compelling business rationale underpinned by tangible and intangible benefits. At its core, empathy fosters a deep understanding of the needs and motivations of employees, stakeholders, and customers alike. This understanding directly leads to increased employee engagement, leading to improved productivity and reduced turnover. The financial impact of retention cannot be underestimated; the costs associated with recruiting, training, and downtime of unfilled positions are significantly reduced when organizations prioritize empathy. Moreover, in an increasingly interconnected and diverse world, empathy leadership facilitates harmonious collaboration between different teams and brings innovative solutions that emerge from different perspectives. From a customer perspective, organizations that consistently demonstrate empathy often deliver superior customer experiences. They resonate with customers more deeply, promote loyalty, and drive repeat business. By recognizing and valuing human emotions and perspectives, companies are better equipped to anticipate changes, respond to challenges, and seize new opportunities, thereby

DOI: 10.4324/9781003413493-10

ensuring not only survival but also sustained growth in today's competitive environment.

Historically, empathy has been largely overlooked and dismissed as merely a "soft skill." Yet, current studies emphasize the need for today's leaders to be more people-centric and proficient at navigating diverse teams, cultures, and backgrounds. A study published in HBR (2017) shows that executives rated managers as exceptional performers when they demonstrated empathy for their teams.

As a supervisor, leading your team with a person-centered focus and genuine empathy creates a positive and inclusive work environment. When you recognize that each individual has different experiences, motivations, and challenges and can empathize with their unique situation, you are better equipped to adapt your leadership style and adapt to his or her specific needs and aspirations.

Have you ever noticed how some people navigate social situations effortlessly, are aware of their own emotions, and react effectively to others, even in tense circumstances? These individuals can quickly gauge a situation, determine what matters most, and respond in a manner that considers everyone involved. They can empathize with others, manage conflict, read social cues, and be sensitive to those around them. Such attributes highlight strong interpersonal skills. Conversely, they can also articulate their understanding of the situation and manage and control their own emotions, even in stressful conditions, demonstrating strong intrapersonal skills. These skills—interpersonal and intrapersonal—encompass effective communication, understanding, and the ability to connect and collaborate seamlessly with others, whether in a professional setting or personal space. Harnessing these competencies, as noted by Spencer and Spencer (1993) and Boyatzis (1982), is pivotal in fostering meaningful relationships and working cohesively with diverse teams.

In Chapter 2, you were introduced to emotional intelligence (EI), emotional contagion, and empathic accuracy. As shown in Figure 10.1 of the *Successful Supervisory Leadership Series Book II Structure*, we will continue to build in the basics and specifically focus on what it means to be an empathetic supervisor. This chapter will review how to refine your interpersonal and intrapersonal skills. You'll learn the distinctions between hard and soft skills, gain a deeper understanding of emotional intelligence, and gain insights to further enhance your interpersonal and intrapersonal proficiency. You will also gain a better appreciation for the value of emotional intelligence in the workplace. As a supervisor, you can use this knowledge to help optimize and manage your team more effectively.

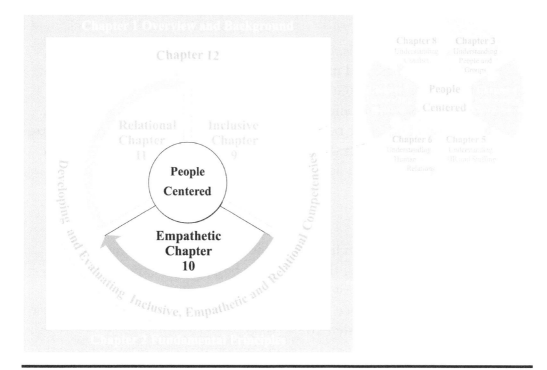

Figure 10.1 *Successful Supervisory Leadership Series Book II Structure.* **Note: Authors' original creation.**

Key Concepts

This chapter will cover the following key concepts:

- What Are Skills and Soft Skills?
- Emotional Intelligence (EI)
  - Empathy and Compassion
- What Are Interpersonal Skills?
  - Top Attributes and Quality of People with Interpersonal Skills
  - Role of Interpersonal Skills in Effective Supervisors
- What Are Intrapersonal Skills?
  - Top Attributes and Quality of People with Intrapersonal Skills
  - Role of Intrapersonal Skills in Effective Supervisory Positions

Definitions

The following definitions of key terms will help to better understand the main elements of this chapter:

Emotional Intelligence

■ Knowing your emotions, controlling them, inspiring yourself, identifying others' feelings, and managing relationships are all parts of having emotional intelligence (Goleman, 2015).

■ An aspect of social intelligence that entails the capacity to keep track of one's own and other people's sentiments and emotions, to recognize the differences between them, and to utilize this information to make informed decisions and actions (Robles, 2012).

Empathy

■ The action of understanding, being aware of, being sensitive to, and vicariously experiencing the feelings, thoughts, and experience of another of either the past or present without having the feelings, thoughts, and experience fully communicated in an objectively explicit manner (Merriam-Webster, 2023a, n.p.).

■ The term "empathy" refers to a wide notion that describes one's cognitive and emotional responses to another person's perceived experiences. The possibility of assisting others and displaying compassion rises when one has empathy (Goleman, 2014).

Compassion

■ "Sympathetic consciousness of others' distress together with a desire to alleviate it" (Merriam-Webster, 2023b, n.p.).

■ The definition of compassion is "to suffer as one." According to academics who study emotions, it is the sensation you have when you witness someone else's suffering and are moved to try to alleviate it. However, despite the notions that they are similar, compassion, empathy, and altruism are not the same (Clarke, 2006).

Soft Skills

■ "Personal attributes that enable someone to interact effectively and harmoniously with other people" (Oxford Languages, 2023, n.p.).

■ Several assigned professional traits are included in soft skills, including "team skills, communication skills, leadership skills, customer service skills, and problem-solving skills" (Charopensap-Kelly et al., 2016, p. 155).

Interpersonal Skills

■ Ability to manage teams and work in groups, develop and coach others to add their roles and tasks, serve customers, negotiate contracts or positions, and work well with people from many origins and cultures (Handley, 2017).

■ While interacting and communicating with people, you rely on your interpersonal skills. They span a range of situations in which collaboration and communication are crucial (Bakhshandeh, 2021).

Intrapersonal Skills

■ Self-awareness, internal attitude, and process control are the cornerstones of intrapersonal skills. Since they make managing your interpersonal interactions easier, your intrapersonal skills are the cornerstone of developing relationships with others (Robles, 2012).

■ Because they deal with one's inner self, intrapersonal skills are self-communication. Therefore, your ability to control your emotions and deal with difficulties at various points in your life depends on your intrapersonal skills (Sheck & Lin, 2015).

Key Distinction among Empathy and Compassion

Compassion and *empathy* refer to a caring response to someone else's distress. While *empathy* refers to an active sharing in the other person's emotional experience, *compassion* adds to that emotional experience a desire to alleviate the person's distress (Merriam-Webster, 2023b, n.p.).

Key Distinction between Interpersonal Skills and Intrapersonal Skills

The phrase "interpersonal skills" is better known than "intrapersonal skills." In contrast to intrapersonal communication, which takes place within your head, interpersonal communication refers to that which takes place between two or more persons. For example, a verbal or nonverbal interchange of ideas can be described as interpersonal skills. Interpersonal communication frequently reduces stress, but intrapersonal communication often increases stress (Goleman, 2015).

Today's Supervisors

In today's organizations, it is not enough for supervisors to do their jobs and attempt to manage their workforces because that will not save the day. In today's fierce competition for a skillful and capable workforce, there is a demand for a powerful supervisor armed with 21st-century competencies and skills that are imperative in developing a productive and high-performance workforce. For that, today's supervisors need to understand, be educated, and be trained in the following skills (see Figure 10.2). Besides the technical skills, which are not a focus of this chapter or book, this chapter covers the rest of these vital skills.

Technical Skills

Proficiencies at work and while performing tasks as supervisors and managing their workforce's productivity for the businesses' success, they fulfill the organization's vision and mission.

Emotional Intelligence Skills

These are skills that provide the supervisors with the ability to develop competencies, attributions, and qualities so they can provide compassion and empathy when leading their workforce.

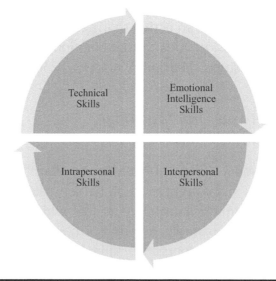

Figure 10.2 Skills of today's competent supervisors. *Note:* **Authors' original creation.**

Interpersonal Skills

These allow supervisors to establish and develop long-lasting and effective relationships with others, including their teams and managers.

Intrapersonal Skills

Supervisors continue their growth in personal awareness and as visionaries with self-confidence and provide leadership to their workforce.

What Are Skills and Soft Skills?

From the beginning of this chapter, we have often mentioned the term *skills*, so we thought to dig in a little further on what we mean by *skills* and *soft skills*, especially when they are used as interpersonal and intrapersonal skills.

Skills

The talent and knowledge needed to carry out a job or complete a task are called skills. Skills are what give people the self-assurance they need to succeed in their endeavors. Almost every ability can be learned, developed, and improved, but doing so requires willpower and practice (Donahue, 2018). According to Rothwell (2015), competence is the capacity to carry out an activity or job with predetermined results within a predetermined amount of time.

Soft Skills

Interpersonal or people skills are included under soft skills. These skills are hard to measure, but in a broad sense, they constitute a person's personality and capacity for collaboration. The ability to think critically, solve problems, communicate effectively, listen objectively, and show empathy and many other traits are among these qualities (see "The Balancing Career," n.d.).

It is unclear where the phrase "soft talents" originated. When Whitmore and Fry conducted a study on leadership in the US Army in 1972, the term was first used (Charopensap-Kelly et al., 2016). Whitmore and Fry (1972) defined the term "soft skills" from a collection of research participants' comments, as stated by Charopensap-Kelly et al. (2016). "Important job-related skills that involve little or no interaction with machines and can be applied in a variety of job contexts" (p. 155).

According to Charopensap-Kelly et al. (2016), several researchers have used and defined the term "soft skills" since the 1990s. Yet, it is evident that emotional intelligence is characterized by five foundations, including "self-awareness, self-regulation, motivation, empathy, and social skills" (p. 155). Moreover, soft skills include some designated professional traits such as "team skills, communication skills, leadership skills, customer service skills, and problem-solving skills" (p. 155).

People Skills as Pertinent to Soft Skills

Robles (2012) used the example of how, in today's culture, the majority of people also use the term "people skills," which are a key component of soft skills, to highlight the connection between soft skills and people skills. Also, Robles (2012) noted that an individual's interactions with other people are illustrated by their people skills. He emphasizes it as one of the most crucial workplace competencies.

Robles (2012) explained, "While many authors equate interpersonal skills with soft skills, interpersonal skills are only one facet of soft skills" (p. 457). In addition to interpersonal skills, soft skills can refer to other personality traits and professional aptitudes, such as a person's time management, personality, and organizational ability (Robles, 2012). In addition, leadership skills, communication proficiency, a collaborative spirit, and a passion for customer service are all professional and career attributes that form the basis of efficient customer service and retention (Robles, 2012).

Emotional Intelligence (EI)

Given that empathy, compassion, interpersonal skills, and interpersonal skills are all elements of four main clusters of emotional intelligence, we thought to start by distinguishing and describing EI or emotional intelligence.

Whether they like it or not, leaders of businesses must deal with the mood of their organizations and all types of emotional outputs from their labor force, from managers and supervisors, and all the way down to the floor staff. The best organizational leaders do this task by utilizing an unusual combination of psychological skills known as emotional intelligence or EI (HBR, 2017). According to the *Harvard Business Review*, these kinds of company executives who are aware of EI competencies state that "they're self-aware and empathetic. They can read and regulate their own emotions while intuitively grasping how others feel and gauging their organization's emotional state" (HBR, 2017, p. 4). EI capabilities are described as "an ability to recognize, understand, and use emotional information about oneself or others that leads to or causes effective or superior performance" (Boyatzis & Sala, 2004, p. 5).

Emotional intelligence inspires businesses, leaders, and personnel to outstanding performance when used thoughtfully and compassionately (HBR, 2017). Our emotions frequently directly impact how we think, even to some extent, how we govern, and how we live our everyday lives (Bakhshandeh, 2015; Hockenbury & Hockenbury, 2007). We make decisions depending on our current emotions, such as sadness, anger, happiness, frustration, or boredom. As a result, we unknowingly select certain responses based on the feelings we are stoking (Bakhshandeh, 2015; Hockenbury & Hockenbury, 2007).

EI has been divided and organized into four clusters and their related competencies (see Figure 10.3) as (1) self-awareness, (2) self-regulation, (3) social awareness, and (4) relationship management.

As an organization executive or a business manager, it is essential to offer training and development in emotional intelligence knowledge, skills, and competencies to supervisors and other employees. This will help them with workforce development and managerial and supervisory skills, which will directly influence their team, group, departments, and people to work with improved behavior and display a positive attitude that will impact their productivity. Those who comprehend and use any of these emotional

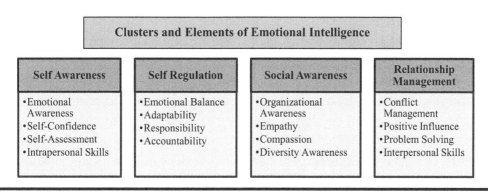

Figure 10.3   Clusters and elements of emotional intelligence. *Source*: Adapted from Bakhshandeh (2021).

intelligence clusters and abilities exhibit a wide variety of traits and attributions. This study highlights three beneficial traits and attributions of those who possess these competencies.

The four emotional intelligence clusters and their pertinent competencies are shown in Figure 10.3, which might enable company executives to implement sets of significant and useful emotional intelligence that would be highly beneficial to train and developing workforces.

Empathy and Compassion

Empathy and compassion are two competencies of the cluster. Social skills are necessary for social awareness. It is not enough for a corporate leader to handle contradictory and challenging situations coming from a lack of social awareness and associated components, even with the capacity to demonstrate understanding, empathy, compassion, and emotional control (Stevens, 2009). This set of abilities applies to workers, customers, and clients of the business. "A person manages to do that by obtaining and maintaining a high degree of emotional intelligence, of course!" (Stevens, 2009, p. 48).

Business leaders may also display social awareness outcomes across organizational awareness by understanding social awareness components like workplace diversity and disparities in the workplace and avoiding preconceptions and generalizations of people (Handley, 2017). According to Handley (2017; referenced in Goleman, 2014) in this regard, "Goleman describes this competency cluster with empathic listening, ability to grasp the others' perspectives, political understanding, organizational awareness, and service to others" (p. 146).

Empathy

The foundation for empathy and the capacity to build personal, social, and professional relationships is the capacity to concentrate on others. The ability to identify common ground with others allows business leaders to focus successfully on them. As a consequence, their thoughts and comments are respected and accepted by their workforce to a greater extent than those of other leaders (HBR, 2017). They are those who, regardless of organizational structure or social rank, emerge as genuine leaders in society and in organizations (Goleman, 2015).

While interacting with people in relation to the current state of their feelings and emotions, one's predisposition to detect and appreciate others' emotional status is important (Goleman, 2015). Understanding others' emotions, recognizing talent, and being helpful to others are some characteristics of empathic people (HBR, 2017).

Compassion

Compassion is the capacity to show empathy, kindness, and understanding for others during their suffering, adversity, and difficulty. Empathy is the awareness of other people's suffering, interests, and goals to make them feel better (Goleman, 2015). Empathy is taken a step further and more deeply by compassion. When they see another individual suffering, someone who has compassion will feel bad and do something to help them. Understanding someone and showing them care are two different things; compassion is one kind of social awareness that makes this distinction (HBR, 2017). A few characteristics of compassionate individuals include putting themselves in others' shoes, actively listening, and accepting others' shortcomings (HBR, 2017).

What Are Interpersonal Skills?

Interpersonal skills are one of the elements and competencies of the *Relationship Management* cluster. Therefore, to better understand interpersonal skills, we shall understand the Relationship Management cluster.

Relationship Management

People's relationships with others impact their quality of life favorably or adversely. Therefore, relationships that don't offer anything and don't provide value to the connection are unnecessary on both a personal and professional level. Individuals who are aware of emotional intelligence are familiar with this important idea (Wayne, 2019; Stevens, 2009).

People must invest in sustaining and working to enhance their relationships in order to have quality relationships in addition to striving for values and building quality. Business leaders need to learn how to use their intelligence effectively to enable them to realize and identify opportunities, effectively communicate, try to solve challenges, and successfully work in partnership with their employees and customers. This is similar to how they would in a personal relationship (Goleman, 2015; Stevens, 2009). Being able to integrate is an essential first step to developing into a capable corporate leader. More specifically, managers have discovered that emotional intelligence is a crucial component of connection-building and dynamic leadership development.

Interpersonal Skills

Being able to integrate is an essential first step to developing into a capable corporate leader. More specifically, managers have discovered that emotional intelligence is a crucial component of connection-building and dynamic leadership development (Spencer & Spencer, 1993; Boyatzis, 1982). While having the right hard skills for the job is crucial to the employees' ability to perform their duties, interpersonal skills such as the ability to work well with others, the ability to communicate clearly, and the ability to project confidence are equally important and can help employees advance in their careers. Some qualities of an individual with interpersonal abilities according to Rothwell (2015) are (a) being aware of themselves and others, (b) being collaborative, and (c) caring about relationships.

The personal traits and actions we exhibit when interacting with others are known as interpersonal skills. Certain personality traits are intrinsic and may be cultivated, while others have been picked up in particular social settings. It's always a conscious decision to use our interpersonal skills in a particular setting, and how well we use them will determine how we affect other people and, eventually, how employable we are. The bottom line will improve if we can get along with our coworkers.

Interpersonal skills are the power behind making things work with others, whether it's settling a problem, earning someone's respect, or understanding what they're trying to communicate. Interpersonal skills are under the category of soft skills, which also include managerial and supervisory operational aptitudes like people management, time management, and organization. Soft skills are social and emotional aptitudes.

Top Attributions and Qualities of People with Interpersonal Skills

Almost all leadership positions, including managerial and supervisory positions, can use interpersonal skills for their benefit and build a relationship foundation with others, including teams and groups. Through decades of research and hands-on experience, professionals have highlighted many qualities and attributions related to interpersonal skills as seen in Figure 10.4.

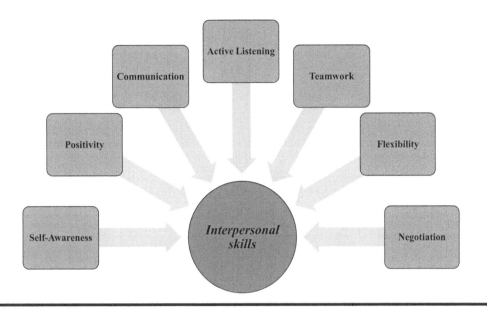

Figure 10.4 Top attributions and qualities of people with interpersonal skills. Source: Adapted from Goleman (2015), Rothwell (2015), Hockenbury & Hockenbury (2007), Spencer & Spencer (1993), and Boyatzis (1982).

Self-Awareness

Self-awareness is the capacity to concentrate on oneself and determine whether or not one's behaviors, ideas, or emotions are consistent with one's internal standards. As a result, you can regulate your emotions, match your conduct with your ideals, and accurately assess how other people see you if you have a high level of self-awareness.

Positivity

Being positive or hopeful in life is a trait or practice of positivity. When we are optimistic, we think positively, feel positive, and act positively by being nice and giving to others. The good effects of all of this optimism, such as better well-being and mental health, are amplified.

Communication

For one to effectively express their thoughts and get appropriate guidance, they must do it in vocal, written, and graphic formats. Each high-performing supervisor must figure out how to get things done with others and the delicate interpersonal skills of persuading and influencing help to make sure that what you say is what others hear and act on.

Active Listening

One of the most effective interpersonal and social skills is listening, intending to act positively. Ask pertinent questions, build a rapport of trust, show compassion for the speaker, and work to get an understanding. Clarifying and replying as the discussion develops is a terrific approach to resolving a challenging issue or coming to an unexpected conclusion. Interpersonal skills such as active listening enable you to interact with the speaker and concentrate on their message.

Teamwork

Understanding the effects of your contribution, relying on others for assistance when necessary, and occasionally taking the lead are all components of teamwork. Several of the other interpersonal skills complement this one. Without great listening and communication skills, collaboration and teamwork are challenging.

Flexibility

Flexibility in the workplace embraces the notion that workers may be effective regardless of when or where they do their tasks. Workplace flexibility recognizes individual requirements and fosters a good work–life balance and worker well-being rather than maintaining a rigid office and workplace atmosphere or timetable.

Negotiation

It is uncommon for two individuals or groups to have identical goals and search in the same direction. Interpersonal negotiation skills are useful when there is a need for concessions, and monetary benefit is at risk. Critical thinking and problem-solving abilities are needed to get to the perfect situation, and the character traits of patience, persistence, and optimism provide all sides the possibility to succeed in a win–win situation.

Role of Interpersonal Skills in Effective Supervisory Positions

Business success depends on being able to get along with people. Interpersonal skills are essential as a supervisor to navigate challenging situations, communicate your requirements, and work together with your team to seize every opportunity (Mutileni, 2020). Interpersonal skills facilitate removing barriers, resolving issues, and surmounting challenges since we all occasionally need a little assistance from our coworkers and team members.

Although people have developed their interpersonal skills since they were little children, it is nevertheless important to consider what they imply when working well in a professional setting. As we have mentioned before, soft skills include interpersonal skills (Neale, Spencer-Arnell & Wilson, 2011). As a supervisor, you employ interpersonal skills when engaging and speaking with others in your workplace to initiate, develop, and maintain connections. As an illustration, a production supervisor facilitates a brainstorming session and purposefully invites involvement from new and more recent team members to allow their ideas and thoughts to stand out. Teamwork, positivity, active listening, and empathy are a few interpersonal skills that are demonstrated in this situation in addition to leadership and motivation.

Table 10.1 is designed for supervisors to self-rate their understanding and level of practicing qualities of interpersonal skills at the workplace and while leading their workforces. Please take time and rate yourself monthly using the following table:

Now use Table 10.2 to formulate a series of actions to increase your understanding of Table 10.1.

What Are Intrapersonal Skills?

Intrapersonal skills are one of the elements and competencies of the *Self-awareness* cluster of emotional intelligence. To better understand intrapersonal skills, we shall examine the Self-awareness cluster.

Self-Awareness

Our awareness is governed by how we see ourselves and other people, and as a result, our awareness transforms into our new reality, which naturally drives our behavior (Bakhshandeh, 2015). According to Goleman (2014), self-aware people understand how their emotions impact how well they perform

Table 10.1 Supervisor's Rating on Understanding and Practicing Interpersonal Skills at Workplace

Supervisor's Rating on Understanding and Practicing Interpersonal Skills at the Workplace						
Supervisor's Name		Date	Supervisor's Manager			
Rating Scale: *1* = Poor, *2* = Marginal, *3* = Acceptable, *4* = Good, *5* = Excellent						
Interpersonal Skills			*1*	*2*	*3*	*4*	*5*
1	Self-awareness					
2	Positivity					
3	Communication					
4	Active listening					
5	Teamwork					
6	Flexibility					
7	Negotiation					
Individual Columns' Totals						
Total of above Individual Columns						
Final Average (above total divided by 7)						

Note: Authors' original creation.

at work, know when to seek help, and know how to concentrate on enhancing their strengths rather than on their weaknesses.

Self-awareness is the ability to recognize and comprehend one's emotions, temperament, and intentions as well as the effects of those emotions on others. Knowing and comprehending our own self-awareness will enable us to notice and comprehend the emotions and mental states of others, as well as how they regard us, how they perceive our actions and attitudes, and how we react to them (Wayne, 2019; Goleman, 2015).

Intrapersonal Skills

You're certainly familiar with the term interpersonal skills, but intrapersonal skills are less well-known. In other situations, intrapersonal skills may be even more important. Spending time developing these skills will improve the bulk of your daily tasks.

Table 10.2   APLI-Connected to Table 10.1

Action Plan for Learning and Improving
Area of Learning and Improving: *Supervisor's Rating on Understanding and Practicing Interpersonal Skills at the Workplace.*
Reference: *Table 10.1*
Three learning and improvement actions for this month that will raise my understanding and awareness regarding *"Supervisor's Rating on Understanding & Practicing Interpersonal Skills at the Workplace"* to enhance my knowledge and clarity by at least one on the next rating:

Action 1:	By When:
Action 2:	By When:
Action 3:	By When:

Note: Authors' original creation.

Self-awareness, internal attitude, and process control are the cornerstones of intrapersonal skills. Since they make managing your interpersonal interactions easier, your intrapersonal skills are the cornerstone of developing relationships with others (Tulgan, 2015). This is the capacity for individuals to recognize and comprehend their ideas, feelings, and emotions. They may use it to plan and manage their personal and business lives (Rothwell, 2015; Cummings & Worley, 2015).

People with intrapersonal skills are adept at reflecting within, probing deeper, and discovering their feelings, emotions, motives, and goals. They have a pronounced introspective and analytical nature and seek self-understanding via self-analysis. Introverted and perceptive people tend to have intrapersonal skills. The majority of their learning is independent and reflective (Shek & Lin, 2015). "Intrapersonal competencies form the foundation of one's development, and they are fundamental qualities of leadership competencies" (Shek & Lin, 2015, p. 255). According to Sheck and Lin (2015), some characteristics of those with intrapersonal aptitudes include (a) understanding and appreciation of themselves, (b) consciousness of their personal agenda, and (c) the ability to remove distractions.

One of the most important aspects of intrapersonal skills is realizing your personal assets and weaknesses. Intrapersonal skills are a form of self-communication since they deal with one's inner self. Part of soft skills is acquired outside of the classroom. Instead, they're the result of an ongoing adjustment of how you present yourself to the outside world, along with introspection and self-reflection. Yet, intrapersonal skills are a crucial component of your professional tools, just as your technical talents (Wall, 2007).

Top Attributions and Qualities of People with Intrapersonal Skills

Intrapersonal skills may be used to their advantage in almost all leadership roles, including management and supervisory positions, to establish a connected foundation with others, including teams and organizations. Experts have emphasized several characteristics and attributions connected to intrapersonal skills through years of research and practical experience. The study served as the foundation for the following list of attributions (see Figure 10.5):

Visionary

A visionary is a person who has a clear sense of the future. The ideas of a visionary may either succeed spectacularly or fail horribly since such visions aren't always correct. However, visionary is often a good term because visionary people are imaginative, look at a bigger picture, are not scared to fail, and always share their vision with others.

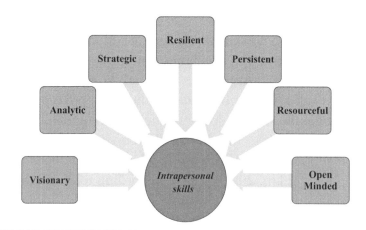

Figure 10.5 Top attributions and qualities of people with intrapersonal skills. Source: Adapted from Goleman (2015), Rothwell (2015), Hockenbury & Hockenbury (2007), Spencer & Spencer (1993), and Boyatzis (1982).

Analytic

What attributes characterize analytical thinkers? An analytical thinker is someone who is curious and driven to investigate issues to find a solution to a problem. Analytical thinkers start by challenging every aspect of the situation rather than making assumptions about it.

Strategic

Strategic thinkers recognize the value of making decisions with decisiveness. They effectively acquire information and then base their decisions on it. They understand that making decisions and drawing conclusions require both information and confidence.

Resilient

The capacity to recover from adversity in life is called resilience. Resilience is a result of the knowledge and abilities we acquire as we mature and deal with all of our challenges, no matter what they may be. Those that are resilient are conscious of their surroundings, their feelings, and the behaviors of others around them.

Persistent

How long you are capable and eager to continue with an activity, no matter how difficult it may be, is referred to as persistence. Some people are prepared to persevere in their efforts even when they encounter obstacles.

Resourceful

Being resourceful involves developing practical and original answers in difficult circumstances. Being helpful implies that your answer is effective and realistic. Being unique denotes an intriguing, original, or creative answer. Being resourceful is when you come up with original answers to challenging problems.

Open-Minded

Being open-minded is actively seeking evidence that contradicts one's preferred ideas, intentions, or ambitions and properly considering such evidence when it is made accessible. Being open-minded does not entail being unsure of one's priorities or being unable to think for oneself.

Role of Intrapersonal Skills in Effective Supervisors

Supervisors with good intrapersonal abilities are more likely to succeed than those without. They often have higher communication and delegation skills to balance competing priorities and handle stressful circumstances better, and they tend to be more self-assured. Everyone wins when businesses help workers develop their intrapersonal abilities.

You take ownership of your own feelings and emotions when you have good intrapersonal abilities. The term "intrapersonal intelligence" also applies to this worldview. You gain the ability to concentrate, create priorities and goals, think critically, and solve problems with purpose. You know how to react when things don't go as planned with a deliberate, intelligent approach to get the desired result (Sheck & Lin, 2015). It's understandable why groups and organizations seek out individuals who can view every difficulty or obstruction as an opportunity for progress. They may remain adaptable, receptive to new ideas, and eager to seek for original solutions to their challenges thanks to their growth attitude. Their internal passion is contagious and emanates from deep inside.

Table 10.3 is designed for supervisors to self-rate their understanding and level of practicing qualities of intrapersonal skills at the workplace and while leading their workforces. Please take time and rate yourself on a monthly basis using the following table:

Now use Table 10.4 to formulate a series of actions to increase your understanding of Table 10.3.

What's Next?

The next chapter, "The Relational Supervisor: Supervising with and through People," looks at the supervisor's abilities to utilize their understanding of being relational, including knowing how to get related, establish a relationship, and build rapport with others. But before moving on, don't forget to review the key takeaways, and take a moment to reflect on what you learned in this chapter by completing Table 10.5, Chapter 10 Discussion Questions and Inquiries.

Table 10.3   Supervisor's Rating on Understanding and Practicing Intrapersonal Skills at the Workplace

Supervisors Rating on Understanding and Practicing Intrapersonal Skills at the Workplace						
Supervisor's Name		Date		Supervisor's Manager		
Rating Scale: *1* = Poor, *2* = Marginal, *3* = Acceptable, *4* = Good, *5* = Excellent						
Interpersonal Skills	*1*	*2*	*3*	*4*	*5*	
1	Visionary					
2	Analytic					
3	Strategic					
4	Resilient					
5	Persistent					
6	Resourceful					
7	Open-Minded					
Individual Columns' Totals						
Total of above Individual Columns						
Final Average (above total divided by 7)						

Note: Authors' original creation.

Key Takeaways

1. Empathy and compassion are necessary elements of emotional intelligence for assisting an effective supervisor in relating and leading their workforces.
2. The personal traits and actions we exhibit when interacting with others are known as interpersonal skills. Certain personality traits are intrinsic and may be cultivated, while others have been picked up in particular social settings.
3. People with intrapersonal skills are adept at reflecting within, probing deeper, and discovering their own feelings, emotions, motives, and goals. They have a pronounced introspective and analytical nature and seek self-understanding via self-analysis.

Table 10.4   APLI-Connected to Table 10.3

Action plan for learning and improving
Area of Learning and Improving: *Supervisor's Rating on Understanding and Practicing Intrapersonal Skills at the Workplace*
Reference: *Table 10.3*
Three learning and improvement actions for this month that will raise my understanding and awareness regarding *"Supervisor's Rating on Understanding and Practicing Intrapersonal Skills at Workplace"* to enhance my knowledge and clarity by at least one on the next rating:

Action 1:	By When:
Action 2:	By When:
Action 3:	By When:

Note: Authors' original creation.

4. Interpersonal skills and intrapersonal skills are two vital qualities sourced from clusters of emotional intelligence. These skills will support supervisors in providing positive and empathetic leadership while working with their people, individually or as a team.
5. Which one of these skills, interpersonal or intrapersonal, is thus more crucial? Your interpersonal and intrapersonal communication skills are closely related. Your capacity to effectively express your wants, objectives, and ideas to people and your emotional intelligence are both influenced by one another. Collaboration, leadership, and influence all depend on your interpersonal skills, but you can't present such attributes unless you have strong intrapersonal ones.

Discussion Questions and Inquiries

Please take a minute to answer the following inquiries and questions in Table 10.5. From your point of view, what have you learned about the following areas?

Table 10.5   End of Chapter 10 Inquiries. Your Perspective on What You Learned in Chapter 10

Your Perspective on What You Learned in Chapter 10	
Area of Inquiry	*What Did You Learn, and How Are You Going to Implement These in Your Position?*
What is emotional intelligence?	
What is self-awareness?	
What is relationship management?	
What is empathy?	
What is compassion?	
What are interpersonal skills?	
What are intrapersonal skills?	

References

Bakhshandeh, B. (2015). *Anatomy of Upset: Restoring Harmony*. Carbondale, PA: Primeco Education, Inc.

Bakhshandeh, B. (2021). *Perception of 21st Century 4CS (Critical Thinking, Communication, Creativity & Collaboration) Skill Gap in Private-Sector Employers in Lackawanna County, NE PA* (Order No. 28841654). Available from Dissertations & Theses @ CIC Institutions; ProQuest Dissertations & Theses A&I. (2577123614). https://ezaccess.libraries.psu.edu/login?qurl=https%3A%2F%2Fwww.proquest.com%2Fdissertations-theses%2Fperception-21st-century-4cs-critical-thinking%2Fdocview%2F2577123614%2Fse-2%3Faccountid%3D13158

Boyatzis, R. E. (1982). *The Competent Manager: A Model for Effective Performance*. Hoboken, NJ: John Wiley & Sons.

Boyatzis, R. E., & Sala, F. (2004). Assessing emotional intelligence competencies. In G. Geher (Ed.), *The Measurement of Emotional Intelligence*. Nova Science Publishers. https://doi.org/10.1016/S0160-2896(01)00084-8

Charoensap-Kelly, P., Broussard, L., Lindsly, M., & Troy, M. (2016). Evaluation of a soft skills training program. *Business and Professional Communication Quarterly*, 79(2), 154–179. https://doi.org/10.1177/2329490615602090

Clarke, N. (2006). Emotional intelligence training: A case of caveat emptor. *Human Resource Development Review*, 5(4), 422–441. https://doi.org/10.1177/1534484306293844

Cummings, T. G., & Worley C. G. (2015). *Organization Development & Change* (10th ed.). Stamford, CT: Cengage Learning.

Donahue, W. E. (2018). *Building Leadership Competence. A Competency-Based Approach to Building Leadership Ability*. State College, PA: Centerstar Learning.

Goleman, D. (2014). What it takes to achieve managerial success. *TD: Talent Development*, 68(11), 48–52. https://www.proquest.com/docview/1643098923/fulltextPDF/33BA6291F86D4459PQ/1?accountid=13158

Goleman, D. (2015). *Emotional Intelligence: Why It Can Matter More Than IQ*. New York, NY: Bantam Books.

Handley, M. M. (2017). An interpersonal behavioral framework for early-career engineers demonstrating engineering leadership characteristics across three engineering companies (Order No. 10666507). Available from ABI/INFORM Collection; Dissertations & Theses @ CIC Institutions; ProQuest Dissertations & Theses A&I; Social Science Premium Collection. (1986249573). https://ezaccess.libraries.psu.edu/login?qurl=https%3A%2F%2Fwww.proquest.com%2Fdissertations-theses%2Finterpersonal-behavioral-framework-early-career%2Fdocview%2F1986249573%2Fse-2%3Faccountid%3D13158

HBR. (2017). *Harvard Business Review Guide to Emotional Intelligence*. Boston, MA: Harvard Business Review Press.

Hockenbury, D. H., & Hockenbury, S. E. (2007). *Discovering Psychology*. New York, NY: Worth Publishers.

Merriam-Webster. (2023a). Empathy. Retrieved March 11, 2023, from https://www
.merriam-webster.com/dictionary/empathy

Merriam-Webster. (2023b). Compassion. Retrieved March 11, 2023, from https://
www.merriam-webster.com/dictionary/compassion

Mutileni, S. (2020). *SOAR with Emotional Intelligence*. New York, NY: BSP Scrolls.

Neale, S., Spencer-Arnell, L., & Wilson, L. (2011). *Emotional Intelligence Coaching*.
Philadelphia, PA: KoganPage.

Oxford Languages. (2023). *Soft Skills*. Retrieved March 11, 2023, from https://lan-
guages.oup.com/google-dictionary-en/

Robles, M. M. (2012). Executive perceptions of the top 10 soft skills needed in
today's workplace. *Business Communication Quarterly*, *75*(4), 453–465. https://
doi.org/10.1177/1080569912460400

Rothwell, W. J. (2015). *Organization Development Fundamentals: Managing
Strategic Change*. Alexandria, WV: ATD Press.

Sheck, D. T. L., & Lin, L. (2015). Intrapersonal competencies and service leadership. *International Journal of Disability Human Development*, *14*(3), 255–263.
https://doi.org/10.1515/ijdhd-2015-0406

Spencer, L. M., & Spencer, S. M. (1993). *Competence at Work. Models for Superior
Performance*. New York, NY: John Wiley and Sons.

Stevens, R. (2009). *Emotional Intelligence in Business: EQ, The Essential Ingredient
to Survive and Thrive as a Modern Workplace Leader*. Middletown, DE:
Self-Published.

Tulgan, B. (2015). *Bridging the Soft Skills Gap: How to Teach the Missing Basics to
Today's Young Talent*. Hoboken, NJ: John Willey & Sons, Inc. https://doi.org/10
.1002/9781119171409

Wall, B. (2007). *Coaching For Emotional Intelligence*. New York, NY: AMACON.

Wayne, J. (2019). *Emotional Intelligence 2.0. A Guide to Manage Anger, Overcome
Negativity ad Master Your Emotions*. Middletown, DE: Self-Published.

Whitmore, P. G., & Fry, J. P. (1972). What are soft skills. In *CONARC Soft Skills
Conference*. Fort Bliss, Texas.

## Chapter 11

The Relational Supervisor: Supervising with and through People

Introduction

As you steer through the complexities of today's global and dynamic work environment, remember that the needs and priorities of your team have evolved. Performance and profit are no longer the sole focus—your team members want more collaboration, meaningful connections, and community, essentially, they want better work relations (Chernyak-Hai & Rabenu, 2018).

In fostering strong relationships, you'll find your team more engaged and innovative. Employees with good relationships with their supervisors typically have higher job satisfaction and a more positive attitude. This improves morale, decreasing absenteeism and workplace conflict while increasing productivity and organizational commitment. However, building effective relationships in the workplace is an ongoing endeavor. It's not a one-time effort but a continuous process that demands persistence and dedication. As a supervisor, you'll find that fostering deep and meaningful connections with your team requires a consistent and proactive approach, and one key element is ensuring trust.

According to Serrat (2017), the emotions associated with trust include "affection, gratitude, security, confidence, acceptance, interest, admiration,

 DOI: 10.4324/9781003413493-11

respect, liking, appreciation, contentment, and satisfaction, all of them necessary ingredients of psychological health" (pp. 627–628). Trust is crucial for team unity. It helps build a sense of belonging and community within the team, which is essential for collaborative success. Trust is not just a nice-to-have quality; it's a strategic asset.

The relational supervisors must be skilled to effectively listen, provide constructive feedback, and engage in respectful discussions that let employees know how important they are to the organization. As opposed to being primarily task-oriented or transactional (focus on procedures and goals), supervisors are relationship-oriented (Yukl, Gordon, & Taber, 2002; Mikkelson et al., 2015). By focusing on relationships, the supervisors can help their employees feel like they are part of the workgroup. Specific relationship behaviors

> can include expressing encouragement to employees, increased levels of trust, respect, and camaraderie between the leader and the employees, and cooperation between employees … take an interest in employees, giving special attention to their individual needs … empowering employees to take initiative, consulting employees for input when making important decisions, and recognizing achievements and contributions … In short, relations-oriented leadership behaviors put an emphasis on treating employees with respect, building relationships, and making the work environment pleasant.
>
> **(Mikkelson et al., 2015, p. 340).**

Embracing a people-centric approach, you can foster meaningful connections rooted in mutual trust. Chapter 2 introduced some fundamental principles on working with and through people, instead of exerting control over them. We examined Social Exchange Theory, which posits that the quality of human interactions is influenced by the balance of perceived rewards and costs. By aligning this understanding with your team's motivations, you gain insights into their needs. We also introduced Daniel Goleman's Social Intelligence (SI) theory, which is closely related to emotional intelligence (EI). This chapter broadens the scope to include relational intelligence, as delineated by Pless and Maak in 2017.

As shown in Figure 11.1 of the *Successful Supervisory Leadership Series Book II Structure*, in this chapter, we will explore the concept of being a relational supervisor, focusing on how to nurture strong connections with your team. We

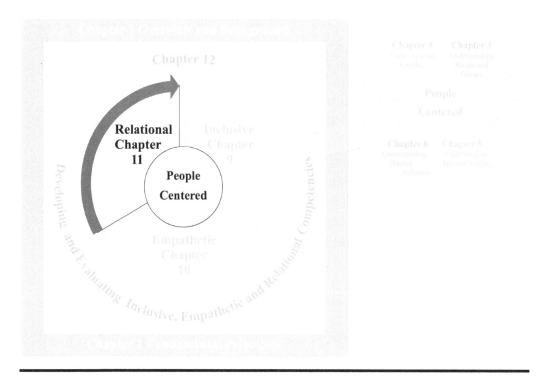

Figure 11.1 *Successful Supervisory Leadership Series Book II Structure.* **Note:** **Authors' original creation.**

will explain what it means to take a relational approach in leadership, understand the importance of relational intelligence in building these bonds, and how relational leadership can create a more cohesive team. Additionally, we'll examine the role of constructive communication in fostering these relationships.

Key Concepts

This chapter will cover the following key concepts:

- Understanding Relational Approach
- Understanding Relational Intelligence
  - Value of Relational Intelligence at Workplaces
- Understanding Relational Leadership
  - Fundamentals of Relational Leadership
  - Advantages of Relational Leadership in Guiding a Team
  - Practices for Developing Yourself as a Relational Supervisor
- Construction Communication
  - Principles of Constructive Communication

Definitions

The following definitions of key terms will help to better understand the main elements of this chapter:

Relational Approach

- Establishing genuine and reciprocal connections with people, as well as in our supervisory interactions, is the goal of a relational approach (Cunliffe & Eriksen, 2011).
- While connecting or talking with people, a relational approach encompasses fundamental principles including respect, inclusivity, honesty, compassion, collaboration, and humility (Relational Approach, 2023).

Relational Intelligence

- The ability to recognize and comprehend one's own and others' emotions, values, interests, and demands, to distinguish between them, to critically consider them, and to use this information to inform one's action and behavior with respect to people is what we refer to as relational intelligence. Relational intelligence is a combination of emotional intelligence and ethical intelligence (Pless & Maak, 2017).
- Relationship intelligence refers to a group of information about a company's common network of business contacts that influence how dealmakers use their time for locating, overseeing, and closing agreements (Jeannotte & Gobeil, 2019).

Relational Leadership

- A leadership style known as "relational leadership" focuses on a person's capacity to forge strong bonds with others within a team or organization (Feistritzer et al., 2022).
- Building relationships at work and utilizing those relationships to work in achieving a shared objective are key components of relational leadership (Jian, 2022).

Construction Communication

- Whether resolving problems or avoiding them altogether, constructive communication is a potent weapon to utilize. This style of communication clearly and constructively handles the problem between the communicators. It increases comprehension, offers adequate information for complete awareness, and conveys the message clearly (Whetten & Cameron, 2002).

Understanding the Relational Approach

There are many various relationship techniques, each of which is tailored to a particular circumstance. To develop and sustain positive connections, the most widely used relational approaches—like active listening and courtesy—are required. More organization and planning are required for alternative strategies. For instance, mentoring or circles can improve current connections and support the resolution of challenging issues (Relational Approach, 2023).

Certain methods are only utilized when there has been a crisis or breakdown in the relationship, and they often require a qualified facilitator to ensure that the discussion between those involved is safe and fruitful. For instance, mediation can end the tension and deadlocks that frequently result from disagreements. When someone has been harmed or wronged, restorative justice can assist to mend such connections (Relational Approach, 2023).

The following competencies and skills are very helpful in resolving issues using the relational approach:

- Interpersonal Skills For Building Relationships
- Effective Communication & Active listening For Establishing Trust and Reinforcing Relationships
- Problem-Solving Model to Create Clarity for Pathways to Resolutions
- Mediation Resolving Conflict

Perceived Organizational Support (POS)

Since it provides an explanation for the link between an organization's treatment of its workers and the employees' attitudes and actions toward their employment and the company, perceived organizational support (POS) is a key term in management literature. Employees' deepest thoughts regarding the organization's consideration and attention are reflected in their level of perceived organizational support (POS). The company is prepared to provide a helping hand in situations where employees need work or life assistance, and employees who have a feeling of POS feel personally acknowledged, cared for, and recognized (Kanten & Ulker, 2012).

Proactivity will be increased via organizational support mechanisms that assist and encourage staff to be self-directed and self-managing. Initiative, such as carrying out a task without being requested to do so, assertiveness, which may be classified as fixing a possible problem by taking control, such as reporting troublesome occurrences, and taking charge in general are characteristics of proactivity at work. The social interactionist theoretical framework that supports proactivity gave rise to the idea of proactive conduct (Kanten & Ulker, 2012).

Understanding Relational Intelligence

Relationships are sometimes viewed as a commodity, something that individuals purchase, sell, and trade for their personal benefit. Relationships are frequently valued for the wrong reasons by people. Relationships can occasionally be helpful for people when they strive to advance their own ambition or feed their own narcissism. This may be because they help them feel encouraged in an environment where they feel helpless or because it can help them get a large promotion at work (Saccone, 2009).

People easily become disposable when we place the incorrect value on relationships or when there is an absence of benefits to be had. But since they have the greatest importance and intersect with the very heart of what it is to be human, relationships cannot be reduced to commodities or treated as disposable. The quality of our human experience is determined by how we choose to relate to one another, which also exposes what we value most. This is the starting point of the relational intelligence journey (Saccone, 2009).

In an interconnected and globalized world, organizations and their leaders (including management and supervisors) confront significant difficulties. Leaders must cope with the challenges of ethics, diversity, business in society, and stakeholder management to effectively navigate the 21st century. These difficulties also influence the relationship aspects of their leadership obligations and positions. The requirement to communicate with diverse stakeholders from varied cultural backgrounds in and outside of the organization, with distinct interests and beliefs, demands leaders to connect and to behave interpersonally and morally competent (Pless & Maak, 2017).

Furthermore, Pless and Maak (2017) described, as a result, that in order to handle the current leadership difficulties emotionally and morally maturely, leaders require relational intelligence. The ability to recognize and comprehend one's own and others' emotions, values, interests, and demands, to make distinctions between them, to critically consider them, and to use this information to inform one's action and behavior regarding people is what we refer to as relational intelligence in this context. Relational intelligence is a combination of emotional intelligence and ethical intelligence.

Pless and Maak (2017) propose and provide an initial moral of relational intelligence based on this notion. Using real-world examples, we demonstrate how relational intelligence, which is influenced by emotional and ethical skills, may direct leadership behavior in encounters, assisting leaders in resolving difficult moral and cultural problems. Relational intelligence can assist global leaders in meeting their leadership difficulties by assisting them in effectively interacting across boundaries and establishing long-lasting connections with numerous stakeholders (Pless & Maak, 2017).

Our capacity as humans to connect with and build trust with others is known as relational intelligence. You might be wondering how emotional intelligence and relational intelligence are related if you've heard of either one before. We believe that high emotional intelligence supports the growth and expansion of relational intelligence. Building relationships is easier when you can recognize and comprehend your own feelings as well as those of others (Cardiff, McCormack & McCance, 2018).

Emotional Intelligence versus Relational Intelligence

Realistically speaking, relational intelligence is the capacity to positively connect with others and create enduring connections, as indicated above. The capacity to comprehend your own emotions, others' feelings, and how to effectively manage emotions is the true definition of emotional intelligence (Jian, 2022).

Value of Relational Intelligence at Workplaces

Organizations and individuals find it challenging to keep up with the rapid changes taking place in the workplace. The question is not if these changes will occur; rather, it is how to cope with them, as Gallup continues to show in their studies (Jeannotte & Gobeil, 2019). Several studies demonstrate that while we are more linked than ever in the digital world, we find it difficult to maintain that connection in our daily lives. The quality of our connections at work frequently dictates the quality of our job and our success, just as partnerships improve our personal life. More meaningful conversations, creative ideas, and ultimately better business outcomes result from stronger connections (Jeannotte & Gobeil, 2019).

Evidence for powerful relationships at the workplace:

a. Individuals and teams gladly exchange knowledge and lessons learned with one another.
b. They are open and honest with one another.
c. They are eager to try new things and think outside the box.

The effect of powerful relationships at the workplace on the organization:

a. Silos are shattered and teams collaborate more quickly and effectively toward shared goals as a result of the absence of fear of failure.
b. Alignment also rises as a result of the absence of the fear of having tough or sensitive talks.
c. There is an increase of camaraderie and teamwork.

Those with high levels of relational intelligence are more likely to be engaged in their work, produce better and more original ideas, collaborate more effectively as a team, and have a greater sense of common meaning and objective. Thus, it is crucial that managers promote and nurture these interpersonal ties both in and out of their team (Jeannotte & Gobeil, 2019).

Understanding Relational Leadership

A leadership style known as "relational leadership" focuses on the efficacy of a leader and how well they can establish enduring bonds with their followers. It also has to do with the process of individuals cooperating to advance society or bring about a constructive change as a group of experts (Lee & Nelson, 2013). Empathy is a powerful tool that relational leaders use to encourage their employees to strengthen their existing talents and learn new ones. The relational leaders' objective is to foster professional development in their team members via encouraging social development and growth in order to accomplish a shared objective (Falls, 2009).

Fundamentals of Relational Leadership

Like any other style of leadership, according to Kim (2022), Cardiff, McCormack and McCance (2018), and Reitz (2015), the relational leadership style has some key fundamental principles as highlighted in Figure 11.2.

Ethical Performance

Ethics are the moral principles that influence a leader's choice or production of a result. Relational leaders frequently uphold high moral standards and follow morally responsible decision-making practices. This leadership approach molds leadership habits through ethics. By employing ethics, leaders may demonstrate behaviors that will inspire their team members, make them feel included, and help them build trust with one another. Relational leaders frequently set the standard for how their team members should behave in order to accomplish their goals successfully through leading by example.

Inclusive and Diverse Leadership

A relational leader encourages diversity, especially when it comes to the thoughts and opinions of the team. Before making a change or making a decision, these leaders take into account all points of view in order to decide what modifications to make. They also take into account any queries and concerns that team members may have. For instance, a relational leader will often consult with their team members before introducing a new policy. A

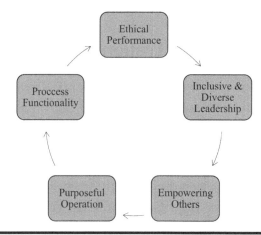

Figure 11.2   Fundamentals of relational leadership. *Note*: Authors' original creation.

relational leader serves as a bridge to enable those team members to make a difference, whereas an inclusive leader fosters an atmosphere where all team members may positively impact a firm.

Empowering Others

It's crucial to provide team members the freedom to make independent judgments and to express their thoughts and opinions freely if you want to be an effective relational leader. By including people in group choices, these leaders give their team members a sense of empowerment. For instance, they may have a team gathering where all are free to voice their opinions and engage in open discussions. Offering team members this amount of autonomy may make them feel as if they're making a difference for the better, which may boost their motivation at work.

Purposeful Operation

A relational leader is intentional in sticking to each objective while establishing connections with other team members. These leaders can assist in arranging the objectives, identifying the shared aims, and predicting how these objectives will turn out. All team members are included in the process of envisioning outcomes by a good relational leader, which gives them a sense of inclusion, importance, and purpose. Before beginning a project, this kind of leader will have individual meetings with team members to make sure they are aware of their roles in achieving the overarching objective. By doing this, each team member will be made to feel important.

Process Functionality

Process functionality describes how a group interacts and works as a unit. A good relational leader recognizes that the journey toward a goal is just as important as the destination. This leadership approach guarantees that every team member knows what to do and when to do it in order to achieve the team's objectives. A relational leader would, for instance, schedule a meeting before the start of a project to make sure team members are aware of their responsibilities, deadlines, and objectives. They keep a careful eye on the procedure as the project develops.

As a supervisor, please use Table 11.1 to rate your participation and use of key fundamentals of relational leadership at your workplace.

Table 11.1 Supervisor's Rating on Understanding and Practicing Fundamentals of Relational Leadership at Workplace

Supervisor's Rating on Understanding and Practicing Fundamentals of Relational Leadership at the Workplace						
Supervisor's Name		Date		Supervisor's Manager		
Rating Scale: 1 = Poor, 2 = Marginal, 3 = Acceptable, 4 = Good, 5 = Excellent						
Fundamentals of Relational Leadership		*1*	*2*	*3*	*4*	*5*
1	Ethical performance					
2	Inclusive and diverse leadership					
3	Empowering others					
4	Purposeful operation					
5	Process functionality and workability					
Individual Columns' Totals						
Total of above Individual Columns						
Final Average (above total divided by 5)						

Note: Authors' original creation.

Now use Table 11.2 to formulate a series of actions to increase your understanding of Table 11.1.

Advantages of Relational Leadership in Guiding a Team

The following are some of the advantages of using a relational leadership style for guiding your team at the workplace, as suggested by Kim (2022), Cardiff, McCormack, and McCance (2018), and Reitz (2015) (see Figure 11.3).

Reinforcing Your Team Morale

By giving your team members more responsibility, you can make them feel important and appreciated and ultimately boost morale on your team. High team morale encourages members to appreciate their work further and work together to accomplish team objectives. By fostering a supportive and collaborative work atmosphere, you may raise team morale. Celebrating both individual and team accomplishments is advantageous. Professionals must also

Table 11.2   APLI-Connected to Table 11.1

Action Plan for Learning and Improving	
Area of Learning and Improving: *Supervisor's Rating on Understanding and Practicing Fundamentals of Relational Leadership at Workplace*	
Reference: *Table 11.1*	
Three learning and improvement actions for this month that will raise my understanding and awareness regarding *"Supervisor's Rating on Understanding and Practicing Fundamentals of Relational Leadership at Workplace"* to enhance my knowledge and clarity by at least one on the next rating:	
Action 1:	By When:
Action 2:	By When:
Action 3:	By When:

Note: Authors' original creation.

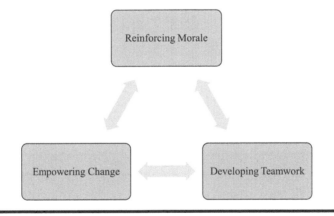

Figure 11.3   Advantages of relational leadership. *Note*: Authors' original creation.

maintain a healthy work–life balance in order to be motivated and remain focused when working.

Developing and Upgrading Teamwork

Team members cooperate to achieve a successful workplace objective in this leadership paradigm. To determine if team members are in roles that are appropriate for their talents, you can develop open feedback and communication. You may build this open conversation if you say that you appreciate constructive criticism, even if it disagrees with your opinions. You might schedule private sessions with them so they can discuss ideas or issues they might be reluctant to bring up in front of others.

Empowering and Enhancing Change

Since it creates a basis for your team in order to collaborate to accomplish a common objective, this leadership style may hasten transformation. Your team might concentrate on working together to accomplish more manageable, shared objectives. You may make sure that all team members are aware of their individual aims and how they participate to achieve the team's goals. This tactic can aid in the group's visualization of more expansive shared objectives and make them appear more doable.

Practices for Developing Yourself as a Relational Supervisor

Here are some simple but effective suggestions for practices that will help you develop yourself as a relational supervisor at your workplace while leading your workforces as suggested by Nicholsen and Kurucz (2019), Lee and Nelson (2013), and Falls (2009).

Be Honest and Authentic

By working with your people in a genuine, honest, and sincere manner, you may help to build trust in the workplace. For instance, you may openly discuss your motivations for achieving the organization's goals with the entire team, share corporate goals and values with them, and invite their input. Gaining the group's trust that you have both the organizations' and their best interests in mind and being honest may help you carry out your obligations to the group.

Establish Meaningful Relationships

Finding significance in your connections may assist you in developing empathy for your peers and employees. You may help your peers and employees advance their talents by being aware of the importance of the relationships you are building. People can develop a strong bond via empathy, which may inspire them to produce great work while pursuing a goal.

Practice Active Listening

Active listening is a crucial skill to develop because it keeps you positively connected with your discussion partner. Active listening is crucial in effective communication. The other person feels heard and appreciated as a result as well. In any situation—at work, at home, or in social settings—this ability is the cornerstone of a successful dialogue.

Get Familiar with Your People

You might set apart specific times to speak with each team member and attempt to comprehend their professional and personal objectives. You may inquire about them and discover how they are now feeling both personally and as a team member. Establishing a personal connection with your team members helps encourage them to perform successfully and efficiently. This can be done by demonstrating that you care about them beyond simply their task.

Give Recognition When It Is Due

There are some quite significant individuals in your company, and many of them are unaware of exactly how significant they are. They most certainly aren't receiving the respect they merit. Consider the range of positions everyone holds at their place of employment. What are their most significant duties? It doesn't matter if the job has the lowest or greatest compensation. Everyone contributes something important to the business, and everyone must work together to advance the organization's vision and goal. They should receive the praise they merit for the distinctive and crucial roles they play inside your firm.

Exhibit Appreciation

Recognizing the contributions that each member of your team has made is crucial for relationship leadership. This acknowledgment might boost morale, which would increase output, revenue, and shared goal accomplishment. You may show your gratitude in a variety of ways.

Provide Positive Feedback

Positive feedback encourages drive, builds self-esteem, and demonstrates your appreciation for others. It aids in understanding and skill development.

The effectiveness of individuals, teams, and organizations are all positively impacted by all of this. Positive feedback is more than merely saying "excellent work," which may occasionally come across as evasive or disingenuous. It's preferable to use the "what & why" strategy instead. The "What & Why" strategy explains to others what about their actions or conduct you found impressive and why what they did was successful. With this method, you may provide feedback that is quite straight and to the point so that the person understands precisely what is expected of them.

Become an Influencer

Seeing oneself as an influential leader is crucial to developing your confidence and being a successful relational leader. This advice can help you take your actions and words seriously since you'll be more aware of how they affect other people. Prominent managers may show their team members the way to success, and because of their assurance, team members may have more faith in their manager.

Use Table 11.3 for rating yourself on practices for developing yourself as a relational supervisor.

Now use Table 11.4 to formulate a series of actions to increase your understanding of Table 11.3.

Constructive Communication

By addressing issues, constructive communication upholds the rapport between the communicators. Conversely, ineffective communication strategies might make issues worse.

The concepts of constructive communication are especially crucial when coaching or advising an employee who has a poor attitude, a personality problem with a coworker, or hasn't performed up to expectations. In these situations, there is a significant chance that the employee will get defensive. In reaction, many managers choose to adopt a "hard-nosed" attitude and forego bothering about employees' sentiments. Many other managers take it a step further and completely avoid dealing with issues (Peterson et al., 2016). Addressing the problem while utilizing the qualities of constructive communication is a superior strategy for handling these circumstances.

By lowering defensiveness, constructive communication helps managers be more effective in coaching and counseling. If they believe they are being

Table 11.3   Supervisor's Rating on Practices for Developing Yourself as a Relational Supervisor

Supervisor's Rating on Practices for Developing Yourself as a Relational Supervisor							
Supervisor's Name		Date		Supervisor's Manager			
Rating Scale: *1* = Poor, *2* = Marginal, *3* = Acceptable, *4* = Good, *5* = Excellent							
Practices			*1*	*2*	*3*	*4*	*5*
1	Be honest and authentic						
2	Establish meaningful relationships						
3	Practice active listening						
4	Get familiar with your people						
5	Give recognition when it is due						
6	Exhibit appreciation						
7	Provide positive feedback						
8	Become an influencer						
Individual Columns' Totals							
Total of above Individual Columns							
Final Average (above total divided by 8)							

Note: Authors' original creation.

reprimanded or threatened by the speech, subordinates frequently respond defensively. While acting defensively, subordinates focus on finding opposing reasons rather than listening. Because of this, positive communication is more effective (Peterson et al., 2016).

Principles of Constructive Communication

When coaching or advising a member of your team, constructive communication is very beneficial. A badly conducted performance review can easily result in defensiveness and even outright rejection of any recommendations for change. According to Whetten and Cameron (2002), the following principles are valuable for managers and supervisors to pay attention to and have

Table 11.4 APLI-Connected to Table 11.3

Action Plan for Learning and Improving	
Area of Learning and Improving: *Supervisor's Rating on Practices for Developing Yourself as a Relational Supervisor.*	
Reference: *Table 11.3*	
Three learning and improvement actions for this month that will raise my understanding and awareness regarding *"Supervisor's Rating on Practices for Developing Yourself as a Relational Supervisor"* to enhance my knowledge and clarity by at least one on the next rating:	
Action 1:	By When:
Action 2:	By When:
Action 3:	By When:

Note: Authors' original creation.

on their minds when they are trying to resolve issues with their employees by using constructive communication.

Problem-Focused Communication

Communication that is problem-focused puts the emphasis on a problem that can be fixed rather than the offender. Person-focused communication places the recipient on guard and concentrates on placing blame rather than preventing or resolving future issues.

Congruent Communication

Congruent communication accurately reflects the speaker's thoughts and emotions. Some circumstances call for prudence rather than complete openness about our thoughts and feelings. But being honest helps us communicate more successfully in the majority of instances. Listeners won't believe what we say if we aren't honest. When we communicate congruently, we are being productive because we are telling the other side the truth instead of taking a misleading approach.

Descriptive Communication

The listeners or their behaviors are subject to judgment in evaluative communication. Instead of speaking in an evaluative way about issues, we should express them objectively if we want to communicate constructively. The listener becomes defensive when you communicate in an evaluative way.

Validating Communication

People benefit from validating communication by feeling heard, appreciated, and accepted. Invalidating communication, on the other hand, treats individuals as if they are unimportant, useless, or estranged. Communication that invalidates is superiority-focused, inflexible, unyielding, and/or disinterested. By validating communication, one avoids becoming obstinate, impermeable, or apathetic toward the listeners or regarding them as a lesser human being. Even when there is a difference of opinion, validating communication demonstrates respect for the other party's opinions and feelings.

Specific Communication

General explanations of issues have two major flaws: they frequently oversimplify and misrepresent problems, and they are frequently too big to be solved. Specific communication will pinpoint the issue at hand and as a result will lead to accessing the actual issue.

Conjunctive Communication

Disjunctive communication can take at least three different forms, including avoiding eye contact and diverting the subject. The other person may believe that their opinions are not being taken into account if there is disjunctive communication. It is not productive to have a debate that veers from one subject to another without concluding on any of them.

Owned Communication

When we completely and responsibly own our communication, we accept accountability for our words and recognize that we, and not anyone else, are the source of our words. When we look for outside persons to hold responsible for our comments, we disown communication. A person who owns their words earns our respect.

Listening

Good and effective listening is actively taking in the information that is being conveyed to you by a speaker, demonstrating your interest and attentiveness, and responding to the speaker so that he or she is aware that the message was understood. While it's sometimes taken for granted, effective listening is an important managerial skill.
(Whetten & Cameron, 2002).

What's Next?

In the end, "Appendix A" reviews sources for education and implementation of practices drawn from the book, which will take you to other sources that can broaden and deepen your understanding of the Inclusive, Empathetic, and Relational Supervisor.

Key Takeaways

1. The relationship between supervisors and their direct reports requires mutual trust. Trust is emotional and does not happen instantaneously.
2. There are many various relationship techniques, each of which is tailored to a particular circumstance. To develop and sustain positive connections, the most widely used relational approaches—like active listening and courtesy—are required.
3. People easily become disposable when we place the incorrect value on relationships or when there is an absence of benefit to be had. But since they have the greatest importance and intersect with the very heart of what it is to be human, relationships cannot be reduced to a commodity or treated as disposable.
4. A leadership style known as "relational leadership" focuses on the efficacy of a leader and how well they can establish enduring bonds with their followers. It also has to do with the process of individuals cooperating to advance society or bring about a constructive change as a group of experts (Lee & Nelson, 2013).

Table 11.5 End of Chapter 11 Questions and Inquiries. Your Perspective on What You Learned in Chapter 11

Your Perspective on What You Learned in Chapter 11	
Area of Inquiry	*What Did You Learn, and How Are You Going to Implement It in Your Position?*
Understanding relational approach	
Understanding relational intelligence	
Emotional intelligence vs. relational intelligence	
Understanding relational leadership	
Fundamentals of relational leadership	
Practices for developing yourself as a relational supervisor	
Construction communication	

Note: Authors' original creation.

5. The concepts of constructive communication are especially crucial when coaching or advising an employee who has a poor attitude, a personality problem with a coworker, or hasn't performed up to expectations.

Discussion Questions and Inquiries

Please take a minute to answer the following inquiries and questions in Table 11.5. From your point of view, what have you learned about the following areas?

References

Cardiff, S., McCormack, B., & McCance, T. (2018). Person-centered leadership: A relational approach to leadership derived through action research. *Journal of Clinical Nursing, 27*(15–16), 3056–3069. https://doi.org/10.1111/jocn.14492

Chernyak-Hai, L., & Rabenu, E. (2018). The new era workplace relationships: Is social exchange theory still relevant? *Industrial and Organizational Psychology, 11*(3), 456–481. https://doi.org/10.1017/iop.2018.5

Cunliffe, A. L., & Eriksen, M. (2011). Relational leadership. *Human Relations, 64*(11), 1425–1449. https://doi.org/10.1177/0018726711418388

Falls, L. (2009). Relational supervision case study. *Psychodynamic Practice, 15*(2), 173–179. https://doi.org/10.1080/14753630902811383

Feistritzer, N. R., Jackson, G., Scott, C., & Willis, P. (2022). Complex relational leadership: Meeting the challenge of post pandemic professional governance. *Nursing Administration Quarterly, 46*(2), 144–153. https://doi.org/10.1097/NAQ .0000000000000519

Jeannotte, J., & Gobeil, V. (2019). How to build great relationships at work with relational intelligence. Officevibe website. Retrieved March 15, 2023, from https://officevibe.com/blog/building-relational-intelligence

Jian, G. (2022). From empathic leader to empathic leadership practice: An extension to relational leadership theory. *Human Relations, 75*(5), 931–955. https://doi .org/10.1177/0018726721998450

Kanten, P., & Ulker, F. E. (2012). A relational approach among perceived organizational support, proactive personality and voice behaviour. *Procedia, Social and Behavioral Sciences, 62*, 1016–1022. https://doi.org/10.1016/j.sbspro.2012.09 .173

Kim, K. (2022). Supervisor leadership and subordinates' innovative work behaviors: Creating a relational context for organizational sustainability. *Sustainability, 14*(6), 3230. https://doi.org/10.3390/su14063230

Lee, R. E., & Nelson, T. S. (2013). *The Contemporary Relational Supervisor*. New York, NY: Routledge.

Mikkelson, A. C., York, J. A., & Arritola, J. (2015). Communication competence, leadership behaviors, and employee outcomes in supervisor-employee relationships. *Business and Professional Communication Quarterly*, *78*(3), 336–354. https://doi.org/10.1177/2329490615588542?journalCode=bcqe

Nicholson, J., & Kurucz, E. (2019). Relational leadership for sustainability: Building an ethical framework from the moral theory of 'ethics of care'. *Journal of Business Ethics*, *156*(1), 25–43. https://doi.org/10.1007/s10551-017-3593-4

Peterson, T. R., Bergeå, H. L., Feldpausch-Parker, A. M., & Raitio, K. (2016). *Environmental Communication and Community: Constructive and Destructive Dynamics of Social Transformation*. New York, NY: Routledge.

Pless, N. M., & Maak, T. (2017). Relational intelligence for leading responsibility in a connected world. *Academy of Management*, *2005*(1). https://doi.org/10.5465/ambpp.2005.18783524

Reitz, M. (2015). *Dialogue in Organizations: Developing Relational Leadership*. New York, NY: Palgrave Macmillan. https://doi.org/10.1007/978-1-137-48912-8

Relational Approach Website. (2023). What is relational approach? Retrieved March 25, 2023, from https://relationalapproaches.com/approaches/

Saccone, S. (2009). *Relational Intelligence*. San Francisco, CA: Jossey-Bass, a Wiley Imprint.

Serrat, O. (2017). Understanding and developing emotional intelligence. In *Knowledge Solutions* (pp. 329–339). Singapore: Springer. https://doi.org/10.1007/978-981-10-0983-9_37

Whetten, D. A., & Cameron, K. S. (2002). *Developing Management Skills* (5th ed.). Upper Saddle River, NJ: Prentice-Hall.

Yukl, G., Gordon, A., & Taber, T. (2002). A hierarchical taxonomy of leadership behavior: Integrating a half century of behavior research. *Journal of Leadership & Organizational Studies*, *9*(1), 15–32. https://doi.org/10.1177/107179190200900102?journalCode=jlob

Chapter 12

Developing and Evaluating Inclusive, Empathetic, and Relational Supervisor Competencies

Introduction

In this final chapter, we synthesize everything and focus on developing and evaluating your competencies as an inclusive, empathetic, and relational supervisor. Think of competencies as the blueprint of an exceptional supervisor, distinct from the mundane checklist of a job description. It's not simply about the task you complete but also about your influence, the passion you bring to work, the camaraderie you foster among employees, and how you energize your team. As a supervisor with an inclusive mindset, ask yourself: Are my actions cultivating a workplace that celebrates diversity, where each member is recognized, and their contributions are leveraged? Do I champion an atmosphere of respect that not only allows but encourages individuals to reach their fullest potential? As an empathetic supervisor, consider whether you are attuned to your team's emotional and intellectual needs. Are you shaping a culture that values understanding and emotional engagement, which encourages everyone but also strengthens team bonds, increases performance, and improves job contentment? Finally, as a supervisor with a relational focus, consider whether you prioritize building robust, supportive relationships with your team members.

DOI: 10.4324/9781003413493-12

This inclusive and empathetic approach to building workplace relationships not only attracts talented and diverse workers but also lowers turnover rates, positioning your organization as a desirable employer. By being able to see the value in different viewpoints and manage interpersonal dynamics effectively, you create an atmosphere conducive to open communication and collaborative problem-solving. This not only refines your decision-making but also turns conflicts into opportunities for growth. By focusing on these skills, you not only create a positive and innovative team culture but also contribute to your organization's success, making it more attractive to potential employees, clients, and investors who value a socially responsible business.

As shown in Figure 12.1 of the *Successful Supervisory Leadership Series Book II Structure*, this final chapter presents a detailed list of key competencies that supervisors can cultivate. It outlines strategic approaches to promote inclusiveness, empathy, and the ability to build meaningful relationships within the workplace. In addition, we will present evaluation instruments to assess both expectations for supervisors and the effectiveness with

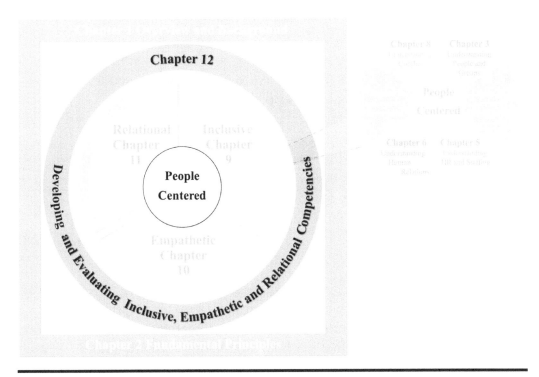

Figure 12.1 *Successful Supervisory Leadership Series Book II Structure.* **Note: Authors' original creation.**

which they meet these standards. Completing the chapter is a concise summary that encapsulates the insights of a people-centered approach to supervision. We conclude this book with a brief overview of "Book III: *Engaged and Organized Supervisor.*"

Key Concepts

This chapter will cover the following key concepts:

- Overview of Inclusive, Empathetic, and Relational Competencies
- Strategies for Developing Inclusive, Empathetic, and Relational Competencies
- Self-Assessment Tools and Reflection Practices
- Preview of Book III: *Engaged and Organized Supervisor*

Definitions

The following definitions of key terms will help better understand the main elements of this chapter:

- **Competencies:** "Competencies are the tools that are used for all performance" (Rothwell et al., 2015 pp. 1–9). They are

  characteristic[s] of an employee (i.e., a body of knowledge, skill, trait, or behavior) that results in effective and/or superior performance....Traits or behaviors can be considered competencies when they can be shown to directly contribute to the successful achievement of one or more job outputs or results.

  (2015, 1-27–1-28)

- **Behavioral Indicators:**

  is a statement of a behavior, action, or psychomotor response that an observer can expect to observe ... that they make the competency "real" or "come alive" ... help all persons correctly understand and learn how to practice the use of the competency for successful performance.

  (2015, 2-55–2-56)

■ **Individual Development Plan (IDP):** "an action plan intended to help individuals narrow performance/development gaps or to leverage their individual strengths" (Rothwell & Graber, 2010, Chapter 3).

Overview of Inclusive, Empathetic, and Relational Competencies

As a supervisor, your role goes beyond task management; it is about fostering a culture in which each team member feels truly valued and supported. You can achieve this goal by promoting inclusivity, exhibiting empathy, and focusing on relationship building. It's about celebrating diversity in identities, experiences, and ideas, which in turn enriches the decision-making process. Proactively challenge biases, encourages open conversations, and implement policies that uphold fairness and equality at the workplace. It is about understanding your colleagues, cultivating trust, and addressing their well-being. Moreover, your relational competencies are the glue that holds the team together. Through clear communication, adept conflict resolution, and an inspiring presence, you can nurture a cooperative atmosphere that primes your team for collaborative success and innovative problem-solving. We recommend reading Chapter 5 of *Book I, Successful Supervisory Leadership: Exerting Positive Influence while Leading People*, to learn more about the essential competencies of a positive and influential supervisor.

The following list (Table 12.1) is a list of supervisory competencies focusing specifically on promoting inclusivity, exhibiting empathy, and building relationships. The first column lists the associated competencies (alphabetical order), based on the previous chapters. The second column lists the corresponding behavioral indicators. Using this list, you can create a plan of action for development and evaluate your progress.

As you utilize this list of competencies, remember that it's neither universal nor exhaustive. You will find that many behavioral indicators overlap between different competencies. Although we have only listed each one once to save space, do not overlook their multifaceted nature. Remember, competencies are inherently personal attributes, not tied to job descriptions. To cultivate your supervisory skills, begin by identifying the unique competencies within your organization through observing those who excel—those who best embody the essence of an inclusive, empathetic, and relational supervisor. Based on your desired competencies, create a development plan and leverage your individual strengths (Rothwell & Graber, 2010).

Table 12.1 Inclusive, Empathetic, and Relational Competencies

#	Competencies	Description	Behavioral Indicators
1	Accessibility and accommodation	Ensure the workplace is accessible to all employees, including those with disabilities. This means advocating for changes that allow individuals with diverse abilities to participate fully in work tasks, communication, and team activities.	Actively seeks and acts on feedback about accommodations, showing a commitment to continual improvement.
			Adjusts information sharing to ensure it is understandable and accessible to everyone.
			Educates the team on the importance of an accessible workplace and how to respectfully interact with colleagues who require accommodations.
			Regularly checks and updates the workplace for barriers and accessibility.
2	Active listening	Listens attentively with feedback or questions for clarification. It involves engaging with the speaker to signal understanding and encourage them to continue speaking.	Asks questions that prompt further discussion and demonstrate they are processing the information and seeking to understand.
			Engages by nodding, facing the speaker, and maintaining an open posture.
			Gives the speaker full attention, avoiding distractions and making eye contact (as culturally appropriate).
			Reserves judgment and allows the speaker to finish expressing themselves.
			Uses paraphrasing or summarizing to confirm understanding and show that they are truly listening.

(Continued)

Table 12.1 (Continued) Inclusive, Empathetic, and Relational Competencies

		Inclusive, Empathetic, and Relational Competencies	
#	Competencies	Description	Behavioral Indicators
3	Adaptability and flexibility	Adjusts management style and approach to the evolving needs and dynamics of the team. Being adaptable, willing to change plans based on team input, and supportive during transitions.	Adjusts leadership style to meet team needs and strengths, fostering a supportive environment.
			Navigates smoothly while considering and responding to team members' concerns.
			Seeks input from diverse team members and adapts plans or strategies to reflect insights.
4	Collaborative problem-solving	Actively involving the team in tackling challenges, leveraging diverse perspectives to find innovative solutions. Encourages team member input to the decision-making process to ensure shared responsibility and commitment to results.	Actively engages different team members in the conversation to ensure a wide range of perspectives.
			Aspires to achieve group agreement by integrating diverse viewpoints and facilitating open discussions that lead to shared solutions.
			Encourages team members to share ideas and builds on their contributions.
			Facilitates conversations to keep the team focused on goals and outcomes.
			Keeps the problem-solving process transparent, updating the team on developments and decisions.
			Remains open to all approaches, avoiding premature judgments.

(Continued)

Table 12.1 (Continued) Inclusive, Empathetic, and Relational Competencies

#	Competencies	Inclusive, Empathetic, and Relational Competencies	
		Description	Behavioral Indicators
5	Conflict resolution	Recognize, address, and resolve disagreements within the team constructively and empathically. Facilitates open communication between conflicting parties, aiming for a mutually satisfactory solution while maintaining positive working relationships.	Focuses on identifying the root causes of conflicts and works collaboratively to find workable solutions.
			Guides conversations toward resolution without escalating tension.
			Maintains an unbiased stance when mediating conflicts, avoiding favoritism.
			Monitors the situation post-resolution to ensure that agreements are implemented, and the conflict does not reemerge.
			Remains composed and can manage emotions, even when conflicts become heated.
			Shows genuine concern for the feelings and viewpoints of all parties involved in a conflict.
6	Continuous learning	A commitment to ongoing personal and professional development as well as encouraging growth among team members. Seeks to expand their own knowledge and skills, but also create opportunities for their team to learn, adapt, and innovate within their roles.	Applies new knowledge and skills to practical work scenarios, demonstrating the value of continuous learning.
			Applies new knowledge and skills to practical work scenarios, demonstrating the value of continuous learning.
			Regularly seeks opportunities for self-improvement and encourages team members to continuously learn.
			Regularly seeks opportunities for self-improvement and encourages team members to continuously learn.
			Shares insights and learning experiences with the team, fostering a culture of knowledge exchange.

(Continued)

Table 12.1 (Continued) Inclusive, Empathetic, and Relational Competencies

		Inclusive, Empathetic, and Relational Competencies	
#	Competencies	Description	Behavioral Indicators
7	Cultural sensitivity	Awareness of and respect for diverse cultural backgrounds, beliefs, and practices. Effectively integrating this understanding into their management practices, ensuring an inclusive environment that acknowledges and values the contributions of all team members.	Demonstrates commitment to learning about the cultures represented within their team.
			Encourages employees to express their cultural identity and integrates cultural traditions into workplace practices where appropriate.
			Includes a range of cultural perspectives when making decisions that affect the team.
			Promotes diversity in the workplace through policies and practices.
			Reflects on personal biases and actively works to mitigate its impact on the team.
8	Delegation	Assigns tasks and responsibilities to employees based on their strengths, skills, and developmental needs. It requires trusting employees in their ability to perform tasks and provide the resources and support they need to promote growth and accountability.	Acknowledges and appreciates employees who take on delegated tasks, fostering a sense of accomplishment and motivation.
			Assigns tasks that align with employees' skills, career aspirations, and developmental needs to enhance their growth.
			Communicates the objectives, deadlines, and performance standards of delegated tasks.
			Encourages employees to take responsibility for their tasks and make decisions within their authority.
			Ensures employees have the resources, information, and authority to successfully complete the tasks.
			Provides guidance and support when challenges arise, without taking over the task.

(Continued)

Table 12.1 (Continued) Inclusive, Empathetic, and Relational Competencies

#	Competencies	Description	Behavioral Indicators
9	Disciplinary action	Addresses employee misconduct or performance issues fairly and constructively, focusing on corrective measures. It requires clear communication about current issues, consistent workplace policy enforcement, and a clear path to improvement and professional growth.	Keeps detailed and accurate records of disciplinary processes and actions for transparency and accountability.
			Explains the reasons for disciplinary actions clearly and directly to the employee involved.
			Addresses disciplinary issues with respect and dignity, preserving the employee's self-respect throughout the process.
			Complies with legal guidelines and organizational policies when taking disciplinary action to avoid potential liabilities.
			Maintains confidentiality and handles disciplinary matters in private settings to avoid unnecessary embarrassment or gossip.
			Monitors the employee's progress after disciplinary action to ensure improvement and provide continuous feedback.
10	Effective communication	Convey information and expectations with team members and ensure mutual understanding. Promotes an environment of transparent and two-way communication through actively listening and assessing the input of others.	Adjusts communication style to meet the diverse needs of team members and accommodate their various communication preferences.
			Delivers messages consistently across all mediums and ensures actions match the words to build trust and credibility.
			Engages in conversations that promote dialogue, not monologues, to enable an exchange of ideas and perspectives.

(Continued)

Table 12.1 (Continued) Inclusive, Empathetic, and Relational Competencies

#	Competencies	Description	Inclusive, Empathetic, and Relational Competencies
			Behavioral Indicators
			Offers timely and constructive feedback, recognizes employee efforts, and guides their improvement.
			Provides clear, concise instructions, summarizes key points, and asks for feedback to ensure understanding.
			Uses inclusive, respectful language, avoids jargon, and translates materials as necessary to ensure everyone understands.
			Uses positive non-verbal cues, such as eye contact, gestures, and body language to reinforce verbal messages.
11	Empathy	Understands and shares the feelings of their employees and recognizes their individual experiences and perspectives. It enables the supervisor to create a supportive and trusting environment where employees feel valued and understood, fostering positive relationships and a collaborative team culture.	Allows employees to express their thoughts and feelings without interrupting or dismissing them prematurely.
			Checks in with employees to show sustained interest and concern for their well-being.
			Demonstrates understanding through body language, such as nodding and maintaining eye contact, which shows attention and concern.
			Offers words of encouragement and support and validates employees' experiences and challenges.
			Recognizes and verbalizes understanding of employees' emotions.
			Remains open to the ideas and perspectives of employees.

(Continued)

Table 12.1 (Continued) Inclusive, Empathetic, and Relational Competencies

#	Competencies	Description	Behavioral Indicators
		Inclusive, Empathetic, and Relational Competencies	
12	Equity mindset	Recognizes and addresses systemic inequalities within the workplace, ensuring all employees have the same opportunities for growth, development, and success. It involves actively working to understand the unique challenges faced by different groups and individuals, and making informed decisions that contribute to a fair and just working environment.	Actively promotes an environment where diverse perspectives are sought, valued, and integrated into decision-making processes.
			Ensures all team members have access to professional development, promotions, and important projects.
			Maintains openness in decision-making processes to build trust and ensure fairness.
			Provides individualized support to employees based on their specific circumstances to help them overcome obstacles to success.
			Sets clear goals for equity and inclusion within the team and stands accountable for meeting them.
13	External awareness	Understands the broader context in which the organization operates, including economic, social, political, cultural, and technological trends. It requires anticipating and responding to external events or changes that could impact the team or organization, ensuring adaptability and proactive strategy alignment.	Keeps abreast of regulatory changes and ensures the team understands and complies with relevant laws and regulations.
			Keeps informed about current and emerging trends, and how they can affect the organization and its workforce.
			Keeps updated on new technologies that could offer opportunities for innovation or pose threats to the organization's operations.
			Recognizes and considers international events and global market dynamics that could affect the organization.

(Continued)

Table 12.1 (Continued) Inclusive, Empathetic, and Relational Competencies

		Inclusive, Empathetic, and Relational Competencies	
#	*Competencies*	*Description*	*Behavioral Indicators*
14	Inclusiveness	Creates an environment where diverse perspectives are essential to success. Consciously involve everyone in discussions, decision-making processes, and opportunities, ensuring each team member feels valued and empowered.	Actively works to create a team that reflects various backgrounds, experiences, and perspectives.
			Encourages equal participation of all team members in meetings, discussions, and decision-making processes.
			Encourages equal participation of all team members in meetings, discussions, and decision-making processes.
15	*Influencing/ negotiating*	Persuades or negotiates effectively with others, understanding their needs and finding common ground. This involves building consensus among diverse stakeholders, facilitating cooperation, and aligning team or organizational objectives with broader goals or individual aspirations.	Articulates ideas and positions clearly and convincingly to win support from others.
			Demonstrates the ability to listen to others, understand their viewpoints, and address concerns effectively.
			Identifies opportunities for compromise that advance organizational goals while meeting the needs of others.
			Prioritizes maintaining and strengthening relationships, cultivating long-term partnerships over short-term gains.
16	Managing diversity	Appreciates and harnesses a team's varying backgrounds, perspectives, and talents to enhance performance and innovation. It requires creating an inclusive environment where differences are celebrated, and every employee can contribute and succeed.	Actively fosters a workplace culture where diversity is celebrated, and all employees feel they belong.
			Adapts leadership and communication styles to meet the needs of diverse team members.
			Creates teams that are diverse not only in demographics but also in thought, experience, and perspective.
			Exemplifies how to interact respectfully with people of all backgrounds.

(Continued)

Table 12.1 (Continued) Inclusive, Empathetic, and Relational Competencies

#	Competencies	Description	Behavioral Indicators
		Inclusive, Empathetic, and Relational Competencies	
17	Mentoring and coaching	Guides and develops employees through the exchange of knowledge, expertise, and feedback that supports their professional growth. It encompasses actively listening to their needs, offering constructive advice, setting developmental goals, and providing the resources and encouragement necessary to advance their skills and careers.	Acknowledges and celebrates milestones and improvements.
			Assists in setting realistic, challenging, and achievable goals.
			Assists in setting realistic, challenging, and achievable goals.
			Conducts consistent and dedicated meetings to discuss progress, challenges, and growth.
			Demonstrates behaviors and attitudes that reflect the values and skills being taught.
			Offers clear, actionable, positive feedback to encourage development and improve performance.
			Provides the motivation and support necessary to address obstacles and build confidence.
18	Motivation	Inspires and energizes employees and fosters an environment that stimulates intrinsic motivation and engagement. This includes understanding individual drivers for each team member and using them to achieve high morale, job satisfaction, and optimal performance.	Actively seeks to understand what motivates each team member and uses that knowledge to inspire them.
			Celebrates successes and acknowledges hard work publicly and privately.
			Demonstrates genuine enthusiasm for the team's goals and visions.
			Demonstrates genuine enthusiasm for the team's goals and visions.

(Continued)

Table 12.1 (Continued) Inclusive, Empathetic, and Relational Competencies

		Inclusive, Empathetic, and Relational Competencies	
#	Competencies	Description	Behavioral Indicators
19	Psychological safety	Creates an environment in which team members feel safe speaking without fear of ridicule or negative consequences, promoting open communication and innovation. It includes encouraging contribution, admitting mistakes, and showing vulnerability, thereby setting a precedent that strengthens trust and collaborative risk-taking.	Fosters a workplace that is energetic, supportive, and conducive to employee well-being.
			Offers feedback that aims to improve performance and motivates employees to take responsibility for their growth.
			Addresses employees' queries and worries with respect and without judgment.
			Encourages team members to take calculated risks in pursuing innovation without fear of negative consequences if they fail.
			Ensures meetings provide everyone with a safe space to speak and be heard.
			Focuses on learning from mistakes rather than assigning blame, promoting a culture of problem-solving rather than finger-pointing.
			Openly acknowledges personal mistakes, modeling transparency and humility.
			Safeguards sensitive information.

(Continued)

Table 12.1 (Continued)   Inclusive, Empathetic, and Relational Competencies

#	Competencies	Description	Behavioral Indicators
		Inclusive, Empathetic, and Relational Competencies	
20	Relationship management	(A component of emotional intelligence-interpersonal skills.) Builds and maintains strong, healthy relationships with team members, peers, and other stakeholders through effective communication, conflict resolution, and interpersonal skills. It requires not only positive management of interactions but also the promotion of a network of cooperation that supports team cohesion and organizational goals.	Actively maintains and expands a network of professional relationships that benefit the team and organization.
			Addresses and resolves interpersonal conflicts constructively and proactively.
			Consistently engages in clear, open, and honest communication that strengthens work relationships.
			Demonstrates reliability and integrity that fosters trust within the team.
			Maintains consistent, fair, and respectful treatment of all individuals, regardless of the situation.
			Provides support and assistance to colleagues and team members, both professionally and personally when appropriate.
21	Responsive feedback	Provides timely and constructive feedback that is receptive to the recipient's perspective and mindful of their emotional state. It is about communicating in a way that supports the individual's growth and development, while also considering the impact that feedback may have on their feelings and motivation.	Balances feedback by recognizing strengths and addressing areas for improvement.
			Checks in after giving feedback to assess progress and offer further support if needed.
			Chooses the appropriate time and place for feedback to respect the individual's dignity.
			Focuses feedback on actionable advice and positive guidance, not criticism.
			Gives feedback and considers the feelings and perspectives of the individual.

(Continued)

Table 12.1 (Continued) Inclusive, Empathetic, and Relational Competencies

#	Competencies	Description	Behavioral Indicators
		Inclusive, Empathetic, and Relational Competencies	
			Gives specific examples to support feedback, making it clear and understandable.
			Provides appropriate feedback in a timely manner to ensure relevance and effectiveness.
22	Self-awareness	(A component of emotional intelligence-intrapersonal skills.) Recognizes and understands one's own emotions, triggers, and reactions—effectively managing behavior and reactions, creating a more empathetic and responsive interaction that resonates with others.	Acknowledges their own errors without defensiveness, viewing them as an opportunity for learning and growth.
			Actively seeks feedback from others.
			Continuously learns more about oneself through new experiences, education, and training.
			Recognizes and acknowledges their emotional state, and understanding how it can affect their decision-making and interactions.
			Reflects on personal biases and takes steps to ensure they do not influence workplace decisions.
			Regularly reflects on their own behavior, emotions, and the results of their interactions.

(Continued)

Table 12.1 (Continued)   Inclusive, Empathetic, and Relational Competencies

		Inclusive, Empathetic, and Relational Competencies	
#	Competencies	Description	Behavioral Indicators
23	*Self-regulation/self-management*	(A component of emotional intelligence-intrapersonal skills.) Controls and appropriately channels one's emotions and impulses in various situations. Exhibits patience and maintains integrity and reliability, creating a stable and trusting work environment.	Demonstrates the ability to resist or delay impulsive reactions or decisions.
			Employs effective techniques for managing stress and helping others manage their stress.
			Exhibits consistent behavior and mood, avoiding erratic or unpredictable actions.
			Maintains composure and calmness in challenging or stressful situations.
			Takes accountability for personal performance and learns from experiences.
			Upholds and models high ethical standards and integrity in all actions.
24	Social awareness	(A component of emotional intelligence-intrapersonal skills.) Empathetically understand and respond to the emotions, needs, and concerns of others. Encompasses perceiving and appropriately reacting to group dynamics and individual feelings within the team, facilitating a supportive and inclusive work environment.	Anticipates, recognizes, and meets the needs of others.
			Correctly reads body language, facial expressions and other non-verbal signals to gauge people's feelings and reactions.
			Demonstrates an understanding of the perspectives and feelings of others without judgment.
			Engages with others in a way that supports and promotes their well-being and professional growth.
			Gives feedback sensitive to individual needs and receptive to the emotional state of others.

(Continued)

Table 12.1 (Continued) Inclusive, Empathetic, and Relational Competencies

#	Competencies	Description	Behavioral Indicators
		Inclusive, Empathetic, and Relational Competencies	
			Respects and values various experiences and practices within the team.
			Understands the organizational dynamics, politics, and cultures that affect the work environment and team morale.
25	Team building	Creates a cohesive and motivated team by understanding and managing the emotions and relationships within the group. Fosters a sense of trust and collaboration among team members, as well as aligning their diverse talents and personalities toward common goals and a shared vision.	Addresses and manages conflicts promptly and fairly, using them as an opportunity for team growth.
			Creates a compelling vision consistent with the goals of the team and the organization and inspires collective efforts.
			Creates an environment in which team members feel safe to express ideas and take risks, knowing that their contributions are valued.
			Establishes and communicates clear, achievable team goals that provide direction and motivation.
			Identifies and leverages the unique strengths and abilities of each team member.
			Promotes cooperative relationships and facilitates the opportunity for team members to work effectively together.
			Recognizes and celebrates team achievements to build morale and promote high performance.

Source: Rothwell et al. (2023), Mohr et al. (2021), Kai et al. (2021), Virtaharju & Liiri (2019), Black & La Venture (2017), Serrat (2017), Harvard Business Review et al. (2015), Creque & Gooden (2011), Goleman & Boyatzis (2008), Chang & Tharenou (2004), Shapiro (2002), Boyatzis et al. (2000).

Strategies for Developing Inclusive, Empathetic, and Relational Competencies

Developing your own plan to become a more inclusive, empathetic, and relational supervisor involves a series of reflective and actionable steps. Figure 12.2 illustrates the recommended steps.

Step 1: **Reflect on Your Current State:** Assess your current supervisory style. Take some time to think about why inclusivity, empathy, and relationship building are important to you and your team. If possible, discuss with your team, your manager, and colleagues about your strengths in terms of inclusivity, empathy, and relationship building, as well as any areas they feel you could improve in.

Step 2: **Identify Competencies to Develop:** Select specific skills that you want to develop based on your reflection. It is generally recommended to focus on developing three to four competencies at a time, allowing for a targeted approach that is manageable and allows you to invest the necessary time and effort for more effective learning and sustainable growth.

Step 3: **Assess Your Proficiency:** Assess your proficiency in the competencies you selected. You can use various methods to measure your ability, such as rating scales, tests, portfolios, or simulations. You can also ask for feedback from your team, manager, mentor, or peers to validate your self-assessment and identify blind spots or biases.

Step 4: **Define Your Competency Gap:** Define the gaps between your current proficiency and desired proficiency for each competency. Prioritize the ones that are most critical for you and your team.

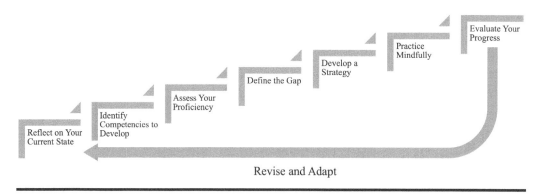

Figure 12.2   Steps to developing competencies. *Source*: Authors' original creation.

Step 5: **Develop Strategy:** Create a development strategy that outlines the measures, resources, and timetables to help you close your gaps. Set SMART (specific, measurable, achievable, relevant, and time-bound) goals related to inclusiveness, empathy, and relationship building. For example,

By the end of the next six months, I will enhance my active listening skills, as evidenced by a 20% improvement in the active listening scores from my 360-degree feedback, by completing a workshop on active listening by the end of Q1 and practicing daily active listening techniques with my team.

Step 6: **Practice Mindfully:** Practice each competence by applying what you have learned in your daily interactions. Be mindful of your actions, reflect on your experience, and adjust your behavior accordingly.

Step 7: **Evaluate Your Progress:** Monitor the effectiveness of your development plan. Track your development strategy against your SMART goals, review formal and informal feedback, and acknowledge your progress.

Step 8: **Revise and Adapt:** Revise and adapt your development plan based on your progress evaluation.

When developing your inclusive, empathetic, and relational competencies, focus on the resources that align with specific behaviors tied to each competency—this approach is often more effective than broad overviews. By focusing on these indicators, you will focus on what is crucial and sidestep unproductive development efforts. For example, if you aim to master "Active Listening," one behavioral indicator linked to that competency is "uses paraphrasing or summarizing to confirm understanding and show that they are truly listening." You should look for resources that show you how to paraphrase effectively. Your development strategy should help you practice and embody these specific behaviors (Rothwell & Graber, 2010). Figure 12.2 illustrates the step-by-step approach to developing your competencies.

Strategies for Developing Inclusive, Empathetic, and Relational Competencies

Strategic development of your inclusive, empathetic, and relationalcompetencies is crucial, because it directly influences the quality of your interactions and the experience of your team. By prioritizing these competencies, you lay the groundwork for a more cohesive, understanding, and effective team dynamic. It's crucial to recognize that such development is not a one-time event but a perpetual progress. Continuously refining these skills ensures you remain adaptable and responsive to the diverse needs and perspectives that you encounter. This ongoing process enriches your personal growth but also supports a workplace culture that values and leverages the strengths inherent in a diverse workforce. As such, it contributes to building a more resilient and innovative organization.

Figure 12.3 illustrates the top ten tactics for cultivating an inclusive, empathetic, and collaborative relationship between supervisors, coworkers, and team members. Tactics like respect, trust, and communication are foundational in developing inclusive, empathetic, and relational competencies, especially in a people-centered approach to supervision. Figure 12.3 illustrates the top ten tactics. By implementing these strategies, you can create an inclusive environment where everyone feels empowered. Cultivating a work atmosphere conducive to inclusivity and empathy and taking a people-centered approach that respects individual differences, builds trust through consistent and ethical behavior, and maintains open lines of communication, you will naturally develop stronger relational competencies within your team. These approaches drive collaboration, innovation, and community, contributing to the effectiveness and satisfaction of your team.

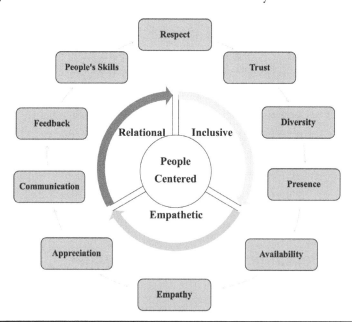

Figure 12.3 Top ten strategies for developing inclusive empathetic and relational competencies. Source: Rothwell, Bakhshandeh, and Zaballero (2023).

According to Rothwell, Bakhshandeh, and Zaballero (2023), the following are top ten strategies to develop inclusive, empathetic, and relational competencies among supervisors:

1) **Respect.** Mutual respect is reciprocal. Reciprocal respect cannot be expected without being selective in its provision. One can demonstrate respect by recognizing the contributions others make to one's life and career, and by carefully examining and embracing their viewpoints and opinions. Furthermore, embracing the variety of others enhances our collective capacity for mutual respect. This method will enhance good, efficient, and fruitful working relationships (Bakhshandeh, 2015).

2) **Trust.** Trust is a crucial component of every relationship. Without trust, it is impossible to develop a functional connection, whether on a personal or professional level. Mutual trust is essential for both parties involved. Trust should be given until there is concrete proof of distrust. Without trust, love, respect, relationships, and effective workability are unattainable (Rothwell & Bakhshandeh, 2022).

3) **Diversity.** Each of us possesses distinct characteristics, such as age, personality, race, education, religion, nationality, sexuality, height, weight, and numerous other personal or professional attributes. Failing to acknowledge and embrace these distinctions, as well as recognizing that individuals possess unique qualities, only complicates the process of building a constructive and impactful connection (Rothwell, Ealy, & Campbell, 2022).

4) **Presence.** When you are in the company of others, focus on being present with them and refrain from fixating on the problems or individuals of others. By prioritizing the needs and concerns of others during discussions, you will foster a favorable atmosphere that will facilitate strong rapport and the cultivation of future connections (Bakhshandeh, 2008).

5) **Availability.** Recognize that your accessibility and mindfulness toward the demands of people for your time is a valuable contribution to them. Being accessible is closely linked to being physically present. In a rapidly changing and high-pressure society, where job demands are intense and the surroundings can be challenging, dedicating your time and making yourself accessible to others helps foster a more robust and constructive connection, while also enhancing your reputation as a leader (Bakhshandeh, 2008).

6) **Empathy.** Empathy, in conjunction with compassion and understanding, fosters robust and mutually respected bonds between individuals. Empathy enables one to understand and connect with the emotions,

sentiments, and challenges of others by connecting to their perceptions and experiences. Engaging in regular practice enhances the qualities of respect and trust (Campbell, 2000).

7) **Appreciation.** Demonstrating sincere thankfulness and appreciation is crucial for maintaining a great connection. Irrespective of the magnitude and proportions of an action, there is always space for conveying gratitude, even by the utterance of a straightforward "thank you." A modest yet sincere demonstration of real respect and gratitude would greatly contribute to fostering a healthy connection and enable others to embrace your influence (Bannink, 2015).

8) **Communication.** Enhancing and honing good communication and active listening skills benefits all parties involved. There are several assumptions made by both parties in the interactions regarding the interpretation and intentions of communications. Enhancing one's communication and listening abilities is a worthwhile endeavor that contributes to the success of personal and professional relationships, ensuring that conversations remain impactful and significant (Rothwell & Bakhshandeh, 2022).

9) **Feedback.** Provide affirming and productive feedback while being receptive to receiving it. Regardless of the approach used, it serves as a valuable instrument for comprehending others and rectifying activities for improvement. Regard feedback as valuable input from someone who is invested, since it may effectively pinpoint deficiencies and areas of oversight while offering a chance to comprehend and rectify them (Lucas, 2020).

10) **People's Skills.** Gaining insight into your own strengths and shortcomings in cultivating interpersonal connections is beneficial. Interpersonal abilities, which encompass people skills, play a significant role in shaping our professional interactions, exerting a substantial influence on our work dynamics. Exhibiting honesty and authenticity, practicing politeness and consideration, and actively listening to others are among the key interpersonal skills (Bakhshandeh, 2002).

Self-Assessment Tools and Reflection Practices

By using self-assessment tools and reflective practices, you can improve your ability to be inclusive, empathetic, and continue to build empowering relationships with a person-centered approach. By reflecting on personal experiences and evaluating your actions, you can identify areas of unconscious bias or lack of knowledge that can affect interactions with others. This practice encourages ongoing development.

Table 12.2 is a checklist for self-assessing your competencies as an inclusive, empathetic, and relational supervisor, and it is sourced and related to Table 12.1. Use this form to self-evaluate your competencies by rating (a) your ability to perform these supervisory competencies and skills and (b) the importance of such skill on the success of your supervisory career.

Now use Table 12.3 to formulate a series of actions to increase your understanding of Table 12.2.

As mentioned at the beginning of this book, you play an important role in creating a people-centered culture in a work environment rapidly changing due to new organizational challenges and technological advances. Valuing your team members can build trust, communication, and morale. You have a unique opportunity to build meaningful relationships with your team members and help them grow and succeed personally and professionally. One of the key factors in achieving success is to truly value the individual strengths and perspectives that each team member brings to the table and to create a safe and supportive environment in which everyone feels heard, respected, and appreciated. Take the time to get to know your team members personally and show genuine interest in their goals, aspirations, and challenges. By fostering meaningful and compassionate connections, you create a firm foundation for building stronger relationships.

What's Next? Preview of Book III: *Engaged and Organized Supervisor*

The next book of the *Successful Supervisor Leadership Series* is Book III: *The Organized & Engaged Supervisor.* Embrace a structured approach to effectively manage tasks, time, and resources while simultaneously committing to the growth and well-being of your team. Organized supervisors are adept at planning, prioritizing, and executing tasks efficiently, which helps them handle their workload and oversee their direct reports' tasks. Furthermore, these supervisors can keep an eye on deadlines and potential conflicts that might arise from multiple projects. On the other hand, engaged supervisors show a clear commitment to their organization's goals and values, and they work to inspire their team members to do the same. They create an environment

Table 12.2 Self-Assessment for Inclusive, Empathetic, and Relational Supervisor Rating Sheet

Self-Assessment for Inclusive, Empathetic, and Relational Supervisor Rating Sheet												
Supervisor:						Month & Year:						
Direct Manager:						Department:						
Directions: Self-evaluate by rating your own (a) competencies as an inclusive, empathetic, and relational supervisor, and (b) the importance of specific competencies for the success of your supervisory career			My ability to perform this competency at my work					How important is this competence to my career success?				
Evaluating Scale			1	2	3	4	5	1	2	3	4	5
#	*Inclusive, Empathetic, and Relational Supervisor*		Ratings from 1(lowest) to 5 (highest)									
1	Accessibility and accommodation											
2	Active listening											
3	Adaptability and flexibility											
4	Collaborative problem-solving											
5	Conflict resolution											
6	Continuous learning											
7	Cultural sensitivity											
8	Delegation											
9	Disciplinary action											
10	Effective communication											
11	Empathy											
12	Equity mindset											
13	External awareness											
14	Inclusiveness											
15	Influencing/negotiating											
16	Managing diversity											
17	Mentoring and coaching											

(Continued)

Table 12.2 (Continued)   Self-Assessment for Inclusive, Empathetic, and Relational Supervisor Rating Sheet

Self-Assessment for Inclusive, Empathetic, and Relational Supervisor Rating Sheet												
Supervisor:						Month & Year:						
Direct Manager:						Department:						
Directions: Self-evaluate by rating your own (a) competencies as an inclusive, empathetic, and relational supervisor, and (b) the importance of specific competencies for the success of your supervisory career						My ability to perform this competency at my work					How important is this competence to my career success?
Evaluating Scale	**1**	**2**	**3**	**4**	**5**	**1**	**2**	**3**	**4**	**5**		
18	Motivation											
19	Psychological safety											
20	Relationship management											
21	Responsive feedback											
22	Self-awareness											
23	Self-regulation											
24	Social awareness											
25	Team building											
Sub-Total (total of each column)												
Total of above 5 rating scales of each category												
Average (above totals of each category divided by 25)												

where employees feel important and supported, which fosters ownership and encourages them to give their best performance every day.

The importance of an organized and engaged supervisor lies in the direct impact of these qualities on organizational performance. As a supervisor, if you are organized, you are more likely to complete projects successfully and meet deadlines, which contributes to the team's productivity. However, being an engaged supervisor complements and amplifies your effectiveness of being organized. While being organized ensures that tasks and resources are managed efficiently, being engaged is what breathes life into these tasks and transforms them into a collective mission.

Table 12.3 APLI-Connected to Table 12.2

Action Plan for Learning and Improving	
Area of Learning and Improving: *Self-Assessment for Inclusive, Empathetic, and Relational Supervisor*	
Reference: *Table 12.2*	
Three learning and improvement actions for this month that will raise my understanding and awareness regarding *Self-Assessment for Inclusive, Empathetic, and Relational Supervisor* to enhance my knowledge and clarity by at least one on the next rating:	
Action 1:	By When:
Action 2:	By When:
Action 3:	By When:

Note: Authors' original creation.

Table 12.4 End of Chapter 12 Questions and Inquiries. Your Perspective on What You Learned in Chapter 12

Your Perspective on What You Learned in Chapter 12	
Area of Inquiry	*What Did You Learn, and How Will You Use Them in Your Position?*
Inclusive, empathetic, and relational competencies	
Strategies for developing inclusive, empathetic, and relational competencies	
Self-assessment tools and reflection practices	

Key Takeaways

1. As a supervisor, your role is to cultivate a workplace where everyone feels valued and supported, emphasizing inclusivity, empathy, and diversity to bolster teamwork and decision-making. Understand and address the needs of your colleagues, building trust and caring for their well-being. It's essential to communicate effectively, tackle biases, foster trust and well-being within your team, and continue to build relationships.

2. Competencies are inherently personal attributes, not tied to job descriptions. To enhance your supervisory skills, start by figuring out which unique competencies are required within your organization. This can be done by observing those who excel at their job—those who best show inclusiveness, empathy, and the ability to form relationships.

3. When developing your inclusive, empathetic, and relational competencies, focus on specific behavioral indicators associated with each competency. This approach is often more effective than a broad overview. By focusing on these indicators, you will focus on what is crucial and overlook unproductive development efforts.

Discussion Questions and Inquiries

Please take a minute and come up with your own answers to these inquiries and questions. After completing Table 12.4 and answering these questions, discuss your learning with your higher manager. From your viewpoint, briefly express what you have learned about these areas. Your discussion with your manager about your new knowledge and understanding would be a great pathway to your development as an inclusive, empathetic, and relational supervisor.

References

Bakhshandeh, B. ([2002] 2008). *Business Coaching and Managers Training.* Unpublished Workshop on Coaching Businesses and Training Managers. San Diego, CA: Primeco Education, Inc.

Bakhshandeh, B. (2008). *Bravehearts; Leadership Development Training.* Unpublished Training and Developmental Course on Coaching Executives and Managers. San Diego, CA: Primeco Education, Inc.

Bakhshandeh, B. (2015). *Anatomy of Upset: Restoring Harmony.* Carbondale, PA: Primeco Education, Inc.

Bannink, F. (2015). *Handbook of Positive Supervision.* Boston, MA: Hogrefe Publishing Corporation.

Black, J., & La Venture, K. (2017). The human factor to profitability: People-centered cultures as meaningful organizations. *Journal of Organizational Psychology, 17*(2), 24.

Boyatzis, R. E., Goleman, D., & Rhee, K. (2000). Clustering competence in emotional intelligence: Insights from the Emotional Competence Inventory (ECI). *Handbook of Emotional Intelligence, 99*(6), 343–362.

Campbell, J. M. (2000). *Becoming an Effective Supervisor.* New York, NY: Routledge, Taylor & Francis Group.

Chang, S., & Tharenou, P. (2004). Competencies needed for managing a multicultural workgroup. *Asia Pacific Journal of Human Resources, 42*(1), 57–74. https://doi.org/10.1177/1038411104041534

Creque, C. A., & Gooden, D. J. (2011). Cultural intelligence and global business competencies: A framework for organizational effectiveness in the global marketplace. *International Journal of Management and Information Systems, 15*(4), 141–146.

Goleman, D., & Boyatzis, R. (2008). Social intelligence and the biology of leadership. *Harvard Business Review, 86*(9), 74–81.

Harvard Business Review, Goleman, D., Boyatzis, R. E., McKee, A., & Finkelstein, S. (2015). *HBR's 10 Must Reads on Emotional Intelligence (with Featured Article "What Makes a Leader?" by Daniel Goleman)(HBR's 10 Must Reads).* Harvard Business Review Press.

Kai Liao, Y., Wu, W. Y., Dao, T. C., & Ngoc Luu, T. M. (2021). The influence of emotional intelligence and cultural adaptability on cross-cultural adjustment and performance with the mediating effect of cross-cultural competence: A study of expatriates in Taiwan. *Sustainability, 13*(6), 3374.

Lucas, M. (2020). *101 Coaching Supervision Techniques, Approaches, Enquiries and Experiments* (Ed). New York, NY: Routledge.

Mohr, C. D., Hammer, L. B., Brady, J. M., Perry, M. L., & Bodner, T. (2021). Can supervisor support improve daily employee well-being? Evidence of supervisor training effectiveness in a study of veteran employee emotions. *Journal of Occupational and Organizational Psychology, 94*(2), 400–426. https://doi.org/10.1111/joop.12342

Rothwell, W. J., & Bakhshandeh, B. (2022). *High-Performance Coaching for Managers.* New York, NY: Taylor & Francis Group; CRC Press.

Rothwell, W. J., Bakhshandeh, B., & Zaballero, A. G. (2023). *Successful Supervisory Leadership; Exerting Positive Influence While Leading People.* New York, NY: Taylor & Francis Group; Routledge.

Rothwell, W. J., Ealy, P. L., & Campbell, J. (2022). *Rethinking Organizational Diversity, Equity, and Inclusion.* New York, NY: Taylor & Francis Group; Routledge.

Rothwell, W. J., Graber, J., Dubois, D., Zaballero, A. G., Haynes, C., Alkhalaf, A. H., & Stager, S. J. (2015). *The Complete Competency Toolkit, Vol I & 2.* Amherst, MA: HRD Press.

Rothwell, W. J., & Graber, J. M. (2010). *Competency-based Training Basics.* Alexandria, VA: ASTD Press.

Serrat, O. (2017). Building trust in the workplace. In *Knowledge Solutions* (pp. 627–632). Singapore: Springer.

Shapiro, J. (2002). How do physicians teach empathy in the primary care setting? *Academic Medicine, 77*(4), 323–328.

Virtaharju, J. J., & Liiri, T. P. (2019). The supervisors who became leaders: Leadership emergence via changing organizational practices. *Leadership, 15*(1), 103–122. https://doi.org/10.1177/1742715017736004

Appendix A: Supportive Resources

Books

Abeni, E.-A. (2022). *Implementing Diversity, Equity, Inclusion, and Belonging in Educational Management Practices*. Hershey, PA: IGI Global.

Bakhshandeh, B. (2015). *Anatomy of Upset: Restoring Harmony*. Carbondale, PA: Primeco Education, Inc.

Booth, W. C. (2009). *The Rhetoric of Rhetoric: The Quest for Effective Communication*. Hoboken, NJ: John Wiley & Sons.

Boyatzis, R. E. (1982). *The Competent Manager: A Model for Effective Performance*. Hoboken, NJ: John Wiley & Sons.

Carasco, M., & Rothwell, W. J. (2020). *The Essential HR Guide for Small Business and Startups*. Alexandria, VA: SHRM-Society for Human Resources Management.

Cohn, R., & Russell, J. (2015). *Hofstede's Cultural Dimensions Theory*. Books on Demand. Online Services for printing books on demand.

Collings, D. G., Scullion, H., & Caligiuri, P. M. (2019). *Global Talent Management*. New York, NY: Routledge.

Commons, J. R. (1893). *The Distribution of Wealth*. New York and London: Macmillan.

Coombs, W. T. (2021). *Ongoing Crisis Communication: Planning, Managing, and Responding*. Thousand Oaks, CA: SAGE Publications.

Cozolino, L. J. (2014). *The Neuroscience of Human Relationships 2e: Attachment and the Developing Social Brain*. New York, NY: W. W. Norton & Company.

Cummings, T. G., & Worley, C. G. (2015). *Organization Development & Change* (10th ed.). Stamford, CT: Cengage Learning.

Davenport, T. H., & Miller, S. M. (2022). *Working with AI: Real Stories of Human-Machine Collaboration*. Cambridge, MA: The MIT Press.

Donahue, W. E. (2018). *Building Leadership Competence. A Competency-Based Approach to Building Leadership Ability.* State College, PA: Centerstar Learning.

Dubois, D. D., & Rothwell, W. J. (2004). *Competency-Based Human Resource Management.* Palo Alto, CA: Davis-Black Publishing.

Fielding, M. (2006). *Effective Communication in Organizations.* South Africa: Juta and Company Ltd.

French, W. L. (2007). *Human Resources Management* (6th ed.). Boston, MA: Houghton Mifflin Company.

Goleman, D. (2015). *Emotional Intelligence: Why it Can Matter More than IQ.* New York, NY: Bantam Books.

HBR. (2017). *Harvard Business Review Guide to Emotional Intelligence.* Boston, MA: Harvard Business Review Press.

Heath, R. L. (2020). *Management of Corporate Communication: From Interpersonal Contacts to External Affairs.* New Jersey: Routledge.

Hockenbury, D. H., & Hockenbury, S. E. (2007). *Discovering Psychology.* New York, NY: Macmillan.

Lewis, L. K. (2011). *Organizational Change: Creating Change through Strategic Communication.* Hoboken, NJ: Wiley-Blackwell.

Lussier, R. N. (2021). *Human Relations in Organizations: Applications and Skill Building.* New York, NY: McGraw Hill.

McCroskey, V. P. R., & James, C. (2019). Human communication theory and research: Traditions and models. In *An Integrated Approach to Communication Theory and Research* (3rd ed.). New York, NY: Routledge.

Meyer, E. (2016). *The Culture Map: Decoding How People Think, Lead, and Get Things Done across Cultures.* NY: Public Affairs.

Mindell, D. A., Reynolds, E. B., Autor, D., & Solow, R. M. (2023). *The Work of the Future: Building Better Jobs in an Age of Intelligent Machines.* Boston: The MIT Press.

Minkov, M. (2012). *Cross-Cultural Analysis: The Science and Art of Comparing the World's Modern Societies and Their Cultures.* Los Angeles: SAGE Publications.

Rothwell, W. J., Ealy, P. L., & Campbell, J. (Eds.). (2022). *Rethinking Organizational Diversity, Equity, and Inclusion: A Step-By-Step Guide for Facilitating Effective Change* (1st ed.). Productivity Press.

Saccone, S. (2009). *Relational Intelligence.* San Francisco, CA: Jossey-Bass.

Serrat, O. (2017). Understanding and developing emotional intelligence. In *Knowledge Solutions* (pp. 329–339). Singapore: Springer. https://doi.org/10.1007/978-981-10-0983-9_37

Siddiqui, H. Y. (2015). *Social Work and Human Relations.* New Delhi, India: Rawat Publications.

Stefancic, J., & Delgado, R. (2010). *Critical Race Theory: An Introduction.* New York, NY: New York University Press.

Thompson, J. R. (2021). *Diversity and Inclusion Matters: Tactics and Tools to Inspire Equity and Game-Changing Performance* (1st ed.). Hoboken, NJ: Wiley.

Tulgan, B. (2015). *Bridging the Soft Skills Gap: How to Teach the Missing Basics to Today's Young Talent.* Hoboken, NJ: John Willey & Sons, Inc. https://doi.org/10.1002/9781119171409

Winters, M.-F. (2020). *Inclusive Conversations: Fostering Equity, Empathy, and Belonging across Differences*. Oakland, CA: Berrett-Koehler Publishers.

Wyer, R. S., Chiu, C., & Hong, Y. (2013). *Understanding Culture: Theory, Research, and Application*. New York, NY: Psychology Press.

Zeigler-Hill, V., & Shackelford, T. K. (2020). *Encyclopedia of Personality and Individual Differences*. Springer International Publishing.

Articles

Adejumo, V. (2021). Beyond diversity, inclusion, and belonging. *Leadership*, *17*(1), 62–73. https://doi.org/10.1177/1742715020976202

Ahmad, T. (2020). Scenario based approach to re-imagining future of higher education which prepares students for the future of work. *Higher Education, Skills and Work – Based Learning*, *10*(1), 217–238. https://doi.org/10.1108/HESWBL -12-2018-0136

Antonacopoulou, E. P., & Georgiadou, A. (2021). Leading through social distancing: The future of work, corporations and leadership from home. *Gender, Work & Organization*, *28*(2), 749–767. https://doi.org/10.1111/gwao.12533

At-Twaijri, M. I., & Al-Muhaiza, I. A. (1996). Hofstede's cultural dimensions in the GCC countries: An empirical investigation. *International Journal of Value-Based Management*, *9*(2), 121–131. https://doi.org/10.1007/BF00440149

Boyatzis, R. E., & Sala, F. (2004). Assessing emotional intelligence competencies. In G. Geher (Ed.), *The Measurement of Emotional Intelligence*. Nova Science Publishers. https://doi.org/10.1016/S0160-2896(01)00084-8

Cardiff, S., McCormack, B., & McCance, T. (2018). Person-centered leadership: A relational approach to leadership derived through action research. *Journal of Clinical Nursing*, *27*(15–16), 3056–3069. https://doi.org/10.1111/jocn.14492

Chao, D., Badwan, M., & Briceño, E. M. (2022). Addressing diversity, equity, inclusion and belonging (DEIB) in mentorship relationships. *Journal of Clinical and Experimental Neuropsychology*, *44*(5–6), 420–440. https://doi.org/10.1080 /13803395.2022.2112151

Charoensap-Kelly, P., Broussard, L., Lindsly, M., & Troy, M. (2016). Evaluation of a soft skills training program. *Business and Professional Communication Quarterly*, *79*(2), 154–179. https://doi.org/10.1177/2329490615602090

Chernyak-Hai, L., & Rabenu, E. (2018). The new era workplace relationships: Is social exchange theory still relevant? *Industrial and Organizational Psychology*, *11*(3), 456–481. https://doi.org/10.1017/iop.2018.5

Chiou, E. K., Holden, R. J., Ghosh, S., Flores, Y., & Roscoe, R. D. (2022). Recruitment, admissions, hiring, retention, and promotion: Mechanisms of diversity, equity, inclusion (DEI) and belonging in higher education. *Proceedings of the Human Factors and Ergonomics Society Annual Meeting*, *66*(1), 135–138. https://doi.org/10.1177/1071181322661026

Clarke, N. (2006). Emotional intelligence training: A case of caveat emptor. *Human Resource.Development Review*, *5*(4), 422–441.

Curtis, K., Tzannes, A., & Rudge, T. (2011). How to talk to doctors – A guide for effective communication. *International Nursing Review*, *58*(1), 13–20. https://doi.org/10.1111/j.1466-7657.2010.00847.x

Delfanti, A., & Frey, B. (2021). Humanly extended automation or the future of work seen through amazon patents. *Science, Technology, & Human Values*, *46*(3), 655–682. https://doi.org/10.1177/0162243920943665

Fallowfield, L., & Jenkins, V. (1999). Effective communication skills are the key to good cancer care. *European Journal of Cancer*, *35*(11), 1592–1597. https://doi.org/10.1016/S0959-8049(99)00212-9

Foy, C. M. (2021). Successful applications of diversity, equity, and inclusion programming in various professional settings: Strategies to increase DEI in libraries. *Journal of Library Administration*, *61*(6), 676–685. https://doi.org/10.1080/01930826.2021.1947057

Greene, J., & Flasch, P. (2019). Integrating intersectionality into clinical supervision: A developmental model addressing broader definitions of multicultural competence. *Journal of Counselor Preparation and Supervision*, *12*(4). https://digitalcommons.sacredheart.edu/jcps/vol12/iss4/14

Goleman, D. (2014). What it takes to achieve managerial success. *TD: Talent Development*, *68*(11), 48–52. https://www.proquest.com/docview/1643098923/fulltextPDF/33BA6291F86D4459PQ/1?accountid=13158

Gundlach, M., Zivnuska, S., & Stoner, J. (2006). Understanding the relationship between individualism–collectivism and team performance through an integration of social identity theory and the social relations model. *Human Relations*, *59*(12), 1603–1632. https://doi.org/10.1177/0018726706073193

Hen, M., & Sharabi-Nov, A. (2014). Teaching the teachers: Emotional intelligence training for teachers. *Teaching Education*. https://www.tandfonline.com/doi/abs/10.1080/10476210.2014.908838

Hofstede, G. (1983). National cultures in four dimensions: A research-based theory of cultural differences among nations. *International Studies of Management & Organization*, *13*(1–2), 46–74. https://doi.org/10.1080/00208825.1983.11656358

Roggeveen, A. L., & Sethuraman, R. (2020). How the covid-19 pandemic may change the world of retailing. (2020). *Journal of Retailing*, *96*(2), 169–171. https://doi.org/10.1016/j.jretai.2020.04.002

Huang, A., De la Mora Velasco, E., Marsh, J., & Workman, H. (2021). COVID-19 and the future of work in the hospitality industry. *International Journal of Hospitality Management*, *97*, 102986. https://doi.org/10.1016/j.ijhm.2021.102986

Jian, G. (2022). From empathic leader to empathic leadership practice: An extension to relational leadership theory. *Human Relations*, *75*(5), 931–955. https://doi.org/10.1177/0018726721998450

Kanten, P., & Ulker, F. E. (2012). A relational approach among perceived organizational support, proactive personality and voice behavior. *Procedia, Social and Behavioral Sciences*, *62*, 1016–1022. https://doi.org/10.1016/j.sbspro.2012.09.173

Kim, K. (2022). Supervisor leadership and subordinates' innovative work behaviors: Creating a relational context for organizational sustainability. *Sustainability*, *14*(6), 3230. https://doi.org/org/10.3390/su14063230

Kunde, N. (2023). Why cultivating 'Belonging' can create a more inclusive workplace. *Research-Technology Management*, *66*(6), 39–42. https://doi.org/10.1080/08956308.2023.2253094

Loosemore, M., & Lee, P. (2002). Communication problems with ethnic minorities in the construction industry. *International Journal of Project Management*, *20*(7), 517–524. https://doi.org/10.1016/S0263-7863(01)00055-2

McFarland, A., & Maniam, B. (2021). A refereed publication of the American society of business and behavioral sciences. *Journal of Business and Behavioral Science*, *33*(2), 11–23.

Mikkelson, A. C., York, J. A., & Arritola, J. (2015). Communication competence, leadership behaviors, and employee outcomes in supervisor-employee relationships. *Business and Professional Communication Quarterly*, *78*(3), 336–354. https://doi.org/10.1177/2329490615588542?journalCode=bcqe

Nasir, S., & Masek, A. (2015). A model of supervision in communicating expectation using supervisory styles and students learning styles. *Procedia – Social and Behavioral Sciences*, *204*, 265–271. https://doi.org/10.1016/j.sbspro.2015.08.150

Pless, N. M., & Maak, T. (2017). Relational intelligence for leading responsibility in a connected world. *Academy of Management*, *2005*(1). https://doi.org/10.5465/ambpp.2005.18783524

Randel, A. E., Galvin, B. M., Shore, L. M., Ehrhart, K. H., Chung, B. G., Dean, M. A., & Kedharnath, U. (2018). Inclusive leadership: Realizing positive outcomes through belongingness and being valued for uniqueness. *Human Resource Management Review*, *28*(2), 190–203. https://doi.org/10.1016/j.hrmr.2017.07.002

Reitz, M. (2015). *Dialogue in Organizations: Developing Relational Leadership*. New York, NY: Palgrave Macmillan. https://doi.org/10.1007/978-1-137-48912-8

Robles, M. M. (2012). Executive perceptions of the top 10 soft skills needed in today's workplace. *Business Communication Quarterly*, *75*(4), 453–465. https://doi.org/10.1177/1080569912460400

Stamps, D. C., & Foley, S. M. (2023). Strategies to implement diversity, equity, inclusion, and belonging in the workplace. *Nurse Leader*. https://doi.org/10.1016/j.mnl.2023.04.007

Van Ruler, B. (2018). Communication theory: An underrated pillar on which strategic communication rests. *International Journal of Strategic Communication*, *12*(4), 367–381. https://doi.org/10.1080/1553118X.2018.1452240

Watkin, C. (2000). Developing emotional intelligence. *International Journal of Selection and Assessment*, *8*(2), 89–92. https://doi.org/10.1111/1468-2389.00137

Yukl, G., Gordon, A., & Taber, T. (2002). A hierarchical taxonomy of leadership behavior: Integrating a half century of behavior research. *Journal of Leadership & Organizational Studies*, *9*(1), 15–32. https://doi.org/10.1177/107179190200900102?journalCode=jlob

Videos/YouTube

AMA (Director). (2021, October 5). *Prioritizing Equity Video Series: Critical Race Theory & Intersectionality.* https://www.ama-assn.org/delivering-care/health -equity/prioritizing-equity-video-series-critical-race-theory

CareerVidz (Director). (2020, December 15). *11 Habits of Highly Effective Managers! (How to Improve Your Management Skills!).* https://www.youtube.com/watch?v =f4CF-qBDu5o

Chartered Management Institute (Director). (2021, October 4). *Intersectionality in the Workplace.* https://www.youtube.com/watch?v=xEQtE6TXR9Q

CNC, K. (Director). (2023, March 29). *Webinar: Exploring How Intersectionality Impacts the Corporate Workplace.* https://vimeo.com/812831822/d48e3daba9

Communication Coach Alexander Lyon (Director). (2017, June 6). *Effective Communication Skills.* https://www.youtube.com/watch?v=6pYSbdGiDYw

Communication Coach Alexander Lyon (Director). (2020, October 27). *What are Communication Skills? Top 10!* https://www.youtube.com/watch?v =xQfYiHbAjJo

EasyMBA (Director). (2021, July 19). *Communication Barriers to Communication.* https://www.youtube.com/watch?v=fhb9u8E2ca0

Galton College (Director). (2017, May 31). *Hofstede Cultural Dimensions Theory.* https://www.youtube.com/watch?v=X5yp8FtKiNA

GreggU (Director). (2015, December 20). *Understanding Human Relations.* https:// www.youtube.com/watch?v=6Tjuh2_kmq0

GreggU (Director). (2020, November 20). *What is Human Relations?* https://www .youtube.com/watch?v=PrUAwXOhVu8

Harvard Business Publishing (Director). (n.d.). *Getting Serious about Diversity— Webinar Recording.* Retrieved November 5, 2023, from https://www.harvard-business.org/insight/getting-serious-about-diversity-webinar-recording/

HBS Online (Director). (2023, June 15). *The Power of Diverse Teams.* https://www .youtube.com/watch?v=lzLtUo9TclQ

Indeed (Director). (2020, November 24). *Top 8 Leadership Styles—Definitions & Examples | Indeed Career Tips.* https://www.youtube.com/watch?v =gvsiYHr573c

Indeed (Director). (2022, February 11). *Relationships at Work: Guide to Networking, Communication & More | Indeed Career Tips.* https://www.youtube.com/watch ?v=SIXrUQgR2cY

Indeed (Director). (2022, August 9). *Top Leadership Skills Explained by tomás mal-donado of the nfl.* https://www.youtube.com/watch?v=_dx55fx87zk

Indccd (Director). (2022, October 11). *How to Communicate Effectively at Work (Tips to Build Your Confidence!) | Indeed Career Tips.* https://www.youtube .com/watch?v=5VOV4C6QuBA

Kamikaze Music (Director). (2023, March 2). *Diversity, Equity & Inclusion. Learning How to Get it Right.* https://www.youtube.com/watch?v=HR4wz1b54hw

Management Courses (Director). (2020, December 21). *Team Building Events: Why, What, and How?* https://www.youtube.com/watch?v=nhwBZ4lssM8

Next Generation Recruitment (Director). (2016, March 30). *How the World of Work is Changing.* https://www.youtube.com/watch?v=HYPxrzHJhF8

Schulich Law (Director). (2016, December 9). *Principles & Commitments.* https://www.youtube.com/watch?v=lm5-Rx0IHgw

Te Tāhū Hauora Health Quality & Safety Commission (Director). (2022, May 17). *Implementing a Relational Approach When Things Don't Go to Plan in the Healthcare Setting.* https://www.youtube.com/watch?v=v1hnIIN2N08

TedX (Director). (2015, May 7). *Interpersonal Communication in the Future World.* https://www.youtube.com/watch?v=KlI2qDO0J6s

TEDx Talks (Director). (2017, May 15). *The Secret to Understanding Humans.* https://www.youtube.com/watch?v=RSlc9IxdBw8

TEDx Talks (Director). (2017, December 13). *6 Communication Truths that Everyone Should Know.* https://www.youtube.com/watch?v=zvcbn6WtJvQ

TEDx Talks (Director). (2020, April 7). *From the Inside Out: Diversity, Inclusion & Belonging.* https://www.youtube.com/watch?v=R9TxD2QmcY8

TEDx Talk (Director). (2021, January 2). *The Art of Effective Communication.* Retrieved November 3, 2023, from https://www.youtube.com/watch?v=2Yw6dFQBklA&t=7s

TEDx Talks (Director). (2022, March 24). *Belonging, A Critical Piece of Diversity, Equity & Inclusion.* https://www.youtube.com/watch?v=2jK0gyQCoTs

TEDxOU (Director). (2019, October 22). *How to Go Beyond Diversity and Inclusion to Community and Belonging.* https://www.youtube.com/watch?v=kZaNa17yeaQ

The Business Professor (Director). (2022, September 30). *Elements of Human Relations Theory.* https://www.youtube.com/watch?v=PcSBhLh4EX4

The Schwartz Center for Compassionate Healthcare (Director). (2015, March 20). *Bridging Difference and Power with Respect: A Relational Approach to Patients, Supervisees and Teams.* https://www.youtube.com/watch?v=1e17cK544OQ

Zikrullah TV (Director). (2022, June 16). *What does the Future of Work Look Like?* https://www.youtube.com/watch?v=k0HMRE-dr-o

Zikrullah TV (Director). (2023, July 27). *The Future of Work.* https://www.youtube.com/watch?v=M9l_lpYnzhI

Blogs/Websites

CHRON. (n.d.). *The Importance of Human Relations in the Workplace.* Small Business - Chron.Com. Retrieved November 4, 2023, from https://smallbusiness.chron.com/importance-human-relations-workplace-23061.html

Deiratani, A. (2021, September 13). *12 Reasons Team Building is Important for Your Company.* TeamBonding. https://www.teambonding.com/6-reasons-for-team-building/

Diversity, Equity, and Inclusion – A Program Action Team of the Extension Committee on Organization and Policy. (n.d.). Retrieved November 3, 2023, from https://dei.extension.org/

Douglas, E. (2023, August 17). *SHRM Essentials of Human Resources—A Solution for Evolving HR Teams*. SHRM. https://www.shrm.org/resourcesandtools/hr-topics/behavioral-competencies/pages/shrm-essentials-of-human-resources-a-solution-for-evolving-hr-teams.aspx

Emerson, M. S. (2021, August 30). *8 Ways You Can Improve Your Communication Skills*. Professional Development | Harvard DCE. https://professional.dce.harvard.edu/blog/8-ways-you-can-improve-your-communication-skills/

Fournier, E. (2022, June 15). *Leadership: Managing Different Perspectives in the Workplace Using Hofstede Dimensions*. Workplace Options. https://www.workplaceoptions.com/leadership-managing-different-perspectives-in-the-workplace-using-hofstede-dimensions/

Fraraccio, M. (n.d.). *Basics of Human Relations Management Theory*. Business.Com. Retrieved November 4, 2023, from https://www.business.com/articles/human-relations-management-theory-basics/

Freedman, M. (2023, October 20). Human relations movement: How it changed management – businessnewsdaily.com. *Business News Daily*. https://www.businessnewsdaily.com/10633-human-relations-movement.html

Grensing-Pophal, L. (2022, March 31). *7 Essential Communication Skills Managers Must Master*. Business Training Experts. https://businesstrainingexperts.com/communication-skills-for-managers/

Haas, M., & Mortensen, M. (2016, June 1). *The Secrets of Great Teamwork*. Harvard Business Review. https://hbr.org/2016/06/the-secrets-of-great-teamwork

Hassan, S. (2022, May 12). *How to Promote Diversity, Equity, Inclusion, & Belonging in the Workplace*. Together Mentoring Software. https://www.togetherplatform.com/blog/how-to-promote-diversity-and-inclusion-in-the-workplace

Indeed Editorial Team. (2023, February 27). *Team Working vs. Team Building: Similarities and Differences*. Indeed.com. https://www.indeed.com/career-advice/career-development/team-building-vs-team-working

Indeed Editorial Team. (2023, July 3). *What are Human Relations Skills?* https://www.indeed.com/career-advice/resumes-cover-letters/human-relations-skills

McKinsey and Company. (2022, August 17). *What Is Diversity, Equity, and Inclusion (DE&I)?* Retrieved November 3, 2023, from https://www.mckinsey.com/featured-insights/mckinsey-explainers/what-is-diversity-equity-and-inclusion

Mind Tools. (n.d.). *Hofstede's Cultural Dimensions—Understanding Different Countries*. Retrieved November 3, 2023, from https://www.mindtools.com/a1ecvyx/hofstedes-cultural-dimensions

Montclair University. (n.d.). *Cultivating Diversity, Equity, Inclusion and Belonging*. Retrieved November 5, 2023, from https://www.montclair.edu/faculty-excellence/teaching-resources/inclusivity-and-diversity/cultivating-diversity-equity-inclusion-belonging/

Petryni, M. (2019, February 1). *The Importance of Human Relations in the Workplace*. Small Business. https://smallbusiness.chron.com/importance-human-relations-workplace-23061.html

Praslova, L. N. (2022, June 21). *An Intersectional Approach to Inclusion at Work*. Harvard Business Review. https://hbr.org/2022/06/an-intersectional-approach-to-inclusion-at-work

Principles of Management. (2015). *12.4 Communication Barriers*. https://open.lib.umn.edu/principlesmanagement/chapter/12-4-communication-barriers/

Robinson, L., Segal, J., & Smith, M. (n.d.). *Effective Communication*. Retrieved November 3, 2023, from https://www.helpguide.org/articles/relationships-communication/effective-communication.html

SHRM. (2023, January 12). *How to Develop a Diversity, Equity and Inclusion Initiative*. SHRM. https://www.shrm.org/resourcesandtools/tools-and-samples/how-to-guides/pages/how-to-develop-a-diversity-and-inclusion-initiative.aspx

The Business Professor. (n.d.). *Human Relations Theory of Management—Explained*. The Business Professor, LLC. Retrieved November 5, 2023, from https://thebusinessprofessor.com/management-leadership-organizational-behavior/human-relations-theory-of-management

Tugend, A. (2018, September 30). The effect of intersectionality in the workplace. *The New York Times*. https://www.nytimes.com/2018/09/30/us/the-effect-of-intersectionality-in-the-workplace.html

VantageCircle. (2019, May 6). *The Difference between Teamwork and Team Building*. Nurture an Engaged and Satisfied Workforce | Vantage Circle HR Blog. https://blog.vantagecircle.com/teamwork-and-team-building/

Willkomm, A. (2018, July 18). *6 Barriers to Effective Communication*. Graduate College of Drexel University. https://drexel.edu/graduatecollege/professional-development/blog/2018/July/6-barriers-to-effective-communication/

Reports/Tools

McKinsey and Company. (2023, July 26). *Gen AI and the Future of Work*. Retrieved November 3, 2023, from https://www.mckinsey.com/quarterly/the-five-fifty/five-fifty-gen-ai-and-the-future-of-work

Minkin, R. (2023, May 17). Diversity, equity and inclusion in the workplace. *Pew Research Center's Social & Demographic Trends Project*. https://www.pewresearch.org/social-trends/2023/05/17/diversity-equity-and-inclusion-in-the-workplace/

The Culture Factor. (n.d.). *Country Comparison Tool*. Retrieved November 3, 2023, from https://www.hofstede-insights.com/country-comparison-tool

Index

Page numbers in *italic* indicate figure and **bold** indicate table respectively

H

I

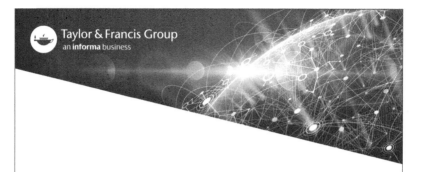